T0284940

More Praise for *The Disengaged Teen*

"*The Disengaged Teen* offers everything a parent or teacher needs to understand, support, and empower a child's learning."

—JENNIFER BREHENY WALLACE,
author of *Never Enough*

"This book gives parents and educators clear, evidence-backed ways to help young people develop the agency they need to navigate our fragile and fast-changing world."

—TODD ROSE,
co-author of *Dark Horse*

"*The Disengaged Teen* may be the most important book of 2025. [It] is a must-read for every parent of an adolescent, or soon-to-be adolescent."

—PAUL LeBLANC,
former president Southern New Hampshire University

"A thoughtful analysis with many wise and practical insights. The authors show, through research and rich storytelling, how recognizing adolescents' desire for autonomy and meaningful contribution can lead to engaging modes of exploration and discovery."

—RON DAHL,
founding director of the Center for the Developing Adolescent
and director of the Institute of Human Development
at University of California, Berkeley

"It's no understatement to say that Anderson and Winthrop have cracked the code for any parent or educator interested in moving kids out of first gear (or reverse), and accelerating learning, growth, happiness, and success. A must-read."

—NED JOHNSON,
co-author of *The Self-Driven Child*

"After twenty years of teaching and even longer parenting, I know engagement is the holy grail of both, easy to identify but almost impossible to find when it's lost. Anderson and Winthrop do a fantastic job of explaining what it is, how to find it, and presenting tools for helping kids engage in school and life."

—JESSICA LAHEY,
author of *The Gift of Failure*

"*The Disengaged Teen* offers specific actions parents and teachers can take right now to make school more meaningful and compelling. An important book, perfectly timed."

—AMANDA RIPLEY,
author of *The Smartest Kids in the World*

"The four modes of engagement offer practical ways for parents to both identify and change the behaviors that get in the way of engagement and deep learning."

—JENNIFER FREDRICKS,
professor of psychology at Union College and
editor of *Handbook of Student Engagement Interventions*

"*The Disengaged Teen* is a compelling read. As a policy maker, educator, and parent, I found it to be rich with insight on how to reset and help our kids who are increasingly struggling with home and school."

—LORD JIM KNIGHT,
former schools minister, UK

"The authors show us, with compelling original stories, summaries of rigorous experiments, and practical scripts of what to say and what not to say, how to: inspire youth to embrace productive struggle (rather than avoid it); harness their stress responses (rather than being crushed by them); focus on broader, self-transcendent purposes (rather than short-term goals), and much more. I highly recommend this book for anyone who wants to get smarter about the wonderful but puzzling world of motivating and engaging the next generation."

—DAVID YEAGER,
author of *10 to 25*

The *Disengaged* TEEN

Helping Kids Learn Better, Feel Better, and Live Better

Jenny Anderson

and

Rebecca Winthrop

CROWN
NEW YORK

Published in the United States by Crown, an imprint of the Crown Publishing Group,
a division of Penguin Random House LLC, New York.
crownpublishing.com

CROWN and the Crown colophon are registered trademarks of Penguin Random House LLC.

Library of Congress Cataloging-in-Publication Data
Names: Anderson, Jenny, 1972- author. | Winthrop, Rebecca, author.
Title: The Disengaged Teen: Helping Kids Learn Better, Feel Better, and Live Better / Jenny Anderson and Rebecca Winthrop. Description: First edition. | New York: Crown, 2025. | Includes bibliographical references and index. | Identifiers: LCCN 2024022928 (print) | LCCN 2024022929 (ebook) | ISBN 9780593727072 (hardcover) | ISBN 9780593727089 (ebook) Subjects: LCSH: Motivation in education. | Stress in adolescence. | Achievement motivation in adolescence. | Education—Parent participation. | Parent and child. Classification: LCC LB1065 .A625 2025 (print) | LCC LB1065 (ebook) | DDC 373.1801/9—dc23/eng/20240821
LC record available at https://lccn.loc.gov/2024022928
LC ebook record available at https://lccn.loc.gov/2024022929

Hardcover ISBN 978-0-5937-2707-2
Ebook ISBN 978-0-5937-2708-9

Printed in the United States of America on acid-free paper

Editor: Leah Trouwborst
Editorial assistant: Cierra Hinckson
Production editor: Ashley Pierce
Production manager: Dustin Amick
Copy editor: Elisabeth Magnus
Proofreaders: Janet Renard and Alison Kerr Miller
Indexer: Ken DellaPenta
Publicist: Tammy Blake
Marketers: Kimberly Lew and Rachel Rodriguez

9 8 7 6 5 4 3 2 1

First Edition
Book design by Aubrey Khan
Illustrations by Bond and Coyne

TO OUR CHILDREN

Ella, Tess, Santi, and Nico

Never stop exploring—in life, in love, and in school.

Contents

Part II

The Engagement Tool Kit

Resources

Authors' Note

We are deeply grateful to every child, parent, caregiver, and teacher who shared their story with us. Every story in this book is real. But in some cases, to protect their privacy, we have changed people's names and identifying details.

Introduction

The Disengagement Crisis

In the world of education, tests rule. They are used to measure what kids know, how much progress they are making, and where they will go to college; it's like a thirteen-year sorting hat exercise. And there is one test that reigns supreme, that measures not just what students know, but if they can think critically and solve problems. This test, given every three years to fifteen-year-olds in about eighty countries, has become a sort of academic GDP: a globally watched measure of the effectiveness of a country's education system. The test is called Programme for International Student Assessment (PISA) and it's been administered by the Organisation for Economic Co-operation and Development since 2000.[1] It originally measured math and reading and science; later tests added new skills such as creative thinking and global competence. The data reveal how well a country's students are developing the assessed knowledge, attitudes, and skills, and, in a competitive twist, how those results compare to other countries.*

For about a decade and a half after the first results were published, PISA scores generally held steady. The knowledge economy needed knowledgeable graduates, and countries spent billions on school

* In 2022 it was taken by 690,000 students, representing a sample of 29 million.

systems. But about ten years ago, something odd happened. In many countries, scores in reading and science started to fall. In 2018, math went off a cliff too. By 2022, the headline for the latest PISA test was resounding: the academic performance of fifteen-year-olds was in free fall.[2]

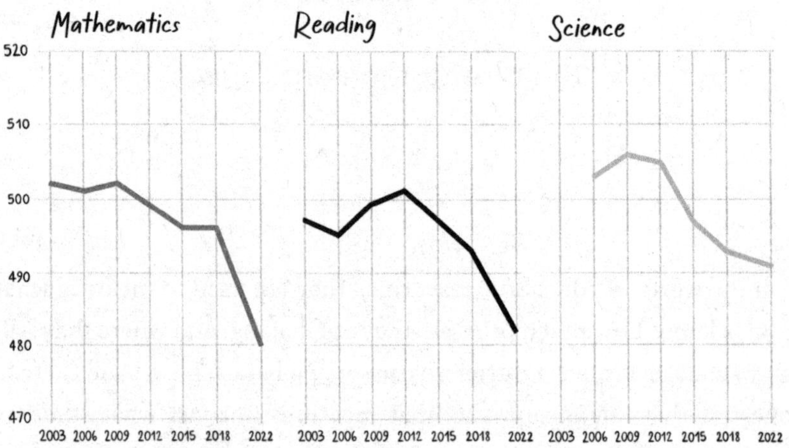

Source: Organization for Economic Cooperation and Development, *PISA 2022 Results*, vol. 1: *The State of Learning and Equity in Education* (Paris: OECD Publishing, 2023).

This drop in scores is not just puzzling—it's alarming.[3] If education today is a leading indicator of a country's productivity and social cohesion tomorrow, PISA is an early signal of what future generations have in store. Well-educated citizens are employable and productive. They can work together to address complex problems, like global warming, polarization, or the downsides of powerful new technologies such as artificial intelligence. Well-educated scientists cure diseases and ease discomfort; knowledgeable entrepreneurs drive innovation; well-trained engineers create beautiful bridges, and make sure they don't fall down. If teens everywhere are losing academic ground, how on earth will we collectively help people live healthier, happier, and more creative and fulfilling lives? Just as a sustained drop in GDP raises alarm bells, the persistent decline in PISA scores raises the question: Why are young people in a learning recession?

The pandemic surely made things worse. Kids missed out on a shocking amount of learning. Being isolated for so long had real developmental consequences, with marginalized young people suffering the most. But the data suggest the problem started well before March 2020. Many blame technology, pointing to the epic distraction of smartphones for hijacking our kids' attention away from sleep, friendships, and learning.

But there's a deeper reason, rarely acknowledged and pernicious: A shocking number of young people don't see the point of school anymore. As a result, they lose motivation and check out. According to the U.S. Census, only one in three students is highly engaged in school.[4] Technology exacerbates this problem but is not the source of it.[5] Kids witness the world around them—wars, social injustice, climate change, disinformation, technology that can write novels and counsel on heartbreak—and wonder why on earth they have to learn the Pythagorean theorem. This is a problem around the world. In the United States 30 percent of students between third and twelfth grade say that what they learn in school feels connected to their life outside the classroom; in Chile only around 20 percent find their schooling useful.[6]

It's not breaking news that most young people don't love what they do in school. The genre of the disaffected tween and teen is a deep and storied one. But the distance between school and life has become a chasm. Imagine for a moment what a teenager's average day would be like for you. You enter work at 9:00 A.M. You sit down in your office, pull out your binder, and get to work on a project. After forty-five minutes a bell rings and you pack up your papers and move to the office next door, where you pull out a different binder and get to work on a different project. You repeat this sequence five or six times a day. For some projects you are allowed to use a computer and the internet. But for others you can only consult your memory and use a number two pencil. How would you feel at the end of the day? How would you feel about your career?*

Parents know something's amiss. When they ask "How was school?" kids deliver the predictable and emotionally flat "Fine." Perhaps because we all don't know what to do about it, or we've heard it for so long, we brush it aside. We've become desensitized to it. We are failing to see it for the crisis it is: Young people, hungry to learn and grow, overwhelmingly associate school with apathy and stress. Trapped in buildings that feel like prisons (teens' words, not ours), they are stressed out by a weird combination of competitive pressures and insufficient stimulation, and they develop a frustration that fuels a pervasive lack of meaning in their daily existence. This is a disaster for kids' mental health. It is bad for countries that need educated citizens. It's also bad for families trying to raise children who can thrive in the twenty-first century.

More than ever before, what kids need now is to become better at learning. Generative artificial intelligence (AI) is accelerating rapidly, and everyone agrees that the pace of change will continue to be dizzying. Uncertainty is the new norm. No one knows exactly what shifts in jobs and society are in store. What can best protect and prepare our kids? Rose Luckin, a British professor and AI expert is blunt: Make them "good at learning." The only thing that can insulate them from rapid change and give them the confidence to move forward is the ability to learn and adapt. Resilient learners are not strong; they are flexible. At a moment when we desperately need them to be firing on all cylinders, engaged with their learning, they do the opposite. Too many young people feel helpless and hopeless when they should feel invincible.

No kid wants to be checked out. Young people are hard-wired for learning, and when they don't succeed at it in school—because it's too easy or too hard, because they have mental health issues or are neurodivergent, because they are not connecting with a teacher, because they experience bullying or discrimination or they don't feel their val-

* We were inspired by Charles Handy's storytelling for this imaginary office in his book *The Age of Unreason* (Boston: Harvard Business School Press, 1989).

ues align with those around them—they respond with the tools they have. They disengage. When that disengagement becomes an identity, their potential and their opportunities get clipped. They miss out on endless chances to learn: about subjects and skills, about themselves and others. Too many are losing at a game they don't want to play and feel angry, sad, or anxious. Meanwhile, plenty of others are winning but are worn out by the relentless nature of a never-ending match.

Faced with this, many parents also feel helpless. You aren't teachers, you're not in classrooms, and you're busy. But just as you support kids with friendships you aren't part of, cheer them on in sports you don't play, and help them find careers you don't do, you can coach them to be better learners without becoming science, math, or English teachers. The tools you need are deeply researched, tucked away in wonky academic handbooks and dense neuroscientific papers. We have spent the last three years distilling them into simple strategies you can use in the car, at dinner, and when your child is cursing their homework.

The science and practice of good learning is called **engagement,** and it's one of the best-kept secrets in education.

More than just grit or willpower, engagement is a complex interplay of emotions, thoughts, and behaviors that ignite a deep, genuine interest in the world around us. When children are engaged, they are energized, not exhausted. They become proactive learners. They ask questions, seek help, advocate for their interests, and learn to set their own goals—whether that's making a video or writing a play in history. They notice if they are ahead or behind in the material and try to do something about it. They become resilient, viewing challenges as opportunities for growth and embracing complexity and uncertainty as natural parts of the learning process. They persist in the face of obstacles, because they know that learning is hard but that effort pays. They seek out resources to deepen their understanding and connect their learning to their lives in creative ways. These curious creatures can be grade-A annoying with their ceaseless questions. But those questions are helping to connect developing networks in their brains in ways that set them up for long-term success.

What sets engaged learners apart is their self-awareness and intrinsic motivation. They walk through the world with a confidence that stems not only from meeting external expectations but also from setting and achieving their own internal goals. They know when to dig deep and when to just get things done. As a result, they are both high-achieving and happy.

If this sounds like some mythical Shangri-la, it's not. Extensive evidence shows that increased student engagement leads to a myriad of benefits that we are neither making up nor exaggerating:[7]

- Higher attendance rates and grades
- Higher achievement
- Higher test scores

- Higher academic aspirations
- Higher graduation rates
- Higher life satisfaction
- More prosocial behavior
- Higher college attendance
- Higher rates of staying in college
- Lower levels of depression
- Lower suicidal thoughts and behaviors
- Less substance abuse
- Fewer delinquency and behavior problems

In other words, more engaged kids learn better, perform better, feel better, and live better.

And yet engagement is rarely discussed in parent-teacher conferences or school board meetings or even at national conferences of education leaders. Engagement is messy and influenced by many factors: parents, teachers, peers, school culture, behavioral norms. Many signals of disengagement can be easy to miss. It is hard to solve a problem you cannot see.

Our offer to you is a simple, clear framework to make what's fuzzy and indecipherable visible and actionable. We will share a map to help you understand and support your child's engagement in their learning, in and out of school. In Part I, you will learn about the four modes of engagement: Passenger, Achiever, Resister, and Explorer. These are not diagnostic labels meant to pigeonhole kids. They are dynamic modes kids move through based on the environments they inhabit.

Once you see them, you won't be able to unsee them.

Kids in **Resister mode** use what power they have to let you, and their teachers, know school is not working for them. They avoid or disrupt their learning, refusing to do homework, derailing class, and skipping school. These signals are usually obvious to see but often mask feelings of inadequacy that can be hard to understand and require work to reverse.

Young people in **Passenger mode** are coasting in low gear, showing up, doing the bare minimum, sometimes bringing home high grades, but never fully engaging in their work. They are uninterested in what is taught, and are at risk of not developing the learning habits necessary to navigate school and work. A lot of kids spend a lot of time here: In our research, we found close to half of middle and high school students primarily operate in Passenger mode.[8] One school head we admire called them the invisible middle in classrooms because overstretched teachers are split between supporting those resisting and, at the other end, the go-getters.

Kids in **Achiever mode** seem like they are at the top of the engagement mountain. They are highly motivated and expend tremendous energy doing well in school, getting top marks on exams, and studying for hours on end. Teachers love them and encourage them. But they are often fragile. Achieving becomes all about grades. So much focus on the destination means they fail to spend any of the journey figuring out what matters to them. Endless praise makes them risk averse. Why stretch themselves if they could fail?

The actual pinnacle is **Explorer mode,** where kids become resilient learners and build skills that help them thrive: They achieve but don't wilt when trying new things or stumbling a bit along the way. They feel confident enough to color outside the lines, flexing their creative skills by proactively generating their own ideas to solve problems in school or on the sports field. They are deeply involved and engaged in their learning, finding meaning amid the hard work.

Exploring is not navel-gazing or prolonged wandering. It is not the developmentally important exploring that toddlers do, which is aimless and joyful. Nor does exploring sacrifice achievement in school. In classrooms where teachers encourage agency, or kids being proactive about their own learning, kids who explore get better grades and exam results.[9] The ability to engage deeply in learning, to have a say in how they spend much of their significant mental energy, is not a nice-to-have but a must-have. It is the price of entry for a meaningful life, whatever they choose that life to be. It is essential for all kids but especially those pushed to the margins of education and society due to racism, limited English language ability, or school funding policies that give the least amount of learning resources to those who need them most. It is, as the careful research of sociologist Anindya Kundu has shown, a key driver in helping them not just succeed in school but to thrive.[10]

The challenge for parents is that most kids are not encouraged to explore in school. Our research found that less than 10 percent of third through twelfth graders strongly agree that their school provides them opportunities to be in Explorer mode.[11] Many schools actively discourage it—often in places where kids desperately need engagement as a counterbalance to hard life conditions. Increasingly, parents are expressing their frustration by leaving. Concerned that their child is not seen, valued, or supported, families are turning to other options, from homeschooling to microschools.[12] This is hardly the first time that many families have felt unwelcome: The United States has a long history of pushing marginalized kids down, not lifting them up. What's changed is that post-pandemic, many more are opting-out.

As a parent, you may think you have little influence here. Your teen is not exactly waiting on tenterhooks for your advice. The bulk of learning happens in classrooms and clubs and on sports fields, right? Wrong. Research confirms that you have tremendous sway. It's as important as the influence of teachers, even in high school.[13] Consider: On average across all OECD countries, students whose parents ask them several times a week what they did in school that day performed 16 points higher in mathematics even after accounting for their socio-economic profile.[14] You are in fact ideally positioned to coach your kid to be an engaged learner. That's because school is by no means the only place kids build Explorer muscles. As we show you throughout the book, the spark to drive a student's learning can come from anywhere. Your job is to know how to look for it, notice it, support it, and connect it to the person your teen is trying to become.

You matter a lot, in what you believe, what you say (and don't say), and what you do. The catch is that to become engaged in learning, kids have to be open to receiving your guidance. We cover that throughout the book. In Part II: The Engagement Toolkit, we draw from the world's best teachers, psychologists, counselors, therapists, school heads, and academics, as well as parents and kids, to offer strategies to help your child navigate the modes and experience more Explorer moments. That means helping kids in Passenger mode get out of neutral and into drive, preventing those in Achiever mode from burning out the engine, and guiding your kids in Resister mode out of reverse and toward their learning again. We show you how Explorers are brave in the face of uncertainty and resilient when they experience failure. We address the philosophical a bit but the practical a lot: tackling procrastination, managing stress, ditching perfectionism and replacing it with excellence, and helping kids focus on who they want to be as well as what they need to get done by Friday.

• • •

The two of us met at an education conference in Bulgaria many years ago. Jenny, a recovering financial journalist, was searching for the powerful data about learning in the same way she had found data so freely available in the financial world. Rebecca helped her find some of it and demystified the very human processes that guide learning, schooling, and education. A few years later, we decided the ideas we talked about at conferences, read about in reports, and wrote about in five-hundred-page studies (Rebecca) and one-thousand-word articles (Jenny) deserved to be more widely known. We created a simple but powerful framework to help you understand your kids as learners. Learning requires courage; we show you how to help them be brave.

Rebecca has spent the last twenty-five years finding innovative ways to improve education. She got her start running education programs in migrant worker camps in her home state of Oregon. Today she is the director of the Center for Universal Education at Brookings and an adjunct professor at Georgetown University. She regularly advises leaders at the highest levels—from the United Nations to the White House to CEOs of philanthropic organizations and Fortune 500 companies. Her work has helped launch new internationally validated tools, new organizations from United Nations offices to funding initiatives, and new education policies in countries from North America to Asia. In 2017, she conducted a global study of three thousand education innovations across 160 countries to help kids leapfrog forward and develop the breadth of skills needed to thrive. But she realized there was a major missing piece of the puzzle: families and parents. She launched the Global Family Engagement in Education Network, an initiative to strengthen the role of families and communities in helping children learn.

Jenny is an award-winning journalist who spent over a decade covering finance and then education at *The New York Times*. Her reporting during the 2008 financial crisis won a prestigious Gerald Loeb Award (and got Merrill Lynch's CEO fired for lying to his board). After she had kids, her obsessions shifted from collateralized debt obligations to how people—and specifically young people—learn. After writing about education for *The New York Times,* she wanted to go deeper into the science of learning and development and connect more of the dots between learning and relationships and technology. In 2015, she joined *Quartz,* a digital media start-up, where she wrote about the future of learning. In 2020, she launched a podcast to interview global education leaders and penned a newsletter for eighty thousand of them.

This book was not easy to write (ask our families). We started three years ago researching and reading everything we could about *what helps kids learn well.* In our search, we found answers everywhere: in classrooms with brilliant teachers and in schools with inspired leadership. We found it in psychology, sociology, neuroscience, learning science, parenting research, and even philosophy. We looked more, in our free time and in our day jobs: Jenny reported hundreds of stories and Rebecca led a global study about how families can work with schools to support children's learning and development.

We analyzed data from surveys of more than twenty-five thousand parents and six thousand teachers conducted in the United States and nine other countries by Rebecca and her Brookings team with their Family Engagement in Education Network partners. In 2024, we partnered with the nonprofit Transcend to conduct two nationally representative surveys in the United States: one with students and one with parents.[15] These Brookings-Transcend surveys dug into what more than sixty-five thousand students between third and twelfth grade say their experience is like at school and what types of opportunities they have to engage in their learning. We compared those to what parents of third to twelfth graders think their children's experience is. Spoiler alert: Parents are in the dark, and the kids are not okay.

We also spent a lot of time talking to young people themselves, the best sources for learning about school today. We interviewed close to one hundred young people from every background we could find: kids in small towns and big cities, kids from wealthy families and from those with limited resources. Half the kids we spoke to were white and half were Black, Latino, Asian, or Native American. We asked about what made them want to learn in school, and what shut them down. We asked about their hopes and dreams for school and beyond. We asked what their parents did that was helpful—or not at all helpful. (We got a lot of cooperation on that one. In case you are wondering, the thing they want most from you is that you listen to them.) We visited classrooms, and held focus groups in schools and in dining rooms from Texas and Tennessee to New York and London. We also spoke with hundreds of parents, teachers, and learning experts.

We are not offering advice from an elevated moral podium. We've also lived through many of the issues we cover in this book. Jenny had a sparky, opinionated kid who was performing well at school until she started fainting, beset by fatigue and an alarming lethargy. A battery of tests over more than a year revealed that her daughter had celiac disease, which was why she was fainting, but also that she had ADHD. Jenny and her husband were stunned. Their daughter had always performed well academically. They realized that no one looks closely at kids who deliver what the system demands, even if there's a cost to them. With the ADHD diagnosis, they suddenly understood so much more about her: why she could hyperfocus and then not focus at all (and why shouting at her never, ever worked). Meanwhile, as Jenny tried to find strategies to get one daughter to focus, she struggled to get the other one to stop studying and go to bed. She knew her daughter's determined drive to perform had risks, but how do you protect against those? The two seemed to need almost opposite things to support their learning, and she felt at sea trying to figure out how to help each of them.

Rebecca, despite being a globally renowned education expert, discovered during the COVID pandemic how little she knew about her own kids' learning. She thought she knew which one was deeply engaged and which one wasn't. She had one son who, until March 2020, had sailed through school with good grades. She thought he would be able to learn independently. That didn't happen. He fell apart. He refused to do any online work because he knew it wasn't graded: "If it's not graded, it doesn't count," he told her matter-of-factly. She saw clearly what his good grades had masked: He wasn't engaged in learning; he was engaged in collecting gold stars. Learning to him was a scorecard and without it he was totally lost. Her other son had suffered in elementary school, convinced he was stupid because he couldn't read. He was eventually diagnosed with dyslexia and ADHD. She worried that he was deeply disengaged from his education and that the pandemic would be a struggle. Instead, she found he was deeply disengaged only while at school. He blossomed during the pandemic: making lists, creating schedules, applying himself to his learning in a way she had never seen him do. He was thriving away from the misery of always trying to keep up and fit into school's narrow definition of "good learner." With all her degrees and policy work, how had she gotten so much wrong in supporting her own sons?

Parenting is hard. Parenting adolescents is even harder. We are with you in the trenches, messing things up every day: yelling and criticizing where we should be recognizing and supporting; moving things along when we should be digging in. We also know we are more fortunate than many. We don't worry about putting food on the table and know our kids are unlikely to be racially profiled when walking down the street.

While our research revealed many struggling kids, it also uncovered remarkable success stories. With the right support from parents, teachers, or their environment, kids who had been hopelessly disengaged, rebellious, depressed, or directionless became engaged and started thriving. All kids are hungry to learn. No kid is a lost cause. Parents are uniquely and powerfully placed to feed that hunger and unleash their potential. We will show you the stories of adolescents who found their way back to learning, or to true engagement with the help of parents,* teachers, other grown-ups, and peers.

This book is for parents, grandparents, aunts, uncles, and anyone else caring for children. We know every young person is wildly different and context is essential, but there are patterns to why kids operate in the modes they do, and we identify those for you. The ideas we offer include actionable strategies and subtle mindset shifts that you can use in the car or at the kitchen table. We show you the neuroscience of why nagging about homework undermines learning—and why enthusiasm and tactics toward tackling hard questions does not. We explain how to decenter your influence (to gain more of it), and why uncertainty about belonging makes learning so hard. In the resources at the end of the book, we tackle technology so that kids start to use it to explore and engage, not distract and detach.

We hope teachers can use this book too. They sit on the front lines of the disengagement crisis, working to find moments of inspiration and ways to tap joy in each child in creative ways (sometimes against all odds). They are stuck in many ways you cannot see, sandwiched between a system that demands preparation for tests, restrictive accountability standards, and parents who insist their kids excel in a system not serving them well. They see the faces of your kids every day and know intimately how many things are not working. Most want nothing more than to help kids engage deeply in their learning. We hope that once they better understand engagement, parents will team up with teachers to boost kids' motivation to learn. Cliché as it sounds, teamwork is

* Occasionally in spite of parents.

golden here. When parents, teachers, school leaders, and students trust each other, schools are ten times more likely to have better learning outcomes, along with a laundry list of other good things.[16]

Finally, this book is for education leaders who have the power to help students become Explorers. Author Annie Dillard writes, "How we spend our days, is, of course, how we spend our lives." We want young people to spend their days learning well. Principals, districts, nonprofits, and philanthropic organizations all play a role in designing more engaging schools. We hope this book helps fuel the movement, already underway, to make school more interesting for our students. We include at the end of the book a list of organizations committed to helping schools across the nation create dynamic learning environments—places like Big Picture Learning, Transcend, and 3DE Schools.

Finally, in the concluding chapter we show how cultivating a love of learning is an integral part of building a meaningful life. Teens are on an intense journey of meaning-making and identity-building. "Adolescence is a period of wanting to stand out and wanting to fit in," says Ronald Dahl, founding director of the Center for the Developing Adolescent at UC Berkeley/UCLA.[17] It is a window of unique opportunity and vulnerability, when the stories young people tell themselves can become embedded in useful and sometimes less useful ways. How kids think about themselves as learners shapes these stories they tell, and you have influence to narrate and model one about growth, malleability, and possibility.

For a fleeting moment you can nudge your teens toward experiences and opportunities to help them understand who they are and who they hope to be. Grades and achieving are part of this; nurturing a robust learner identity—that is, developing Explorer muscles—is essential yet, alarmingly, overlooked. Becoming better learners will help kids accelerate toward goals they care about, unstoppable where they were once stuck.

Our hope is to help young people move from languishing to thriving, from being checked out and stressed out to knowing how to drive their own learning, one of the most important parts of a fulfilling life.

We do that by empowering you, with language, knowledge, and strategies. Your own relationship with learning—your willingness to grow, change, and model the qualities of an engaged learner—directly influences your child's journey. We'll challenge you to step outside your comfort zone, to ask questions, and to seek out new knowledge alongside your teen. We'll encourage you to embrace the discomfort of not having all the answers and to demonstrate the resilience and adaptability you hope they one day embody. Learning is an essential part of thriving. It is also essential to your teen cultivating hope—hope that they can make their way through a messy world and contribute to improving it.

And who doesn't want a little more hope these days?

PART I

The Four Modes of Engagement

1

The Power of Engagement

Unlocking Every Kid's Potential

When Kia was in kindergarten in Hunter, North Dakota, she was the smartest kid in her class. She'd finish her homework during school as soon as it was assigned and never have to take anything home. In her free time, she tore through all the Percy Jackson books. She played the saxophone and piano before taking up guitar. At her dad's suggestion, she taught herself songs such as Jack Black's "Tribute." There were fewer than four hundred people in her rural town, but she was always busy. She'd spend her evenings with her dad, reading, playing, or listening to music.

But in fifth grade, the homework picked up, and Kia, who is white, started to lose interest. The issue wasn't just that it was harder; the curriculum was often rigid and standardized, failing to capture her imagination or tie into her passions for reading, drawing, singing, and playing music. Kia found it particularly challenging to focus on repetitive tasks that didn't engage her creative side. The traditional classroom setting, with its emphasis on sitting still, listening quietly, and completing worksheets, felt stifling to her. She saw no reason to put in effort to do something that felt meaningless.

At age twelve, she was diagnosed with ADHD, like her dad, and while it helped her understand her school-related challenges, it didn't help her get any more motivated. She got a phone at age thirteen and spent far more time obsessively scrolling than doing her homework. She stayed in her room, watching videos and glued to social media. She left the house less and less and stopped talking to people. She gave up reading, walking, and all of her other hobbies. When COVID struck and Kia had to learn at home, things didn't get any better. Even though her school was well set up for online learning, she, like many other teens, did nothing. She nearly failed ninth grade, in 2020–21, and insists that she passed only because everyone passed. "School went from being fun to being a chore—a chore I would never complete, and then I would get stressed because it was never done," she told us.

The school knew Kia was in trouble. "We're losing this kid, she doesn't want to do anything, won't do homework, won't engage," Tom Klapp, one of her teachers at the time, remembers thinking. She was known to staff and educators as a nice kid, "someone you can have a really good conversation with, very articulate," with a talent for writing and a passion for reading. But it was evident to all involved that school was not working for her. Her teachers would say, "Write this down," and she would just refuse, Klapp said. "She didn't find value in any of it."

Kia didn't like not trying. When she started giving up, she felt ashamed and guilty. She was angry that getting things done seemed so easy for others, and she started to feel stupid. But it was her dad, Lee, she felt worst about. Lee had dropped out of college and had worked at the local grain factory for twenty years, now as a manager. He had always pushed Kia to do well in school so that she would have better options than he did. Imparting knowledge to her, he once told her, was how he showed his love. When Kia pulled back from learning, he stayed connected to her and encouraged her to keep asking questions. "We talked for hours," she told us. Her dad was the smartest person she'd ever met, and she hated letting him down.

In tenth grade, a teacher noticed that Kia had some strong opinions about the futility of school and suggested she be part of a learner advisory panel going to Fargo. Would she go and talk to the school board about how legislators and educators could make school more engaging? "It was a moment in which my brain went from 'This is useless, and I hate everything' to 'Hold on, maybe I have a say,'" Kia explained. "So I said yes, of course."

The group went to Fargo and testified. Kia was nervous. She hadn't had much practice speaking in public, and she had so much she wanted to say. Because she and the other students were there to answer questions, she couldn't really prepare. At first, she answered the board's questions—"What are you worried about for the future?" "What changes should be made to make things better?"—by trying to sound as official as possible ("long-winded sentences that don't actually say anything," she explains). But then it occurred to her that she should stop trying to sound smart and just focus on communicating her message. She needed to be crystal clear.

Finally, when the board asked whether she had anything else she wanted to say, she saw her chance. She told them that school simply did not feel relevant to kids—sitting at desks, ingesting narrow content rather than doing things related to problems outside their door: climate change, underemployment, rising mental health problems. You can't force kids to learn, she said. They have to want to do it. But when they do—when they get truly *excited* about learning—they will be unstoppable.

After speaking up, she felt a wave of relief. She had said what she came to say. They had heard her. She felt powerful.

At that board meeting, Kia was speaking for countless other students. According to a survey conducted by her school, in 2021 just 34 percent of students found school relevant—a figure in line with national averages. "We ask honest questions—'Who are we?' 'What is our purpose?'—and instead of answers, we're given an equation," Kia wrote after visiting Fargo in an essay summarizing her testimony. "We want the chances to discover our passion, to find ourselves."

Learn Well, Be Well

Being a teen has never been easy. But misery levels are out of whack everywhere—in studies, in the news, in our own homes. In the years between 2011 and 2021, rates of depression among high school students jumped to more than 40 percent. A tragically high percentage of high-school-aged kids are also at risk of dying by suicide: In 2021, 22 percent said they'd seriously considered attempting suicide; 18 percent had made a suicide plan; 10 percent had attempted suicide.[1] Among those, LGBTQ+ teens were more than twice as likely to make a suicide plan.[2] This was not just the pandemic: between 2007 and 2017 suicide rates increased by more than 56 percent.[3] The youth mental health problem in the United States is so serious that the U.S. surgeon general issued an advisory in December 2021 calling it "the defining public health crisis of our time" and elevating it to the level of a national consciousness.[4] Young people are lonelier than they have ever been and lonelier than any other age group, an anomaly in history. Kids have fewer friendships, are having less sex, and are drinking less—the last two things we could chalk up as a victory if not for the alarming malaise that seems to have replaced it.[5] They are even avoiding the one place they are still meant to gather together: More than a quarter of America's school-aged children were absent from school 10 percent or more during the 2022–23 school year.[6]

There are many well-documented potential causes: The isolation and anxiety caused by the pandemic. Social media and smartphones. Increasing inequality, with wealthy kids anxious about getting into elite colleges and low-income ones worrying about where their next meal will come from. Climate change, mass shootings, and Americans' seemingly endless capacity to be divided—all of it weighs heavily on the shoulders of young people.

But too often we overlook another pervasive cause: *Students just don't like what they do in school.* In elementary school, three-quarters of kids are enthusiastic about school. By high school, that figure has flipped—more than 65 percent report feeling checked out of school.[7]

Worst of all, they feel like there's nothing they can do about it. They feel helpless and hopeless. They are hungry for ways to contribute and have an impact on their world—in school, with their friends, in their communities—and they are not able to. Instead, most days, they shuffle between classes where they sit passively at their desks listening to adults. Some are so busy trying to win the race—to be extra-amazing at everything and get to the best college possible—that they fail to consider what race they want to be running. Others think the race is dumb and so don't even lace up. As parents, we shrug, maybe empathize, but assume there's not much we can do. A high school diploma is non-negotiable today, and high school is, well, high school. *Just get through it.*

That message is not working anymore.

The pandemic taught us a lot of things, including the obvious fact that kids need to be well to learn well. An anxious or depressed child will struggle to learn algebra. But more than thirty years of scientific studies on learning, longitudinal epidemiological studies, classroom experience, and common sense shows the inverse is also true: When kids learn well it helps them to feel well.

Engagement sits at the core of what it means to learn well. Feelings, thoughts, and actions work together to influence whether kids dig in when things get hard or give up; whether they try to make sense of something or let it go; whether they ask for help and marshal resources for what they care about or passively comply with what's on offer. When kids are disengaged, they flounder, like Kia in middle school. They lose motivation, check out of school and retreat into themselves (and their phones), or act out in despair. They don't want to be this way—like Kia, they are eager to learn things that feel meaningful. But disengagement stifles them. It is deeply corrosive to their well-being.

Here's the good news: With the right support, all kids can become engaged.[8] It's not rocket science, but it does require unpacking some science, which we do for you. Understanding engagement will help you see and understand your kid's learning much the same way a coach sees and understands an athlete. That coach measures the athlete's fitness levels, sets ambitious but realistic targets, develops strategies to get stronger, and assembles a support team to drive improvement. When you do this with engagement, young people perform better and feel better.

Unfortunately, parents way underestimate just how disengaged their kids are. They see some apathy or stress but assume it's normal. Our research found that students' love of school takes a nosedive after third grade. In the Brookings-Transcend report *The Disengagement Gap: Why Student Engagement Isn't What Parents Expect,* we found that by twelfth grade fewer than 30 percent of students love school, while parents think more than 60 percent of their children do.[9]

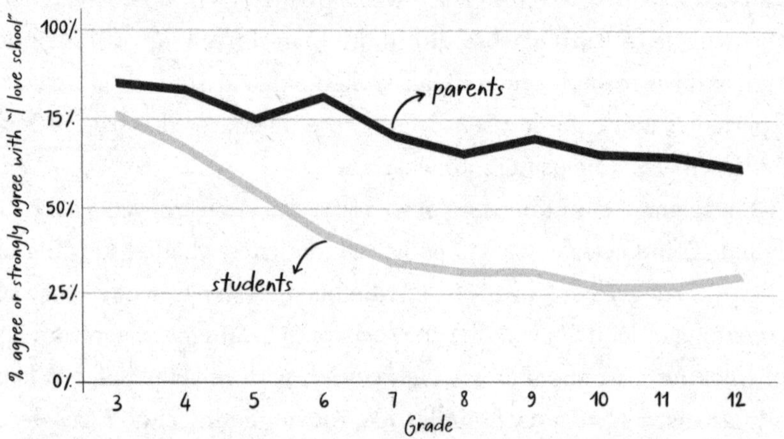

Source: Rebecca Winthrop, Youssef Shoukry, and David Nitkin, *The Disengagement Gap: Why Student Engagement Isn't What Parents Expect* (Washington, DC: Brookings Institution and Transcend 2025).

Decoding (Dis)Engagement

It's no surprise parents don't understand the full scope of this crisis. It's not just what kids *do:* go to school, turn in homework, take tests. This is what parents, and teachers, can easily see. But it's also about how they *feel:* ideally safe, like they belong, interested in what they are

WHAT YOU SEE

WHAT THEY FEEL AND THINK

doing. This influences how they *think.* Without those feelings, students find it hard to focus on learning—making connections between calculating the area of a rectangle and painting the fence in the backyard, seeing links between the Industrial Revolution and the origins of pollution. Engagement is also about students *initiating* their own learning, from asking their teacher if they can write an essay on Manchester United to diving into YouTube videos to learn everything about cooking eggplants.* Engagement explains why some kids can come home

* What kids do, feel, think, and initiate corresponds to what researchers call behavioral, emotional, cognitive, and agentic engagement.

with straight As but are actually deeply disengaged in their learning, while others can struggle in class but develop excellent learning skills outside of it.[10] It's also why it's so hard for parents and teachers to know what to do. If they can't see many parts of students' disengagement, they can't do much to counteract it.

Engagement and disengagement can take many different forms, and kids can switch between them with confounding speed. If you have more than one kid, or you're a teacher, you know well that kids approach their learning in many different ways. They can coast, showing up and rushing through assignments without much thought. They can do all the work with determined intensity—but then suddenly burn out. Or they can take initiative to find ways to make things interesting for themselves, emailing a teacher to ask to read a book that is not on the prescribed reading list. A single kid can shift through all of these states in the course of a day depending on whether they click with a teacher or are inspired by an assignment. They can be engaged one minute and disengaged the next, fired up in English and despairing in math. Or they can be disengaged for all of high school and suddenly become engaged in college—or like Kia, they can be a medley: passively engaged in elementary school, deeply engaged in learning music at home with her dad, totally checked out in middle school, and completely dialed in for the second half of high school, supported by her dad, her school, and the Fargo school board.

Learning Environments Drive (Dis)Engagement

Scholars of education have long understood that how people engage in their learning is of immense importance. In ancient Greece, Socrates was perhaps the first known thinker to discuss student engagement. He famously refused to write any of his teachings down, believing the written form was less dynamic, less personal, and less likely to lead people to wisdom.[11] He preferred spirited dialogue with his students: questioning assumptions, exploring possible answers, and contrasting perspectives. He promoted active hands-on learning, famously saying "All

I do is ask questions," and encouraged students to search for the answers for themselves.[12]

By the Middle Ages, however, this form of engaged learning no longer played such a central role in education in the West. The Catholic Church was the guardian of tradition and knowledge in Europe.* The center of learning no longer was in town squares but in monasteries, where monks preserved and passed down knowledge by meticulously copying religious manuscripts word for word and reading them for personal spiritual reflection.[13] Many of today's school practices derive from these monastic traditions: transmitting knowledge rather than challenging or applying it, with writing as the preferred medium. This works for some kids; it does not work for many. Today's learning scientists confirm what the ancient Greeks knew: that most humans need active inquiry and lively discussion to fully engage in their learning.

Today, engagement is most commonly discussed not in schools or universities but by Big Tech. We'd argue these companies have a warped and myopic definition of engagement—more hijacking our kids' attention and monetizing their time and data, less getting them excited about learning new things. Tristan Harris, a former design ethicist at Google turned anti-tech crusader, explains it this way: "When you wake up in the morning, you have certain goals for your life or for your kids. But when you open YouTube, it doesn't know any of those goals, it has one goal: to make you forget your goals and to keep you watching as many YouTube videos as possible."[14] Learning can happen on YouTube and connection can be fostered on Snapchat, but these apps are designed to hook you and keep you, not actually engage you.

In recent years, our understanding of engagement has skyrocketed, and we have come to see just how important it is for learning. At the

* We are sharing the arc of education across the Western world, but there are of course different histories of education across the globe. For example, during the Han dynasty (206 BCE–220 CE) in China, the emperor established a "university" to train a bureaucratic elite to administer the empire, founding perhaps the first high-stakes testing regime in history. Today, alongside other features of globalization, school systems are incredibly similar in their fundamental design in every country of the world.

same time, we've arrived at a deeper understanding of the elements needed for kids to unlock their engagement. We recognize now what seems an obvious pattern: when students disengage, parents and teachers only make things worse by treating them as "problem kids." When disengagement becomes a character flaw, kids know little is expected of them; they try even less and achieve less, and everyone's assumptions are confirmed.

But disengagement is not pathological. It is not a personality trait or an identity. Instead, it is the product of a kid's interaction with their context, their environment. That means by changing a student's environment, we can unlock their motivation and engagement.

One of the best examples of this comes from a famous study published by David Yeager, a psychology professor at the University of Texas at Austin, and colleagues in 2014. It tested two ways to give feedback to middle school students to see which motivated them more. Group one got their essays with detailed comments and an offer to let them incorporate the feedback to try to get a better grade. Group two got the same detailed comments but a different message—"I'm giving you these comments because I have very high expectations and I know that you can reach them." They too could revise the essay to try to get a better grade.[15]

The group that got those nineteen words were twice as likely to revise their essays, and they fixed twice as many mistakes. The kids most likely to do so were the most disengaged students. It was a breakthrough in understanding the importance of how teens receive feedback—often not well—and what power adults have to influence that (the researchers called it "wise feedback"). The study reveals how hard it can be to simultaneously criticize someone's work and motivate them, because criticism can feel devastating to young people's confidence. And it shows the solution is not lowering expectations but keeping them high while offering support to meet them.

"The secret sauce in wise feedback wasn't what was written on the note. It was the dignity and respect afforded to young people at a time when they were vulnerable," Yeager says.[16]

Building Engagement Beyond the Classroom

Parents, in particular, have tremendous influence to create and cultivate environments that unlock their child's engagement. One of the keys is that you *believe* they can grow—their disengagement is not a character flaw but a sign that they need our help. Another key ingredient is how you speak to them, in ways that convey status and respect, not frustration or contempt. Discussion is to adolescent development what cuddles are to infants: foundational to building healthy brains. Through discussion you can deploy your own version of wise feedback, setting (appropriately) high expectations and backing them up with deep support. With it, even kids who seem completely stuck can turn things around.

Disengagement is not an individual act of defiance or protracted plot to annoy you. As we said, it's a response to a specific context, a way to signal something's wrong. What we see—a kid refusing to do work, forever procrastinating, rushing through homework, cheating, always choosing friends over studying—is the outcome of a set of feelings and experiences. It is not the starting point. You may need to deal with the consequences of it—kids need guardrails, and accountability matters. But you also need to look at the why: What's driving the disengagement?

Smartphones, gaming, and social media are often painted as the prime culprits in kids' unhappiness. Tech is a powerful distraction, or a "race to the bottom of the brain stem," as Harris often calls it.[17] Mindless videos and endless group chats are simply easier and more fun than slogging through Shakespeare. But tech is merely exacerbating the underlying problem of disengagement. Teens have been disengaged from learning for longer than smartphones have dominated their lives. The core problem is that most schools do not provide the opportunity for the type of deep, interesting learning students crave. What's changed is that they now have something powerfully entertaining and addictive to fill the gap that school leaves. Tech monopolizes their attention and offers a Xanadu of distractions.

Kids also disengage for reasons related to the core experience of being an adolescent. They don't feel they belong; they feel overwhelmed or have fallen behind and can't see a way out; they face emotional headwinds they don't feel they can manage. In addition, there are far too many kids who face significant obstacles to engaging, from being hungry, to living without a home, to dealing with the death of a caregiver, to trying to survive amid violence. School, a place where they spend a lot of time, often feels anonymous, standardized, and irrelevant. Not being excited about school when the future looks bright is a drag. Not feeling good about school when the future seems grim is soul-deadening—especially when the energy required to compete is so much higher than it used to be.

For Kia, the obsessive scrolling was the symptom, not the problem. It was only when she was given a voice to express her deep frustrations with her learning environment that her engagement started to improve.

The Four Modes of Engagement

To help parents demystify engagement, we developed the **four modes of engagement.*** We created them not to label and categorize young people, but to help parents understand and coach their kids' learning.

Many kids in Passenger mode are bored because school is too easy, while others are overwhelmed because it's too hard. Either way, they check out, engaging *just enough* to get by. When young people are in Achiever mode, they work hard and aim high, tallying their achievements and soaking in the praise of parents and teachers. But too often they fail to figure out what they care about, opting instead to keep feed-

* We used four steps to develop the four modes of engagement. First, we reviewed the myriad ways academics defined and measured student engagement. Second, we examined teachers' perspectives on student engagement through Amy Berry's Continuum of Engagement. Third, we analyzed students' perspectives on their learning through our in-depth discussions with almost one hundred students representing a wide variety of demographic characteristics. Finally, we tested the modes with students, parents, educators, and academics to see if they made sense, resonated with their experiences, and were helpful in understanding children's engagement.

ing the insatiable demands of the system. They become risk averse and worn down. In Resister mode, kids use their voice to signal something isn't right. They disrupt class or avoid school and learning completely. They are often a massive headache for parents and teachers. Finally, kids in Explorer mode do well academically because they are engaged, but they don't rely solely on our scorecards. They are confident because they are doing something they care about. Progress *and* performance matter. They take risks and mess up, collecting critical self-data from both. Explorers do better in college and life because they have developed the mindsets and strategies to navigate their learning independently (which helps when no one is there to tell them what to do).

As we said, these four modes are states, not traits, and change in direct relationship to the conditions of learning in which kids exist. Resisting often becomes Exploring when schools or parents help catalyze change. Teens in Passenger mode often coast at school and thrive at something else, like sports, cooking, or band. Achievers can quickly move to resisting when the challenge gets too great. Kia was in Passenger mode in elementary school (coasting by with little effort, but getting straight As because she could do the work in fifteen minutes). She began resisting in middle school (checking out completely, to the point that it disrupted her learning). When she decided to go to the school board meeting in Fargo to speak out on an issue that she cared about, she was experiencing the first flickers of Explorer mode. (Spoiler alert: Kia's passion and performance started to take off from there.)

Once you have language to understand what you are seeing, you will be able to support your kids as learners, which is to say as humans. When you recognize what mode your kid is in, there are specific strategies and tools you can use to help support them, and ultimately to help them spend as much time as they can in Explorer mode.

Unlocking the Explorer in every child is not about curating the perfect mix of extracurriculars and academics or finding the right tutor. It doesn't require demanding As. It's about being present and having conversations—about the substance of their learning, and the hard things they face, and the weird things that matter to them. It's not about being a teacher, but rather about being a learner.[18] When you focus on growth as much as performance, and on mattering as much as outcomes, it shows. It's the way you react to the small things, life's micro-moments, as well as the big ones, both in school, where so much of their lives take place, and outside, where opportunity abounds. It's how you invest in and model good relationships, which play a starring role in children's flourishing, the definition of which includes not giving up in the face of setbacks and being curious learners. Christina Bethell, a professor of public health at Johns Hopkins University, found that children with strong relational health—strong relationships with parents or neighbors or teachers—are twelve times more likely to flourish than those without it.[19]

"We are the medicine," she says. That doesn't mean we have to do the right thing to save them; it means we have everything we need to help them grow and thrive.

Relational health is income agnostic: Kids who faced no adversity but had low levels of relational health with adults in their lives flourished *less* than kids who experienced significant adversity—from homelessness to exposure to violence to death in the family—but had high levels of relational health.[20]

In other words, you matter a lot.

Agents of Their Own

What Explorers have that the other modes lack is not just engagement but **agency,** the ability to set meaningful goals and marshal resources to meet them. Agency isn't just having a plan, it's being able to plan and execute that plan even if it means overcoming barriers along the way. It requires tapping into internal resources, like effort, and external ones, like experts (teachers, parents, neighbors, pastors).

Agency is critical to learning. It requires knowing yourself—*How do I learn best? What distracts me? What motivates me? What do I care about?* Kids develop it by pursuing goals they care about (improving at math, getting a scholarship, finding a better friend group, improving at basketball). It often requires asking for help along the way—*Who can give me advice on my next step? Who or what can help me overcome the obstacle in front of me?* With agency, kids have fuel to move forward and are less likely to feel oppressed by school. They find ways to make it through difficult periods because they are not afraid to ask for help or try a different route. Adults support kids' agency when they resist the urge to solve the math question, rewrite the essay, or hire a tutor without first doing some simple sleuthing. Instead, they ask respectful, curious questions, such as "What do you think is holding you back in this class? What kind of support would be most helpful for you?" Critically, these parents, coaches, mentors, relatives, and teachers listen to the answers and act on them.

Agency isn't magic. There are always hurdles that appear along any journey that's meaningful. Some may be too significant to overcome. But adolescents, like adults, need to feel some control, to know they have a say in their future. It turns out that this feeling makes all the difference when trying to overcome challenges.

Not all kids have access to agency the same way. When Black and brown students exercise agency in the classroom it can be interpreted as defiance and met with harsher discipline than when their white peers show the same behavior. Teachers and school leaders may not do this intentionally, but unconscious or implicit bias creeps in.[21] This can hurt students. Verone Kennedy, executive director of knowledge management at New York City's Department of Education, is emphatic that Black and brown families want their children to have agency—to be Explorers in learning—just as much as any others. The difference is they face extra burdens such as worrying about how to keep their children safe alongside giving them opportunities to explore.[22]

It is easiest to think of a child's approach to learning placing them somewhere on a two-by-two matrix (see page 18). On the horizontal axis we have engagement in learning. The vertical axis represents agency. We want all kids aimed at the top right corner because when a kid is fully engaged and has agency, they will explore. Researchers call this "agentic engagement."[23] Take away agency and deep engagement, and they are in the bottom left corner, coasting, in Passenger mode. In Resister mode, up on the top left, kids have agency: They are making it clear that they are not happy. Those achieving are engaged—they work hard, getting good grades—but their fear of failure means they often lack the bravery to forge their own path.

THE FOUR MODES OF ENGAGEMENT

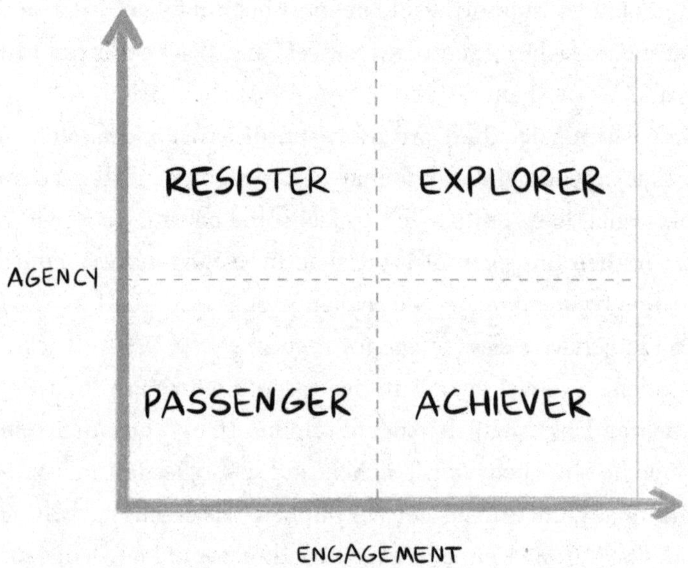

Engagement: what kids think, feel, and do. Agency: what kids initiate.

The Age of Achievement

A major reason kids do not explore is they are not given opportunities to do so. In the introduction we said that less than 10 percent of students have the opportunity to explore in school. But our research shows that number drops to less than 4 percent when we look just at students in middle and high school. For them, only a small handful report a learning environment that regularly lets them:

- Develop their own ideas
- Learn something they are interested in
- Choose how to do their work
- Have a say about what happens to them[24]

Excellent teachers strive to provide these opportunities, but they are often held back by the traditional school system, which is designed to transmit knowledge and to sort and rank. The system directly affects the choices kids and teachers make. Consider some examples: An eleventh grader wants to learn about carbon markets and the green economy but is discouraged because it is not likely to be on the AP Macroeconomics exam. A teen loves baking but knows that won't look good on a college application, so gives it up to found a club to curb social media use. Better to be safe than provocative, to comply with what's expected rather than venture into the unknown.

This can be a very difficult balance for teachers. Teachers need to get a wildly variable group of kids to the same exact place at the same time, defying all logic about human ability and motivation. In a typical classroom teachers face students whose abilities can span three to five grades.

Carole Basile, the dean of Arizona State University, one of the most innovative universities in the United States, tells a story about a five-year-old that highlights the problem. The child, her granddaughter, was desperate to read *Itty Bitty Princess Kitty*. Her teacher told the child she wasn't ready. So Basile took her granddaughter to the library, checked out one of the books, and the two sat to read it together. Her granddaughter struggled with a few words but managed most of it. By the third time through, not only had her granddaughter learned the tricky words, but she was over the moon to have mastered the book. She had experienced success reading something hard and wanted to do more.

When Basile told us this story, she noted that many of us were probably thinking *what a terrible teacher* stifling her granddaughter's ambitions. But when Basile's daughter asked the teacher why she had discouraged the text, the teacher was honest. The issue wasn't the girl's reading level—it was that the teacher couldn't sit and help her read that book. There were too many other kids in the class with too many needs, and she didn't want the girl to get frustrated.

"This job is not humanly possible," Basile said. "This structure—one teacher, one classroom—it's a model that has to change."

There are subtle and effective ways to improve classrooms within the system we have (we highlight those later). But the unfortunate truth is that today most schools are not designed to help all children grow and thrive and meet their potential. As education grew from one-room schoolhouses in the early 1800s to a public system for all, a key function of schools was selecting those who should go on to the already long-established universities. Today, at their core, most schools still are designed to produce education winners and losers, with less advantaged kids too often losing out.

As schools expanded access—a good thing that has driven up income and skills for many—more kids entered the race to be sorted and ranked, the hoops to jump through got higher, and more were created. A lot of kids worked harder to get through each one—better grades, higher SAT/ACT scores, more extracurriculars, more competitive scholarships.[25] Admissions rates dropped by 45 percent between 2006 and 2018 at the top fifty most competitive US colleges. At the most elite ten, the figure plummeted from 16 percent to as low as 3 percent.[26] We call this decades-long educational arms race the **Age of Achievement.** Because the hoops entailed a narrow set of goals, the Age of Achievement demanded kids work harder to meet each one. Stamina was a key ingredient. The system was simply not designed for individual growth or exploration.

This is a terrible shame for the lives of the kids around us.

Teen brains undergo an ambitious and exciting renovation process fueled by learning. In childhood, networks of the brain become specialized at specific tasks. In adolescence these networks become more intricately wired together: the patterns of connectivity are crucial for managing increasingly complex tasks and adapting to changing environments. Along with these changes, they are increasingly able to use their brain to evaluate their own thinking, rather than just doing things. Brains develop as they are used.

Just like pregnant women crave what their bodies need, teens crave what their brains need during this epic rewiring. And what teens seek is respect. Hormones and neurological changes make them particularly averse to shame, criticism, and social pain and highly motivated to find ways to gain admiration and praise, what one academic calls social success. They experience a surge in sensation seeking, which many link to recklessness but which better explains why falling in love for the first time feels so thrilling or having a fight with your best friend feels so devastating.

Emotions are amped up in ways that may present as unreasonable to us adults until we consider the formidable developmental challenges adolescents face: separating from their caregivers, finding a mate, and living independently. To gain the skills to do this, they scan the savanna, look for danger—especially as it relates to their status—and seek ways to contribute. To secure their place in society, they seek meaningful experiences that win them respect. The key is, we cannot give that respect to them; they have to earn it. Cultural anthropologists call the process of gaining that status "earned prestige."[27]

As the *Age of Achievement* increasingly focused on academic proficiency, broader opportunities to earn that prestige were sacrificed. A false bargain emerged: Kids must choose between exploring or mastering academic skills. But it is the very act of exploration that engages students and makes them better thinkers. Exploration fuels the executive control network (ECN) of the brain, or the taskmaster network, which is rapidly developing in adolescence. Primed to evaluate and take in everything—emotional, environmental, practical—its data collection helps the ECN get better connected to the rest of the brain. Meanwhile the default mode network (DMN) is also developing. It is relevant to the reflective, meaning-making processes of the brain that allow young people to look at the bigger picture and be creative. If teens don't explore when they are most primed to do so, fewer connections are forged. That doesn't mean it can't happen later; brains are malleable and can grow and change. But adolescence is a period that shapes motivations. It is why our memories from middle and high school are so powerful, from sitting alone at lunch to being authentically recognized by a teacher you love.

The obsession with academics at the cost of everything else is the equivalent of training your left leg to get stronger for soccer and ignoring your right one. You need both legs working together in coordinated ways to play well. When we ask kids to ingest more content by remembering and analyzing it, harking back to the transmission approach to education, it crowds out time to reflect on why it's important in the first place. They miss out on exploring ways that knowledge can be used to solve today's problems, or create new solutions through dialogue and debate rather than just getting the right answers—all the skills Socrates helped his students develop. Kids want experiences and opportunities to contribute, to be social, and to solve problems. Instead, we ask them to study more so that we can rank and sort them.

The most common response we parents get to all this is "I'm bored." Developmentally, it's natural that teens feel so bored. With puberty comes a craving for high-intensity and novel experiences. School, which is repetitive, seated, and predictable, is not this. But boredom is more than a lack of stimulation. It's also a crisis of agency. Eager for real experiences and unable to make them happen, kids shut down. Academics who study boredom (yes, these people exist) define it as "the aversive state of wanting, but being unable, to engage in satisfying activity."[28] The problem is not nothing-to-do; it's feeling helpless to change things. They lack agency to move and explore in directions that make sense to them. The opposite of boredom is not being busy; it's being interested.

The Age of Agency

The solution to kids' boredom is not to ask kids to work harder or jump higher. It's to give them some choice over how they spend their days—in and out of school. It's building the self-awareness and skills to pick the goals that matter to them. This is the **Age of Agency**: not just jumping through pre-set hoops, but also knowing the hoops that matter and investing accordingly. In it, students have more of a say about what they learn, how they learn it, and how they demonstrate mastery of it. This requires a better understanding of what successful learning looks like.

You are ground zero of how broad or narrow that definition will be. Math is important. Math and the agency to know what you want to do with it is twenty-first-century gold.

This means shifting from a narrow focus on easy-to-measure outcomes to a broader menu of learning experiences for young people. As one education expert often warns, if we are not careful, we will educate "second-class robots and not first-class humans."[29] With more engaging opportunities to contribute in their classrooms and beyond the walls of their schools, parents and teachers can help develop not just academic skills, but all-important human ones, like empathy, communication, and collaborative problem solving. This will not detract from kids thriving in the transition between the ages of achievement and agency; it will make them stand out.[30]

A lot of this requires education systems to change. But a huge amount of it requires parents to change, supporting growth and learning and not just outcomes and grades. For a time, you help shape your kids' values and habits. Is learning a game to be played or a value that underpins a good life?

Signs of the emerging Age of Agency are everywhere. In the 1970s, employers in the United States regularly stated that the top three skills they were looking for were reading, writing, and arithmetic.[31] Schools at the time did their part, delivering at scale instruction to the country's young people in all three. But the world has changed considerably. In a recent global survey of employers, the skills they most value today include analytical and creative thinking, resilience and flexibility, motivation and self-awareness, curiosity and lifelong learning.[32]

For decades, the Age of Agency has been embodied in alternative school models on the margins of education systems: from Montessori to EL Education schools. But this new era is now quickly moving to the center of education systems. During 2023, in the space of a year, some of the most influential architects of modern schooling announced some major refurbishment plans. In the spring, the Carnegie Foundation for Teaching and Learning teamed up with the Educational Testing Service (ETS), one of the largest testing companies in the United States, to announce that it would begin to assess, through more than just tests, a wider range of skills, including critical thinking, communication, and creativity. In addition to assessing knowledge, they will find ways to measure progress in developing "underlying skills that are actually going to have relevance for the world of work and in society," said Amit Sevak, the CEO of the ETS.[33]

Over at the College Board, which administers the SAT and the Advanced Placement tests, CEO David Coleman called attention to the "quiet crisis" of boredom in American classrooms. Education needs a better invitation to students to *want to* participate in learning. "I think what we need to do is deeply change—what we cover, and how we do it," said Coleman. It has created new interdisciplinary tests and classes, like AP Seminar, which lets students pursue independent projects in subjects they are interested in.[34]

These changes may seem incremental; they are not. "Change assessment, you change teaching," Randi Weingarten, the head of the American Federation of Teachers, told us.[35] If you assess a broad range of skills and not just a narrow set of academic markers, you get a richer picture of what a kid can do, and over time, hopefully, that kid develops a broader sense of what they want to do.

In the Age of Agency, kids will need to rely on more than just academic heft. They will need self-awareness, and the ability to generate new ideas, build off old ones, and communicate their ideas effectively.

In other words, they will need to be creative and self-driven. Like all skills, kids aren't born with these Explorer skills; they develop them through practice. If we don't create places and spaces for them to train, the muscles will atrophy.

Kia was lucky to have a school that asked her what she thought about learning. Thanks to creative teachers who began reflecting on ways to boost engagement through seminars with the local university and work with Transcend, a nonprofit that works with schools to support student agency, the school did more than ask students for their input. It began a trial with six-week studios, self-directed courses that students pick but that must align with core subjects (science, math, English, social studies) and state standards. In one studio, Kia produced a podcast on culture and mythology and the role of storytelling, which fulfilled English and social studies requirements. In another, fulfilling history and science requirements, she designed an elaborate escape room, with a game based on the assassination of a president. She researched the assassinations or attempted assassinations of John F. Kennedy, Abraham Lincoln, and Ronald Reagan. Clues involved anatomical files explaining how the bullet went through the body. The studios were perfect for her. Her grades soared and her interest in her own learning skyrocketed.

"I am learning something I am interested in," she said. "Compare that to eighth-grade me, who would not do my algebra homework."

The real test came in her senior year, when she enrolled in four traditional dual-credit classes, including in two subjects she used to hate: history and math. She found she loved both because she had figured out how she learned best and how to motivate herself. "The studios rewired something in the way that I treat tasks that I have to do," she told us, weeks away from graduation. Now whenever she has a problem or task, she asks herself, *How can I make this enjoyable?* She doesn't necessarily want to do it. "It sucks," she says. "But I know how to make myself like it now."

What exactly had she learned in the studios that magically made boring material fascinating? "I learned that you can learn anything. You just have to know how you work and how to teach yourself. And that was that skill that I did not have."

In sum: Kia developed the skills and mindsets of an Explorer.

In math, her main struggle is not the problem sets; it's getting started. She learned she loves teaching other people, so she waits until others are struggling and swoops in to help, which motivates her to get the work done. In history, quirky interests bring old, dead presidents to life. She is currently writing a massive paper on the birth of bureaucracy under Harry Truman's administration—a topic she refers to as "fascinating." It is powerful evidence that some choice in learning is not an add-on but necessary for building Explorer muscles.

When you ask Kia what made the biggest difference, she talks about her studios and connecting with her teachers in her college-level courses. But she also mentions her dad, who always encouraged her to be curious, pushed her to think about things, stuck with her when things got hard, and made sure she grabbed every opportunity she could.

"He answers every question I give him with a genuine response," she told us, pride in her gaze. Why water towers are round. Why car engines click and hiss when they cool down. Why she needs to know the word *pedagogy* if she's giving a presentation on how learning in school needs to change.

"No matter how stupid the question," she says. "Because of the way he encourages me, I'm still asking those questions."

2

Passenger

Quietly Quitting

During middle school, Mateo couldn't stop poking other kids. He'd be sitting in class, listening to the teacher; then, without even realizing it, he'd find himself stretching out his arm and poking his friend in the back. He was a sociable kid, and not being able to talk in class bugged him. He'd sneak his phone under the table, text his friends, and then pass them a note. There was always so much to discuss. "No matter where you send me, I will find conversation with somebody," he tells us.

His teachers would have to shush him a lot, but he didn't get into serious trouble. He wasn't trying to be disruptive or mean-spirited. It's just that he was desperate for something, *anything,* interesting to happen.

Though talkative, Mateo appeared to be a good student in many ways. He had straight As and played volleyball. He took theater for his elective and was active in drama club, rehearsing songs with his cast-mates during recess. He took all the advanced classes his school offered: prealgebra in seventh grade and algebra and geometry in eighth. But he found all of them easy. In elementary school, he had come home with an honor roll award and told his parents they had to buy him ice cream as a reward, because that's what other kids' parents did. They did, even though they didn't really understand why—they had moved to Providence, Rhode Island, from the Dominican Republic when Mateo was four and didn't speak much English. His parents didn't pressure him by demanding perfect grades, but they made it clear they expected him to do well because they needed him to succeed in the United States. He was the only one of their three boys who showed interest in school. He helped them navigate everything, from calculating how to pay their bills to translating anything they needed into Spanish.

Despite his good grades, Mateo was deeply disengaged. When the teacher introduced a new unit with new concepts and material, he paid attention only for the first few minutes. He usually got it right away. Then, for the rest of the lesson, Mateo's active mind would search for something to do. He would pull out the homework due in his next class and finish it. Once that was done, he would lean over and whisper a joke to the student next to him, or flash his winning smile at a peer across the aisle. In geometry class, his teacher rewarded extra credit points for each task completed in an online math program you could do at home. Mateo quickly calculated that he could pass the class with extra credit points alone. He never did a single geometry homework assignment. He just raced through the online math program every evening. He still received an A. "I didn't really understand it," he says now. Why would the teacher make it so easy to *not* do the work? All Mateo had to do was master the art of coasting.

As seventh grade wore on, poking classmates wasn't enough to keep his attention. One day, he and his friends decided not to go back into class after recess. They went to the lunchroom instead. They felt like rebels, walking quickly in the hallway and laughing when no one noticed. The next week, they tried it again. Soon they were skipping classes two to three times a week.

Mateo's grades never slipped—his teachers spent so much time reviewing material, he had no problem keeping up. But Mateo's parents started getting regular calls home from the teachers whose classes he skipped. Mateo told them the school was wrong. "I was there," he would tell them. "I don't know what that teacher is talking about." Mateo's parents didn't speak enough English to get the full story from the teacher. Plus, his good grades bought him cover. "They didn't know better but to believe me," he says.

Mateo and his friends decided to take it up a notch. One morning, instead of going to school, they settled themselves on the black swings of the playground next door. They stayed there kicking the brown wood chips covering the ground and talking until about 1 P.M., when they got hungry and tried to sneak back into school for lunch. But not before a teacher looked out her window and caught them. "This time, I did get in trouble," he says.

Mateo realized he was disappointing his parents, which felt terrible. Money was especially tight at home, as his grandmother was sick and needed financial support. Even still, his parents had always been there for him, sacrificed for him. When he wanted to go to the movies with his friends, they always found a way to put together twenty dollars for him. He was beginning to understand what it meant to have his family need him to be successful. His friends, on the other hand, never studied and lacked ambition. He only went along with them because he had nothing else to do—he preferred being bored on the playground to being bored in class.

Gradually, in eighth grade, he started to spend more time alone, isolating himself, unhappy and unmotivated. He stopped hanging out with his friends, so he didn't have a group to socialize with in the lunchroom or at recess. "I felt like a loner," he says. That year, the only person Mateo was having substantive conversations with was his drama teacher, who had initially disliked Mateo—he was always goofing off in class—but had come to see he would put in effort if someone in school showed they cared about him. At the time, she seemed the only one.

Passengers: Coasting in Neutral

Mateo looked engaged to most people around him, at least until he started skipping school. He was in drama club, getting straight As, and, until eighth grade, surrounded by friends. He was **behaviorally engaged.** It's what kids everywhere do every day—what teachers ask of them.

But below the surface, Mateo was deeply disengaged. He thought school was a waste of time, nothing more than busywork. He didn't think it was important or valuable. He lacked **emotional engagement** with what he was being asked to do every day.

Finally, Mateo didn't really process much of what was happening in school because he wasn't challenged. Schoolwork was easy and rarely sparked his interest. His goal wasn't to find connections between his learning and his life. His goal was to find the shortest route to good grades, the most efficient hack to what teachers were asking of him. He wasn't **cognitively engaged** in his schoolwork.

In other words, for most of middle school, Mateo was in Passenger mode—coasting along in neutral and unwilling to put the car in gear. Passenger mode is characterized by bare-minimum, surface-level engagement. Kids in this mode go through the motions. They turn up, do their homework—though usually not well—and appear happy to just skate by. They are complying, which means they are behaviorally engaged (until, like Mateo, they start skipping school). But they aren't invested in what they're learning, nor are they interested in trying to make sense of it, meaning they are not emotionally or cognitively engaged. For these kids, the general reaction to school is "Meh." They are passive participants in their education. They may have a select few classes or activities that get them really jazzed, while others completely shut them down.

Some signs your kid is in Passenger mode:

- They comply with school requirements but never do more than what is asked of them.
- They focus on the minimum requirements of assignments and not the content.

- They show little interest in what they are learning about (or why).
- They spend more time finding shortcuts than on actually learning.
- They race through homework with no interest in doing it well or checking it.
- They regularly procrastinate doing homework or school assignments. Most kids procrastinate some (as do most adults), but if it is every night, do you know why? Do they not know how to get started? Do they feel lost? Or are they simply bored by it?
- They love going to school to see their friends but dislike classes.
- They are distracted by family problems (parents going through a divorce or losing their job), love (a new relationship beginning or an old one ending), or issues with friends (being cut out of an activity, being canceled online, fighting with a best friend), any of which may shift their attention away from schoolwork.
- They declare everything "boring."
- They have endless energy for *Fortnite* but not one bit left for science.
- They frequently use "fine" to answer the question "How was your day?"

Passenger mode is everywhere. As we mentioned in the Introduction, according to our student survey, it is the most common mode of engagement, with almost 50 percent of young people from sixth to twelfth grade saying their learning experiences at school inspire coasting.[1] Teachers and parents see it all the time, but they often don't consider it a problem. That's because kids in Passenger mode are not the "problem kids" who require significant time and attention from adults around them. Nor are they the go-getter, high achieving kids you will meet in chapter 3, who also soak up (positive) time and attention. Their behavioral engagement masks a deep-rooted emotional and cognitive disengagement. Meanwhile, parents may see the apathy but too often assume it's normal or will pass. *Things will surely turn around,* they tell themselves. There are no serious problems, so it seems there are no problems at all.

But there are real risks for kids staying in Passenger mode too long.[2] While some coasting can be strategic, allowing teens to allocate their resources and focus their energy on the things they care about rather than the things they don't, too much surface-level learning means Passengers develop poor learning habits and miss out on the myriad benefits that come from digging in and taking risks with their learning. According to Johnmarshall Reeve, a professor at Australian Catholic University who has been researching student engagement for the last twenty years, students in this mode are "wasting their time developmentally" when it comes to building good learning skills.[3]

Mateo was delivering good grades, rarely getting into serious trouble, starring in the school play, and saying hi to peers in the hallways. Even when he missed school, no one worried too much. His grades—the number one signal parents rely on to gauge whether students are succeeding in school—didn't tell the full engagement story.

But we *should* worry about Mateo. The warning signs were clear to those paying attention: Mateo was losing interest in school. Sometimes, when that apathy intensifies, it becomes an identity. At that point it becomes much harder to turn around.

The Zone of Proximal Development

"Bored" is the go-to description for students in Passenger mode. Daren Dickson, head of culture at Valor Collegiate Academies in Nashville, Tennessee, says the number one thing disengaged kids tell him is "'I'm just bored' or 'It's so boring.' 'The subjects are boring.'"[4]

When kids say they are bored or school is boring, it can mean a lot of different things. They can be checking out because of fear of failure, because of frustration with low expectations, because of perceived pointlessness. "It's boring" could simply mean they don't see the point of what they are studying in school. They know generative AI can write most papers, do most math assignments, and outdo them on the SAT or ACT. So why *not* spend time doing things that are more fun?

One of the most common reasons kids say they're bored is that they find school too easy—like Mateo. But they can also say they're bored if they find school too hard: calculus may seem boring to a fifth grader—because a fifth grader doesn't have the skills or development to succeed at it—but fascinating to a high school student. When it's too hard to keep up, many disengage.

This is because they are not in their **zone of proximal development** (ZPD). Introduced by Soviet psychologist Lev Vygotsky in the 1920s, the ZPD is the sweet spot for learning: where a student does not find it so easy that they lose interest and not so difficult that they give up. Instead, it is just challenging enough that with the right support from teachers, peers, or technology, they can dramatically accelerate their learning. Vygotsky was one of education's most influential thinkers for his work uncovering how interactive learning really is, and the critical role guidance plays in learning. Unlike psychologists of the day who embraced the idea of learning through individual exploration or discovery, Vygotsky emphasized how much we learn in interactions with others. Learning is social. We learn most when we are stretched to reach a goal but also have support to get there, when something is challenging but achievable.[5]

Key to that stretching is something called *scaffolding.* In construction, a temporary scaffold holds a building up until it is structurally sound, at which point it can be taken away. Similarly, when a teacher explains persuasive writing to a child, she doesn't just say, "Try it!" She tests out what the learner knows. She explains the goals of persuasion. She uses sample essays to show how it's done. She takes apart and introduces the components: thesis statement, supporting arguments, evidence, and counterarguments. She brainstorms ideas and then asks the student to try to develop a thesis statement. The two discuss strategies to improve it. They talk about organizing ideas. The teacher offers support until she sees the student gaining proficiency, at which point she allows the student to work more independently.

The scaffolding is key. It can be teachers, parents, peers, or sometimes even YouTube and AI: anything that is more knowledgeable than the learner and can help them reach greater understanding. All kids are like Goldilocks: They need to find their learning sweet spot, or ZPD. For this, they need help.

In the United States, a shocking amount of time in school is spent on mastering basic information and skills, which leaves armies of kids like Mateo way below their ZPD. A well-respected survey of 1,600 tasks at six middle schools found that only 4 percent of tasks asked students to operate at high levels of complexity. Conversely, 85 percent asked them to recall basic information or apply basic skills.[6] The opposite is also a problem. Naturally, some kids need more support than others. Too often a kid struggles to master a concept before the teacher moves on, leaving him stuck trying to work above his ZPD. Learning builds on itself; when kids don't master fractions before they start multiplying and dividing them, they easily become overwhelmed and many check out. What they need are ways—learning strategies—to help break things down, organize the content, and catch up. (Good news: We offer guidance on building these in chapter 7.)

In fairness to teachers, who know all about the ZPD and use it to design lesson plans and tests, it is a monumentally hard task to help every student learn within their ZPD. It is not something teachers can measure at the beginning of the year and be done with it. A lot of learning and growth is subtle, making it hard to identify when students' skills vary so widely, with multiple grade levels represented in many classrooms. What we ask of teachers would be like asking a doctor to see her patients in groups of thirty, diagnose their individual problems within forty-five minutes, and then prescribe effective, personalized treatment plans that constantly evolve in real time as each patient's health changes.

So teachers do their best, trying to help those who are behind by reviewing material but also trying to get through required concepts and state standards for each grade. This leaves lots of kids bored to tears, hanging out below their ZPD, while others are completely lost, stuck above it. The great promise of AI applied to learning—one that has not yet been realized at any scale—is that the AI will help identify where each student is and provide support and challenges within their own personal ZPD. This will allow kids to learn more than they would in a classroom where teachers have to navigate multiple ability levels.*

A teen's ability to engage in learning and operate in their ZPD is for any given class or day shaped by a myriad of factors. Did they have enough to eat before coming to school to learn? Students who are hungry, as an unconscionably high number are in the United States, will have a hard time learning that day. Do they have a place to live or are they stressed because their family has recently lost their home? Do they feel safe at school? Kids who worry about bullying use much of their focus and attention to avoid abuse, leaving little to absorb what they are being taught. Do their natural abilities predispose them to better understanding the lesson, placing them ahead of many other students? Do they learn differently from the average student? Do children with learning differences have the specific supports they need to get into the zone? Do they have parents or other adults at home supporting their approach to learning? The majority of what influences children's skill and ability is their experiences and relationships in life.** What are those experiences and relationships?

Often students can move from above to below their ZPD all in the same day depending on the class. Take the case of Stella, whom you will

---

* To date, technology has not radically transformed schools in a way that significantly improves learning. There are notable exceptions, such as inclusive technology helping dyslexics read and write in school; virtual reality experiences boosting first-year college students' active learning experiences and test results in introduction to biology courses, and adaptive learning literacy programs helping children learn to read in overcrowded classrooms in Malawi.

** And how these relationships and experiences regulate gene expression.

meet again in subsequent chapters as she traverses through the modes. A senior in her competitive public high school in Philadelphia, Stella has very fond memories of her early education. Her white, middle-class parents opted for the progressive elementary school in their neighborhood. From kindergarten through sixth grade, Stella recalls creative activities, learning experiences that she found meaningful, and teachers who were accepting and supportive. Even though she struggled with spelling and writing, she was hellbent on becoming a journalist. Talking to Stella now, it's easy to see all of the ways the profession would suit her: She's articulate, insightful, and intensely curious, and her eyes light up whenever she says something funny, which is often. But in middle school, she began to feel overwhelmed by English. The work suddenly seemed redundant, and she felt unable to connect with the lessons. Her essays started to come back to her marked in red, but she didn't have any sense of how to improve them. Ever since then, knowing she won't understand it anyway, she hasn't tried much, and she finds English class overwhelming and boring. She's been stuck above her ZPD in English and ended up squarely in Passenger mode in the class.

"It doesn't feel like you're learning anything," she says, exasperation spilling out in her voice. "You're reading a book to answer questions that we either (a) don't go over or (b) we just turn them in for you to tell me they're all wrong. And we move on. And by the time we get them back, we're so far away from the passage that I forget what I read and I'm like, 'I don't know what that's about.'"

Stella doesn't feel very capable. She wishes she could have a refresher on writing—she insists she hasn't learned much since fifth grade, when she was meant to master the essay. But she doesn't know how to ask for help on such a fundamental skill. She's meant to know how to write by now, right?

She also feels her teacher doesn't have much faith in her. Because Stella knows she expects little of her, she satisfies that low expectation regularly, handing in suboptimal work. She told us about one essay that had "no thesis and BS evidence." Stella was as annoyed that she didn't get marked down for the lack of thesis as she was irritated that her teacher actually bought her BS evidence. Was the teacher even paying attention?

Stella regularly shops online during class, or texts her longtime girlfriend. She reads the book on her own at home and cuts corners where possible, like cheating on the questions assigned as homework. Clearly Stella isn't always doing her best work. But when she has tried, and failed, she hasn't received feedback that makes her believe she can improve or gives her an incentive to do so. She's fed up, convinced English is not her subject.

In math class, Stella has the opposite problem. She's in her second year with the same teacher, and she's figured out how to get good grades. The teacher has specific routines, ways of assigning homework, and expectations for quizzes and tests that make sense to Stella.

The problem is that many other kids in her class are struggling with math. A lot of times, Stella's math teacher frequently takes the time to explain things to her peers that Stella already knows. Stella is empathetic—she knows what it is like to not to understand a subject. But it does mean she is below her ZPD, not being challenged given her skill level, and bored. So Stella sits in the back of the class and does the homework for the next day, which she finishes quickly. That usually leaves her twenty minutes to burn. She unlocks her phone and spends the rest of the class scrolling on social media.

Stella says parents should believe their kids when they say they did nothing in school. Some days "we sit in class all day doing nothing, they ask nothing of us." Her parents have a hard time believing that is true. Maybe they were never asked to do nothing in school when they were young. But she recently skipped school the last four Fridays and missed—wait for it—nothing at all.

In English, Stella is above her ZPD and overwhelmed. In math, she's below her ZPD and bored to tears. Stella shows us clearly how a teen can be *both* bored and overwhelmed, often all before 10 A.M. This makes Passengers possibly the most rational learners we have: They are responding to an under- or overwhelming environment by doing what they have control over. They check out.

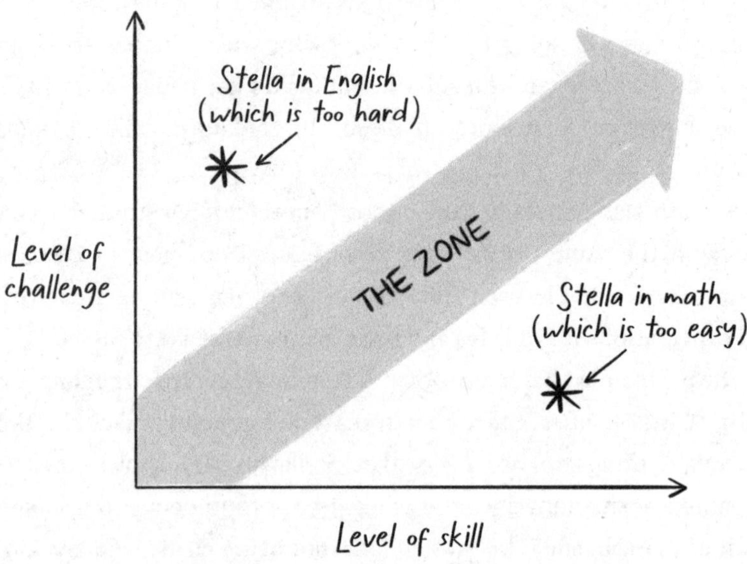

Source: L. S. Vygotsky, *Mind in Society: The Development of Higher Psychological Processes* (London: Harvard University Press, 1978).

Getting into the Zone Can Be Tricky When Kids Have Learning Differences or are Neurodivergent

Getting into the zone is hard for any kid. For those with learning differences, it can feel Herculean, with school becoming deeply demotivating. For example, children with dyslexia usually excel at pattern recognition but struggle to learn to read, especially if they are taught the alphabet right alongside neurotypical students. We spoke to several students with dyslexia who thought they were stupid because they couldn't master what other students so easily picked up. Before they were diagnosed, they decided it wasn't worth trying (better to not try than feel dumb). But once they were diagnosed and received specialized supports, including learning their letters in a different order (e.g., *t, d,* and *n* all go together because they require the tongue to touch the roof of the mouth), they could succeed in school and also lean into their strengths. One student reminded us that half of all self-made millionaires have dyslexia.[7]

Adolescents who are neurodivergent often need specialized supports and creative solutions to get into the zone. Take the case of Emily. She was always a precocious child, an early talker who loved to chat. She's still bubbly today and eager to share her thoughts with others. Sometimes she jumps up to draw on a whiteboard to illustrate her point, her long blond hair flowing behind her. Her energy draws us in. We imagine her in the future leading a team doing important things in the world.

But for many years, Emily struggled with school. She lives in Berkeley, California, with well-off parents who initially enrolled her in their community's bilingual, public Montessori charter school. She could not find her groove. She was always interested in what every other kid was doing even though she was meant to be focusing on her own independent work. Her parents switched her to their local neighborhood public school, where she started to get in trouble for interrupting class. She had her own take on the world and sometimes struggled to communicate it. One year she showed up on her first day wearing pointed fairy ears. She is social and wants to connect with others but finds it difficult to read people, which can be exhausting in school, where reading the emotions of so many kids consumes a lot of brain power. She struggled mightily with memorizing multiplication tables. Her father, James, would try to help her. "You don't know how to explain it in a way that I understand it!" she would tell him through tears. Emily was their first child, so they didn't know how school worked. Should they be worried?

Her parents decided to get her tested to understand why she was struggling. In fifth grade she was diagnosed with level 1 autism spectrum disorder, the mildest form.[8] It gave Emily and her family a new perspective on why she was struggling and what support she needed to get into her ZPD.

Neurodivergence is not an abnormality. It is part of the beautiful diversity that makes up the human race.[9] In fact, what we diagnose today as neurodivergent—children such as Emily with autism—reflects more what we value in our society than anything else. Schools are traditionally institutions that cater to the middle, which can make learning hard for those on either end of the spectrum in any given dimension, be it autism, ADHD, synesthesia, or sensory processing differences. Often neurodivergent children begin to feel frustrated, embarrassed, and angry, which causes them to disengage. If their needs go undetected, they may develop a learner identity built on the premise that school is not for them.[10] Alexander the Great, who historians note likely had ADHD from the accounts of his behavior, was lionized for his indefatigable energy, drive, and focus. By age thirty, he had built one of the largest empires in history. Today, he would have most certainly been told off for not sitting still in class.

When given the supports at school and at home, neurodivergent kids can thrive.* The fact that they are wired in a way that makes traditional school hard may also make them exceptionally good at some things. Creativity, spotting patterns, intense focus, keen powers of observation, visual-spatial thinking, incredible memory, and novel problem-solving are some of the many skills associated with kids who have ADHD, ASD, and dyslexia. This is why organizations such as NASA and various US national security departments regularly recruit neurodivergent people.[11] Parents have an important role to play in helping neurodivergent kids learn well, from advocating for evaluation and supports to recognizing both the difficulties their kids face and the strengths they have. This even includes getting behind wild solutions their kids may propose.

When Emily was in fifth grade, every time her teacher asked the class to work independently, she couldn't do it. It wasn't that she struggled to understand the assignment—it was the ASD. There was so much to look at! The big blue-and-white carpet next to a shelf of books;

* This is not to say it is easy, or that any parent will automatically know what to do.

red, purple, and orange thinking strategy posters on the wall; tables in the middle of the room; boxes of markers and crayons and papers by the teacher's table. "You have a race-car brain and everything is just whizzing by and you just need a place to stop and look around," Emily explained to us.

One day that year, after she'd been struggling to focus, Emily's gaze landed on the floor cabinets lining the left-hand side of the classroom. They were filled with art supplies, books, pens, and snacks. The one under the sink was mostly empty. Emily decided she could fit inside. In fact, it seemed perfect. A place that would allow the world to stop.

She approached her teacher, Mrs. Kennedy, with an unusual idea. What about making the cabinet under the sink her place to go when she needed to focus? Mrs. Kennedy was pretty sure that the principal of her traditional public school would not approve. *A student studying in the cabinet under the sink? It seemed so Harry Potter but not in a good way.* But more than anything, Mrs. Kennedy wanted Emily to be able to succeed. Plus, the other options Emily had tried before—a desk at the back of the class, sitting in the hallway—hadn't worked. She told Emily she was game to try it as long as she kept the cabinet door cracked open. The message to Emily? We all support you.

Mrs. Kennedy let Emily's parents' know the plan, and they got behind it. Then she did what most are unlikely to: She cleaned out the cabinet under the sink and bought a little battery-powered light and stuck it on the inside of the cabinet wall. Emily loved it. She would take her work into the cabinet and the buzz of the classroom would become muffled. "It would be like, you're alone. You can finally take a deep breath," she explained. "And when I was done, I would just walk out of the cabinet."

Boys Struggling to Get into the Zone

In nationally representative surveys, boys are consistently a bit more disengaged in school than girls.[12] As we interviewed students for this book, we often noted that it was much easier to find boys than girls who spent much of their time operating in Passenger mode. The gendered nature of disengagement shows up in the disparity between boys' and girls' grades. In 2019, the United States, the most common high school GPA of boys is 3.00 and of girls is 3.23.[13] American boys are not the only ones falling behind. Across the United States and in more than eighty other countries, boys are 50 percent more likely than girls to get a failing grade in math, reading, or science, three core classes in virtually any high school around the world.[14] Girls are graduating from college at far higher rates: In 2019, there was a 15 percentage point gap between boys and girls receiving a bachelor's degree.[15]

What we heard from Thomas, a fifteen-year-old boy from Boston, was similar to stories we heard from many boys and their parents. Thomas loved his weekends, hanging out with his friends and playing soccer. But when Sunday afternoon would rolled around, he always felt slightly sick to his stomach. Mr. White's seventh-grade Latin class was one major source of the problem. Mr. White would cold-call on the students with questions about the latest homework assignments. Every other kid seemed to perk up when they were called on and reply quickly with the answer. Not Thomas. When Mr. White called on him, he would freeze up. "I was the dumbest person in the class," he said. He was failing. He was also the new kid. He had transferred to the small, academically rigorous private school in the middle of middle school. All the other kids had already taken Latin for a year.

But while Thomas was bombing Latin, he was a star in the school's sports teams. His blue eyes sparkled every time he talked about Lionel Messi or Kylian Mbappé. Thomas operated in Passenger mode most of the time. Often this was because he struggled to get into his ZPD. He had ADHD and found it hard to concentrate on homework in the evening when his medicine wore off. He would procrastinate a lot, even though he didn't want to. Plus, he hadn't been taught *how* to study, which made it hard to master content he found confusing. It seemed easier to do the minimum to get by, and a lot more fun to focus on sports and friends.

We heard versions of Thomas's story so many times: *Why can't I get my son to do his homework? Why doesn't he care more?* Or from the kids: *Why can't my parents just lay off the nagging?!*

One explanation for this comes from biology. In *Of Boys and Men: Why the Modern Male Is Struggling, Why It Matters, and What to Do About It,* Richard Reeves, president of the American Institute for Boys and Men, argues for holding boys back one year when they start school. With boys' prefrontal cortex—the air traffic controller of the brain—developing about two years later than that of girls, he argues, adolescent boys don't have the level of "impulse control, planning, [and] future orientation" that girls do.[16] This becomes especially detrimental when they start high school and need to buckle down, study more, and play less. Girls are simply at an advantage due to the average timing of their natural brain development.

There's a difference between holding boys back at the onset of their education versus having them repeat a year because of low performance once they've started. Studies suggest that holding kids back doesn't have significant short-term academic benefits and hinders long-term outcomes like graduation rates and college enrollment.[17] Students who have to repeat grades often feel ashamed; the repeated material just makes school more boring and does little to boost their engagement.

Other forces are also at play. "Boys don't gain social status from achieving academically," says Jordan Shapiro, a professor at Temple University.[18] Remember, adolescence is a time of "wanting to stand out and wanting to fit in."[19] Teens are beginning to forge their own identity by separating from their parents, looking for unique ways to contribute to their tribe (peer group). When boys struggle in class, they look for other ways to distinguish themselves. Like Thomas, they search for an identity that makes them stand out. Not trying and not caring—or pretending to not care—can start off as a way to look cool but can soon become a self-fulfilling prophecy. As one ninth-grade boy we spoke to said, "In eighth grade, I pretended I didn't know what was going on. But now I really don't know what's happening in school." The more students don't try, the farther behind they fall, and the more they find other ways to gain social status.

Thomas's mother has tried everything she can think of to help her son boost his academic performance: extra tutoring, locking his iPhone from six at night to six in the morning, reaching out to his school to request assistance, sitting next to him when he studies. But mainly, she says, she wants him to know that it takes effort to succeed. "I keep telling him that all his friends who get good grades are only pretending like they don't study," she says. "I don't think he gets that you actually have to put in the effort to reach the goal."

Sparking an Interest

There's good news here. Passengers don't have to stay stuck in neutral. In his last year of middle school, Mateo took a robotics class. When he first stepped into the room, he didn't see a teacher holding a textbook at the front of the room, assigning tests, quizzes, and classwork. No one was seated. Instead, big blue boxes spilling over with wires and circuit boards were scattered around the classroom, and a teacher invited him to pick things up, move around, and explore.

"It was the coolest thing ever," he says. "It made me think, it made me be creative. . . . It was the only class where there was really no right answer." It was a welcome break from the rest of his day, which he describes as "just lecture after lecture." For the first time, he was really challenged, getting into his ZPD, or stretch zone. He started spending his free time learning everything he could about how to code his robot to make it go through a maze or navigate across uneven terrain. And the energy he invested in robotics class began to spill over into the others. He was so animated and working so hard—on weekends, during the evening, with no prompting—that the robotics teacher asked him to help other students.

Robotics didn't automatically transform everything about school for Mateo. It didn't make him love English. But it gave him enough of a

KIDS IN PASSENGER MODE: ABOVE THEIR ZPD

THINK	FEEL	DO (AND SAY)
I can't do this!	Overwhelmed, don't know how to do what is asked of me, ashamed, I can't focus	School is boring.
I need to look cool, let me see which friends I can hang with at lunch/after school.	Uninterested, schoolwork is hardly the most important thing in life	School is boring.

KIDS IN PASSENGER MODE: BELOW THEIR ZPD

THINK	FEEL	DO (AND SAY)
I learned this last year.	Frustrated, annoyed, trapped, like school is a waste of time	School is boring.
What is the point of this?	Punished by busywork, question the relevance of the curriculum, complain about teachers	School is boring.

spark to get moving and reengage with his learning. This shifted the direction of his life: He began a virtuous cycle of effort and learning. His identity began to slowly change from the "rebel skipping school" guy to the "coding is my thing" guy. He distanced himself from his friends who he felt were going nowhere fast.

He also had a new goal: to get into a good high school. The Met, a Big Picture Learning public school that gives students freedom to pursue their interests through internships two days a week throughout their whole high school career, seemed especially cool.[20] If he could get in, high school would be way more hands-on and interesting. This thought made the easy and boring classes more tolerable. He sent in his application and waited anxiously to see if he would be accepted.

For some students, it's not just that they're outside their ZPD, finding school too easy or too hard. It's that they don't see the relevance of what is being taught to their life and their ability to solve problems in the world. Math becomes a series of formulas to memorize instead of tools to use to build new technology to solve climate change. History becomes a series of dates to remember rather than the forces that shape our current politics. Mateo found school too easy and was *also* simply uninterested in the material being taught through traditional lectures. It was only when he discovered robotics that he became interested in school.

Interests are to adolescents what chew toys are to puppies: necessary for development, fun, and a useful way to avoid boredom. Teachers support students' interests less by adding entertainment to their lessons (videos! quiz games! prizes!) and more by giving students choices over what and how they want to learn. Students have to master Civil War history? Let them choose which period to write about for their end-of-term essay. Better yet, let them choose to either write an essay, write a play, design a graphic novel, or make a podcast about it.

Of course, not everything in school needs to be riveting. Plenty of kids would opt out of taking algebra or ever writing an essay. Both are necessary to learn. But helping students find something that piques their curiosity and excites them is one of the best antidotes to disengagement. When young people are engaged in one part of their lives—a class or an extracurricular activity—it spills over to other areas.[21]

One teen we met, Charlie, found school easy to the point of boredom and didn't spend a lot of time doing his homework. But outside of school he loved watches. He would drag his parents to watch shops anytime they went to the mall. He knew every kind of watch there was and could tell you how they were made. He was fascinated by their internal mechanics. His parents were happy to see him light up at something, anything. After several years of watch obsession, he started getting interested in computers and then plane engines. In high school, he asked for computer parts and proceeded to build his own PC, which he uses to this day. (Steve Wozniak, cofounder of Apple, also famously built his own PC, which was the first preassembled PC brought to market.) Next came an interest in plane engines. Today Charlie is training to be a pilot.

Enlightened administrators know the power of interests. When Kaya Henderson, the former chancellor of the District of Columbia Public Schools, took the helm it was the worst-performing major metropolitan school district in the United States. Her first strategic plan in 2012 laid out some of what you might expect: increase academic achievement, especially in the lowest-performing schools, and increase graduation rates. But she knew that tapping into kids' interests was key to getting them engaged and learning. "It was as important for us to develop kids' talents as their test scores," Henderson told us. She asked every school to offer a wide variety of interesting clubs, activities, and classes.[22] Soon students were in one of the fastest-improving districts in the country.

All interests start from an interaction with people (parents, friends, teachers, wacky uncles) or the environment (objects, tasks, listening to music, dancing with friends, concerts, museums, staring out the window, watching grandpa grill). This is the first step in the four phases of **individual interest development,** a framework developed by two of the world's leading experts on the intersection between interests and learning: Suzanne Hidi and Ann Renninger, from the University of Toronto and Swarthmore College, respectively.[23]

The process of interest development goes like this. First, something grabs a young person's attention. They are curious and begin to engage. This triggers a "situational interest." For instance, a student perks up when her teacher talks about tornadoes. As she leaves the classroom, she thinks about them a bit more than anything else the teacher talked about but doesn't dig in yet. Someone or something enters to support her continued involvement—a teacher, family member, coach, or mentor. That social support helps to build the interest, moving it from triggered to sustained. At this point she might Google tornadoes or ask generative AI some basic questions: How much damage do they do? Was the one in *The Wizard of Oz* true to life? Now, over weeks and months, she's digging in, eager to learn more about tornadoes, hurricanes, and cyclones.

Finally, you know your child has a "well-developed individual interest" when she obsesses over extreme weather events and eagerly seeks new knowledge, pestering you and the rest of the family with nonstop information about wind loads and tornado-proof housing construction. She picks studying weather over TikTok and persists when something difficult appears, like understanding the calculus behind the meteorology. Through the process of developing her interest, she learns to regulate her thinking, persisting with a weather-related task instead of toggling between things. Learning about it feels valuable and brings joy. It becomes part of her identity—a kid who is seriously into weather and will often show off that expertise unprompted.

Parents play a huge role fanning the flames of situational interest and moving kids along the way to an individual interest. Charlie's parents asked him questions, quizzed him on different watches, pointed at pictures of watches in magazines. You do not need to know a lot about the content of your kid's budding obsession. In fact, kids love it when they know something and their parents don't. Asking probing

HOW INTERESTS ARE DEVELOPED

1 **TRIGGERED** SITUATIONAL INTEREST

Something grabs our attention.

2 **MAINTAINED** SITUATIONAL INTEREST

We keep our attention on the object or topic, attempting to resolve curiosity.

3 **EMERGING** INDIVIDUAL INTEREST

We may return to it of our own accord and seek more info or the help of others.

4 **WELL-DEVELOPED** INDIVIDUAL INTEREST

The interest is integrated with our identity; we independently seek mastery and generate our own questions.

Source: Developed based on Suzanne Hidi and K. Ann Renninger, "The Four-Phase Model of Interest Development," 2010.

questions that give your kids a chance to teach you about their interest does wonders to cement their knowledge about it and deepen their enthusiasm for it.

The late Peter Benson, a pioneering practitioner in positive youth development, worried about young people who didn't find their "spark," which he described as "discovering what's deep inside you so that you're less blown around by external pressures and distractions."[24] Decades of research show that interests or sparks fuel positive, productive youth identity but also confer some protection in the roller-coaster ride of adolescence.[25] It doesn't matter what a teen's spark is, as long as it isn't harmful to themselves or others.

The goal for young people in Passenger mode is to turn a few situational interests into individual, well-developed ones. Multiple studies show that interests are a powerful energy source for learning. The intersection of young people's interests with their learning increases a host of learning superpowers: memory and attention, emotional regulation, voluntary focus, self-efficacy, and perseverance. (Again, we are not exaggerating this list at all.)[26]

Interests can be energizing in school. Academics call this the "replenishment effect." In studies, when students are interested in something, their ability to persist with cognitively repetitive and exhausting tasks doubles. For example, students spent time on a difficult but mind-numbing task and were then given a short break to read or write about something that interested them. When presented with another boring and taxing task, their persistence was boosted by 30 percent because they were "replenished" by the interesting thing.[27] Their energy did not run out; it was refueled. If homework seems draining, do an interesting and cognitively engaging activity. Then jump back into the boring stuff. One study we like was done by Ulrich Trautwein and five of his colleagues, who studied 5,528 German high school students to see what role being interested had in learning. The group included both disengaged students expending minimal effort and more engaged high-effort students willing to slog through.[28]

Trautwein and his colleagues found that when interested in the class, the low-effort students applied themselves *as much* as the diligent high-effort students. Interest boosted effort and engagement for the coasting students by more than one standard deviation in the subject they were interested in—which, in nonmathematical terms, is a lot.

Another study found that when college students majoring in life sciences (including biology) took a required, and often dreaded, physics class, they performed as well as the physics majors when the professor reverse-engineered Trautwein's conditions for learning.[29] The professor's secret? Illustrating the physics principles with biology examples.

The trick for teachers is figuring out how to get a sea of checked-out students interested in what's being taught. Mateo's robotics teacher didn't only give a theoretical lecture on the principles of robotics, but let the students get their hands dirty. He gave young people the opportunity to exercise some choice and agency over their learning—a key feature in Big Picture Learning schools where students develop skills inside and outside the classroom through workplace experiences each year.

Mateo was accepted to the Met, the Big Picture Learning school, where he thrived. The school gave him ample space to pursue his curiosity and interests. During COVID, he helped reform the school's mental health support system, channeling his conversations with his peers into concrete recommendations for the principal. He was able to make choices about what he learned. Every semester, he picked an internship and spent two days a week learning in the workplace. He saw math formulas in action and learned how to interact in a professional setting. His senior year, he interned in the IT Department at the University of Rhode Island. The experience clinched his interest in going to college to study computer science.

In the midst of his senior-year application frenzy, his computer science teacher pulled him aside and suggested he apply for an engineering scholarship connected to Amazon. Mateo didn't think he had a shot, and he was overwhelmed with getting all his other applications in. But his teacher encouraged him, and in November he applied right before the deadline. Then he went back to studying for his classes.

On a breezy day in May, at the end of his senior year, he sat in a conference room at the University of Rhode Island before his last exhibition. At the Met, students have to present what they have learned every semester to their teachers, parents, internship mentors, and peers. They have to really know their stuff, as people ask questions and they have to respond cogently. It's much harder than guessing on a multiple-choice test. Mateo took a deep breath and launched into his presentation. The audience members peppered him with questions, and at the end of the session he was relieved. He felt he had handled things well.

Then his adviser stood up, holding a small cardboard box. Mateo was confused. This wasn't a normal thing that happened at the end of exhibition presentations. His adviser said he wanted to present Mateo with a special award and handed him the box. Sitting at the front of the room, Mateo opened it and started sifting through the large pile of blue shredded paper. When he saw what was in it, he burst into tears. In the box was an oversized check for $40,000 made out to *Amazon Future Engineer.* The room burst into cheers. His parents, teachers, and friends rushed over to him and enveloped him in a collective hug.

When we last checked in with Mateo, he was nearing the end of his freshman year in the honors program at Clemson College with a full scholarship and a living stipend. He was adjusting to life in South Carolina. He had discovered that he didn't like grits, and he was trying to understand the distinctions between different types of fried chicken. But he was loving school, putting his social skills and curiosity to good use. He had just been elected to the Student Senate, where he was working on making the school feel more welcoming, especially for kids of color. He was having fun in his computer science classes and diving into antitrust law in his political science seminar because he was curious to understand how it applied to the tech companies he was interested in working for. He had a 4.0 GPA and was off to spend the summer in Seattle at Amazon headquarters for an internship with a software engineering team. He was planning to go a week early so he could explore the city.

Takeaways

1. When students say school is *boring,* it can mean many different things: classes are too easy, too hard, disconnected from things they see and experience in their daily life, and/or uninteresting.
2. The *Zone of Proximal Development* is the learning sweet spot for every kid, where, with support from others, like a teacher or a peer or maybe even an online video, they can master new knowledge and skills.
3. Many schools struggle to get all kids into the zone, including students with learning differences, students who are neurodivergent, and frequently boys as they enter middle and high school.
4. When students develop a "spark" or strong interest they can pursue, it boosts engagement: They have more energy, they pay closer attention, they try harder, and they are more motivated to learn.
5. Operating in Passenger mode from time to time can be a useful strategy to balance a demanding workload. But when students spend most of their time here they can start to develop a Passenger identity and lose out on the valuable skill building needed to operate in Explorer mode.

3

Achiever

The Perils of Perfection

Stella first signed up to take French as an elective her sophomore year. Her French teacher, Ms. Roberts, was young and dynamic—she was only seven years older than Stella, but she told her students that she'd been teaching a while and had become a French teacher because she hated how she was taught French. "She has all the same ideals as me, because she grew up kind of in the same time," Stella says.

Over the course of the year, Ms. Roberts got to know her students, including Stella. She knew who Stella's friends were. She knew what extracurricular activities they took part in. One day, Stella and her friends had a free period. Instead of going to the library, they went to Ms. Roberts's classroom to visit her and ended up hanging out. This soon became a habit. It's where Stella and her friends leave their sports bags in the morning and where Stella comes during study periods to hang out and chat with her teacher—to talk about issues with her friends or her girlfriend, to tell her a funny story about losing her keys, to share a new song she loves. In her senior year, Stella began fighting with one of her good friends. Ms. Roberts noticed; she suggested that they listen to each other and mediated between them. The classroom felt like home to Stella.

Stella is emotionally engaged in French: She feels connected to her teacher and peers, and feels that her time is being well spent. She is also cognitively engaged, monitoring her learning and looking for gaps and ways to improve her skills by asking questions and probing her knowledge. She wants it all to make sense because it feels good to master something. She also wants to impress her teacher, whom she adores. Her emotional and cognitive engagement intertwine, building off each other, fueled by her relationship with her teacher.

The classroom has an environment of high expectations and academic rigor but also warmth and genuine support. "When she says there is no such thing as a stupid question, she means it," Stella says. This is relationship gold for Stella, who has *a lot of* questions and, like most humans, does not want to feel like an idiot for asking them. It used to be that when Stella raised her hand to ask a question, she started it by saying, "This might be a stupid question," but Ms. Roberts was always quick to say, "There is no such thing as a stupid question." This was a major improvement from some of Stella's other teachers junior year, who often replied, "We'll see."

Ms. Roberts takes Stella seriously, and Stella is eager to return the respect. Stella gives French her all. She asks questions when she doesn't understand the lesson and tries to answer questions even when she doesn't know if she's right—"something I don't usually do," she admits. She isn't afraid to look stupid in front of her peers, so she inquires when she's confused or maybe missed something when she was daydreaming, which happens. "I love French so much," she gushes, her eyes lit up and her energy palpable. She describes her experience of French class as being like when you are into a movie and you are not thinking about anything else but the movie; you aren't thinking about needing to text your friend or dad or about something you want to buy online. This is a decidedly different experience from her other classes, especially junior year.

Ms. Roberts's students know she cares about them. She asks about them. She will go out of her way to help them. At the end of that first year, Ms. Roberts confessed to the class that it wasn't true what she had told them at the beginning of the year: She hadn't been teaching for a while. This was actually her first year. But by then, all the kids loved her. Stella has taken French with her three years in a row.

The Beauty of Happy Achievers

Stella during French class represents Achiever mode at its very best. She turns up ready to engage in all the teacher has to offer and to excel at everything she's asked to do. Those in Achiever mode invest in their learning. They develop excellent skills, such as planning and discipline, and an impressive ability to juggle an array of things. They are driven by winning and feel good when the accolades come in from parents, teachers, and deans' lists.

Kids in Achiever mode:

- Show up, work hard, get good grades.
- Ask questions and seek help to ensure they do the assignment the right way.
- Excel at expectations set by school, parents, and coaches.

The world loves kids operating in Achiever mode. These folks populate the world's top banks, schools, law firms, construction companies, hospitals, and nonprofits. They relish clear goals, always hoping not just to hit them but to surpass them. Young people in Achiever mode have internalized that doing well at school is important, and it has become a central motivation for them. Thus they build excellent work habits and real-life skills: time management, getting things done, doing things well.

Teens who value school and are engaged—feeling like they belong, enjoying being part of their school community, participating actively in class and extracurricular activities, and interested in what they are learning—perform better and feel better. They graduate at much higher rates and have higher grades. They are happier and are less likely to have problems with alcohol and drug abuse.[1] They love the feeling of accomplishment, and they love the results of their hard work: Who doesn't love getting a hoard of accolades?

The habits those in Achiever mode develop are life-skills gold. Indeed, all of the kids we interviewed for this book who existed mostly in Achiever mode were a damn impressive lot. They accomplished so much! They performed so well! Teachers adored them for their diligence and high standards as well as their modeling of exemplary behavior for others.

Unlike students in Passenger mode, who are only behaviorally engaged, kids in Achiever mode are also *cognitively* engaged. They think and process, trying to connect the dots with their learning and make sense of the tasks they face. They organize themselves to get through demanding things: a set of tough exams or the drudgery of reviewing the conditional perfect tense in French. And many high-achieving kids—the ones we call happy Achievers—are also *emotionally engaged.* They feel like they belong in the classroom or school. They are interested in and enjoy their lessons. This comfort helps them ask questions even when they are confused, like Stella in Ms. Roberts's class (counter-intuitive as it may seem, kids tend to ask fewer questions the more confused they are). In Achiever mode, kids at their best are excited by learning what's in front of them and willing to do what it takes to master it well.

This would seem the pinnacle of engagement: kids turning up, focused and outcome oriented. They are cognitively, behaviorally, and emotionally engaged. But there is another side to Achiever mode, when everything that feels positive and future-proof can turn dark and sometimes toxic. Sometimes teens operating in Achiever mode only respond to the demands made on them rather than considering what direction they want to move in. Often they perfect the art of following. The system, of course, rewards this. But the cost to kids of becoming good at satisfying a system with bottomless demands is missing out on learning about themselves.* What interests them? What annoys them? Without opportunities for reflection, they cannot chart their own path because they have no idea what that path might be. They've got Waze and they are following it, rather than looking up or considering that there might be another way to get somewhere.

Kids who spend too much time in Achiever mode risk failing to develop their own creativity. It's hard to think of an original way to do something when so much energy is spent getting the "right" answer. This focus on being right works for some and can work for a while. But in an age where AI can come up with complex answers in a nanosecond, humans will need to hone their creative problem-solving. When students spend too much time in Achiever mode, it can become an identity. Being the "smart one" translates to a certain confidence. But there can be an unexpected downside, when too much achieving makes kids fragile, unwilling to take risks for fear of failure. While there are plenty of kids who are happy achieving, there's an increasingly large share of unhappy ones, kids who run themselves into the ground trying to nail the perfect GPA, get into the best college, get a good scholarship, and juggle a dizzying array of demands from volunteering to producing original research to excelling on the sports field.

These kids in unhappy Achiever mode are missing an essential piece of the puzzle. They are not emotionally engaged. They know how to play the game and sacrifice a lot to play it well. But they are empty inside, unsure of why it matters or who they are aside from their academic and extracurricular accolades. Surprisingly, these unhappy Achievers often have worse mental health outcomes than kids who are highly disengaged. They are at serious risk of being overwhelmed by stress, burnout, depression, anxiety, and are more likely to cheat.

We call this the **Achiever Conundrum,** the frustrating reality that something we all want for our kids—a strong work ethic and pride in

* There are exceptions here: schools where students are required to explore and take the lead in their own learning to succeed. These schools put student agency at the center of their design, but, unfortunately, they are still the exception rather than the rule.

doing well—could also harm them. This is thorny terrain for parents and educators alike. We all want kids to push themselves and achieve. We don't want them to break.

The Fine Line Between Achieving and Falling Apart

The first time we meet Amina, a radiant, twenty-year-old Nigerian American, she talks so much we barely have time to ask questions. We transcribe all of our interviews, and typically we speak 25 percent of the time and young people speak 75 percent. Amina speaks 89 percent of the time, covering topics from computer languages to achievement culture, the Kumon curriculum, how to nail a college application essay, Gen Z's proclivity for a new kind of work, the perils of too much travel, and the merits of failure therapy. Her language is precise, intense, and thoughtful: When she leaves an idea unfinished she always remembers to come back to it, as if she's got an automated checklist of topics running in her head.

Amina grew up in Atlanta. Her parents came to the United States from Nigeria for graduate school, her father becoming a lawyer and her mother an engineer. They were hard-charging immigrants who expected their kids to excel at everything: Kumon, school, clubs, sports. They had the financial resources, so they enrolled her in a top private school. Amina did not disappoint. Here's her high school résumé: Straight-A student. Student council president. Mock trial president. Athlete (soccer, rowing, basketball). Checkout worker at Chick-fil-A. Member of the CoderSchool, an after-school program to build coding and character skills. Volunteer: for a church community serving HIV+ individuals and a nonprofit that helps low-income immigrant families settle (fourteen hours short of the Presidential Service Award, which requires one hundred hours).* By her account, she loved it.

"I love praise. I loved being praised. I loved being complimented. So I really loved being called out by my teachers for being so smart, for being so diligent," she tells us, speaking at approximately twice the pace of other people her age. She loves being a winner, she says. It shows in her intensity.

Her goal, from elementary school, was to get into a great college. Her parents liked this plan and helped her, signing her up for Kumon to get a leg up. She muscled through the entire Kumon program—each level being a curriculum of two hundred pages. The program required doing homework, getting it checked, and revising errors until there were zero. Some nights she would cry, staying behind to correct her math while her brothers would go home, leaving her alone. But she said getting through the curriculum then made high school easy (at least until Calculus II). Kindergarten through eighth grade was a breeze, and high school was easy as long as you paid attention in class and did your homework.

What drove Amina? So many things, she tells us. She doesn't like having her choices curtailed. If you are going to do something, why not do it well, she says to us a few times. She likes being in charge, and people put top performers in charge. Occasionally, when she didn't like a teacher, spite fueled her. She found her high school biology teacher

* There is not one iota of embellishment here.

confusing and unhelpful, a damning combination in Amina's mind. "I was like: I'm going to pass this class, just because I don't like you," she told herself, then went to every one of that teacher's student hours after school.

But mostly what drove her was that smart and driven became her identity.

"There's a sense of validation. I don't know when it becomes tied to identity, but you do start thinking of yourself like 'I am smart, and I am gifted, I am a top student, I am a learner,' and you just kind of have to keep doing those things."

Applying to colleges was fun for Amina. "I pride myself on my ability to do a great college application," she says. She knew she was an excellent candidate. She applied to nine schools and got into all of them, including Stanford—her first choice. She even got into Harvard, which she didn't think she would because she didn't like the essay prompts in the application. She ultimately picked Yale (her dad thought it was best). She was confident she would succeed. It was all she'd ever done.

Soon after Amina got to Yale, things started to unravel. There were a lot of other smart people, and classes were significantly harder. She was majoring in computer science and struggled mightily with the math. Homework assignments took way longer than they used to. Classes covered way more content. She was not used to struggling and started to check out because she felt so at sea with new feelings of uncertainty and self-doubt. "My usual systems from high school are no longer working for me in college. And I don't really know how to pivot because what's worked in high school has kind of always worked." She stayed busy—joining crew while balancing her courses and telling herself it would all be okay in the end. She'd figure it out because she always did.

By sophomore year things started to really fall apart. She dropped crew to focus on studying. She took a course in discrete math for computer science, which did not go well. She got caught up in the social scene of Yale, taking on too many extracurriculars without realizing that in college you go deep and not wide. She had no idea what to go deep on. Some clubs she applied for—the Yale entrepreneurial society, its investment group club—rejected her. It was her first time experiencing failure, and it deeply destabilized her self-confidence. If she was a winner, why did no one want her in their clubs?

She was exhausted—even though she was getting back from class at 1:30 P.M. She suddenly could not motivate herself to do anything. She started skipping class, ignoring professors' emails, staying in bed much of the day while enjoying being with her friends at night. She had no idea who she was, only that it all felt uncomfortable.

Having mastered so many things, from Advanced Placement courses to college essays, Amina was well programmed for hard work but had never contended with real struggle and failure so had no understanding of it and no skills for coping with it. "I didn't know what to do," she says. "And I didn't want to seek help. Because it felt like I was admitting that I had a problem, and smart kids don't have problems."

She'd make sporadic attempts to get support, usually after a "stern talking to herself." She got some tutoring, went to office hours. But "student who needs help" didn't match the story she had told herself her whole life. She didn't tell anyone at home what was happening. "I'm a go-getter, goal setter, high achiever," she says, "and so when they still think of me in that way, and I feel like I'm falling apart over here, I didn't really know what to do. I didn't want to let anybody down." She beat herself up, thinking, "I'm not even at Stanford, which has a way harder computer science program, and I am struggling!"

As the Christmas break approached, she knew she needed to do something. She was about to fail her classes. She went to talk to her adviser, who suggested a gap year. She didn't love the idea. "It felt like quitting," she tells us. But after mulling it over for a while, assessing her poor grades and downward spiral, and having a few more conversations with her adviser, she decided it was better than flunking out of college. She filed the paperwork with a heavy heart and then went with her family to Nigeria for Christmas break.

She couldn't bring herself to tell her parents when she was with them. She couldn't face the disappointment in their faces. If she felt like a gap year was the same as quitting, she knew her parents would see it that way. They had invested so much in her. How could she break their hearts?

Her mom kept pestering her to get a ticket back to New Haven after the break. She was running out of time. She canceled going to a concert out of town and used that to set a deadline for herself. She texted her parents to set up a meeting in the evening, asking that her dad not work late. "I let them eat dinner so they would not be hangry," she recalls. Then she told them. Everyone cried. They were angry. "How could this happen? Why didn't you tell us? Are you sure you can't go back?" She was clear: It was done. She had filed the paperwork.

It was particularly hard on her dad, who reminded her that he had come here to give them a better life and that they had cousins back in Nigeria who would love the opportunities she had. He reminded her that he had come to the United States alone and that he did not get to see his family in Nigeria much. Then he said something that made her heart sink: "I am disappointed," he told her.

She went back to school after break to pack up her dorm room. And then she turned around and went home.

Amina felt checkmated.

She had gone from spending all her time in happy Achiever mode to getting stuck in unhappy Achiever mode in the space of a year and a half. Unable to succeed, she felt disconnected from learning and at a loss to figure out how to reset. She wished she had had "rejection therapy" in high school so she would be prepared to fail and would know it didn't mean she herself was worthless, which was how she felt now. Her goal had been to get into a good college. She had done it. "What's the next big thing?" she asked herself. "What's the next goal? I don't know what it is that I'm supposed to be working toward. Now that I'm here, especially when you're at like an Ivy League, like Yale, what do I do next?" The idea of getting a good job didn't inspire her. "No eighteen-, nineteen-, or twenty-year-old is inspired by work," she explains. Grad school seemed like more of the same. She hadn't had the time to develop the self-knowledge to pick her own goals now that no one was telling her exactly what to do to succeed. She was out of ideas and out of gas.

We found young people walking this tightrope all over the country, in small towns and big cities, in competitive public schools and in elite private ones. They told us that sometimes when things get really busy, they feel like they can't breathe. They worry endlessly about letting people down—their teachers, their parents, themselves. They berate themselves for many things like getting less than a perfect score or wasting time when they took a break to mindlessly scroll on TikTok. We also spoke to kids who had walked the tightrope and fallen off into a world no parent or educator wants for their children: cheating, panic attacks, depression, self-harm, a sense of a meaningless life, suicidal ideation.

All parents, and teachers, want their teens to achieve in school but not at the expense of their well-being. And yet a lot of young people in the United States and around the world find themselves operating in unhappy Achiever mode, sacrificing health and happiness for good grades.[2] Research shows that how young people approach their learning has an impact on their happiness—and operating primarily in unhappy Achiever mode can be detrimental. Researchers Ming-Te Wang and Stephen Peck conducted a longitudinal study of more than one thousand students at twenty-three public schools and analyzed data across ninth grade, eleventh grade, and one year after expected graduation to assess how young people's level of engagement affected their mental health, school success, and future aspirations.[3] The results revealed that the teens with the greatest increase in depressive symptoms were those who were cognitively engaged but emotionally disengaged, in other words kids in what we are calling unhappy Achiever mode. They were even more depressed than their peers who were hardly engaged at all, students we describe as being in Resister mode, who were, unsurprisingly, experiencing a fair number of mental health challenges themselves. Further, Wang and Peck found that demographic differences (ethnicities, genders, parental income levels) or preexisting depression made no difference. Regardless of any of these differences, the group of emotionally disengaged, high-achieving students *were the most depressed.*

The study results highlight that for students, doing well on paper doesn't always correlate with doing well psychologically; in fact, the opposite is often true. The kids in unhappy Achiever mode in the study *looked great:* working hard, taking part in activities, turning in high-quality work, making connections between what they learned in school and other things they knew about. Their average GPA was a very high 4.1. But they were deeply unhappy: Their level of depressive symptoms on a scale of 1 to 3 was a full point greater than that of emotionally engaged kids in what we call happy Achiever mode and Passenger mode. These students in unhappy Achiever mode didn't like school, they didn't find it interesting, and they did not enjoy being there. And while 80 percent of these teens had enrolled in college, their enrollment rate tanked from 80 percent to 50 percent after the first year, falling to the same level as that of the most disengaged, Resister mode students in the study.

The Achiever Conundrum is widespread. Across seventy-two countries, from the United States to Europe to Latin America and Asia, the more wealthy a country is, the happier its adults are. But not so its adolescents. Life satisfaction actually goes down as income levels rise. Researchers who spotted this trend find that it is the intensity and competition of adolescents' education that is to blame.[4]

In the United States, there is an additional burden for Black and brown students striving to excel. Multiple studies have shown that the extra energy minority teens spend worrying about stereotype threat (the risk of confirming negative stereotypes about race, ethnicity, gender, or a cultural group, which increases cognitive load and reduces academic performance) is mentally exhausting and adds a layer of stress that white students do not have to deal with.[5] In one study of students, the majority of whom were Black and faced multiple forms of adversity, it was the students who were doing *better* at school who had higher levels of anxiety and depression compared to those students who were not doing well.[6] The authors concluded that this counterintuitive finding was because the high-performing students were carrying the extra weight of keeping it all together while dealing with challenges and mentally fighting back against stereotypes.[7]

Not only are many students in unhappy Achiever mode suffering from poor mental health, but they feel so compelled to perform that they take some big risks. Some schools call this *academic dishonesty;* most of us think of it as cheating. Since 2018, Denise Pope, cofounder of the nonprofit Challenge Success, and her team have documented alarmingly high levels of it, with three out of four teens reporting they engaged in behaviors that are considered cheating (working on assignments with others that they were meant to do alone, for example) in the month prior to taking the survey.[8]

Frantically focused on mastering the present, teens in Achiever mode crowd out the time to consider who they are or who they want to be—critical questions teens need time and space to contemplate. Leaving these questions unanswered can cause problems down the road, just as it did for Amina. A hyperfixation on jumping through the hoops put in front of them means never asking themselves, *What am I interested in?* When you ask students in Achiever mode for input on what interests them about a lesson or where they would like to start the discussion or how they would like to move forward, often they can't answer. But one day they will have to. "When they look inside themselves, there is nothing there," says Johnmarshall Reeve.[9]

Reeve does not mean that children who can't figure out what direction they want to take in learning when given the opportunity are devoid of substance. He does worry that they haven't invested enough time wondering what they care about to be able to take the initiative when the opportunity arises. Many of those busy achieving operate dangerously close to losing themselves in a system whose demands are endless. They're at the ready with the correct answer to a question, but balance is not part of their lexicon. What is enough studying? How many extracurriculars are enough? Who even has time to self-reflect?

We all want young people to succeed in school. But at what cost? Achieving opens doors. But it can also mask a lot of misery and, ironically, diminish a lot of motivation. For parents this is especially tricky territory. Clearly, we want to instill high expectations and strong values around the merits of education. But we don't want to overdo it. One way is to closely monitor that very real but hard-to-see line between happy and unhappy achieving. The charts below and opposite are a place to start.

KIDS IN UNHAPPY ACHIEVER MODE

THINK	FEEL	DO (AND SAY)
I can't believe I missed one question!	Angry, disappointed in themselves	I could have done so much better. I studied really hard and only got a 97. I thought I would get a perfect score.
I have three more hours to learn this. Keep going, don't quit.	Stressed, tired, depleted	My day was fine.
I can't do this anymore. I wish I could just disappear and no one would notice.	Numb, sad, alone, helpless, on autopilot	My day was fine.

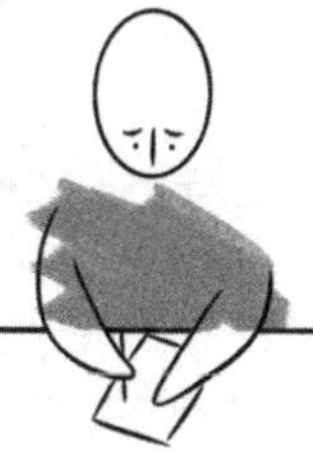

One way parents, and even teachers, can manage the Achiever Conundrum is to help students take it down a notch. Striving for excellence is a good thing but not if it pushes kids over their limits. In this case, a happy kid coasting in Passenger mode is better than a deeply anxious kid stuck in unhappy Achiever mode.

KIDS IN HAPPY ACHIEVER MODE

THINK	FEEL	DO (AND SAY)
Nice! I nailed that.	Accomplished, proud, confident	I got an A on my test.
I didn't know that before, how interesting!	Curious, energized	Did you know that when the US Supreme Court was founded, the judges had a hard time getting people to show up to their trials? Can you believe that?!
I don't know exactly what I have to do for this assignment.	Worried about letting others down (family, self, peers), fearful about not doing everything right	I need to go talk to my English teacher after school about my assignment, so I will be home a bit late.
I can't wait to go to band and see my friends!	Seen, connected, important to others	I do not want to be late to band.

Sometimes a Little Passenger Mode Is a Good Thing

No one can drive in the fast lane 100 percent of the time.[10] Sometimes you need to switch lanes and slow down to successfully navigate your way around unexpected obstacles. In an age of teen mental health problems, being in Passenger mode for a time can be self-protective.

One self-described kid in Passenger mode we spoke to is Diego, a carefree, quick-to-laugh fourteen-year-old boy in a competitive STEM public charter high school in Tucson, Arizona, that prides itself on putting kids through a grueling, military-like pace of eight advanced classes a day. "No one in my school is an Explorer," he declares. "My school would never allow it." The way Diego sees it, from 8 A.M. to 4 P.M. he is on school duty, a job he needs to do but doesn't necessarily care about. He likes seeing his friends, enjoys being on the basketball team, finds some classes interesting, and basically maintains a B average by doing what he needs to get by. He often whizzes through homework, crams the day before for tests (sometimes), and from time to time doesn't turn in his assignments.

"I don't let my school life interfere with my personal life," he declares authoritatively. If it's time to go to bed and he hasn't finished his homework, he just goes to bed and doesn't worry about it. Maybe he will quickly finish it before class the next day, maybe a friend will give him some of the answers, and maybe he just won't turn it in. No biggie. (This is not an unhappy Achiever response to a missed assignment, which, depending on the kid, can range from sullen withdrawal to tears to anger.) Diego prioritizes friends, after-school activities, and the thirty minutes of *Zelda: Breath of the Wild* that his parents allow each day. Plus, he loves investigating anything to do with flight—he makes intricate paper airplanes and tests them in his house, in the park, from the top of the public library's stairs.

"Do you have to be an Explorer *inside* school?" he asks us.

The answer is no. It doesn't matter where—in or out of school—teens are building their skills to drive their own learning and, importantly, to figure out healthy ways to get themselves out of being bored.

A kid who operates mainly in happy Passenger mode while still getting decent if not great grades so as not to foreclose their options for higher learning or future careers is in many ways preferable to one stuck in unhappy Achiever mode and suffering from anxiety and depression. This is Diego's philosophy at least. He would put many of his friends in the unhappy Achiever category. He knows that some kids really need medication for anxiety, but he also sees the toll that stress takes on his peers. "A full third of the kids in my class just need to get their lives together," he says. "They are so stressed about being perfect at school, and sometimes their parents are so intense about it, that they stay up till 11 P.M. doing homework, and then they need to relax, so they go on social media until 2 A.M., and then they wake up at 7 A.M. and have like two Red Bulls. They are so unhappy all the time."

The Fragility of Kids in Unhappy Achiever Mode

Most teens in happy Achiever mode have a healthy view of achievement: They want to do well because it feels good and because it will help them get where they want to go. They see achievement as excellence, which is obtainable, versus perfection, which is not.

But the curse of unhappy Achievers *is* perfectionism, striving for flawlessness in all realms, an impossible goal that no one can achieve. Who can blame them? Perfectionism is the "weakness" we all love to tout (especially at the end of an interview when asked to cite a personality weakness). "It's everyone's favorite flaw," says Thomas Curran, an assistant professor of psychological and behavioral sciences at the London School of Economics and Political Science who studies perfectionism.[11]

It is easy to fall in love with perfectionists. They do such good work! They care so much! They try so hard! But in a bid to avoid failure, perfectionists are setting themselves up for it. At their core, perfectionists are fragile. To build the muscles of an Explorer, young people need to practice trying things, falling down, reflecting on why they fell, and getting back up and trying again. That is how any child learns to ride a bike. But with kids in unhappy Achiever mode, it is as if they, and often their parents and peers around them, have forgotten that they can recover from a fall. The intense stress of worrying about potential failure breeds competition with their peers; it makes school a place where they experience isolation and anxiety not growth and enjoyment.[12] These feelings do not fuel engagement with their learning, they hinder it. Disconnected, stressed, and unhappy students struggle to concentrate on the interesting aspects of learning. Homework and tests become meaningless gauntlets they have to run through every week. They do what they must to come out on top, but they are not enjoying the process. Some have a name for themselves: "robostudents."[13]

Curran is quick to point out that this is bad news. There are lots of kinds of perfectionism: expecting others to be perfect; expecting yourself to be perfect. But the kind that is rising most dramatically—and has pernicious consequences—is **socially prescribed perfectionism,** the belief that one's worth or value is contingent on meeting the perceived expectations of others (for example, everyone on Instagram).[14] Amina's fear of rejection or criticism and her sense of inadequacy stem from this form of perfectionism. It's highly correlated with "psychological distress, including anxiety, depression, suicidal ideation, and anorexia," Curran explains.[15]

In our research, we heard about perfectionism everywhere. Carter is a clean-cut, middle-class kid with closely cropped blond hair. He's a junior at a high school in a small Tennessee town where his parents are managers working in local government. By all external measures he is a grade-A Achiever. But he periodically suffers from panic attacks, which can come at any time. He describes what these feel like as follows: "It feels like I'm coming up against a wall and there is no way out." He says his parents just tell him to do his best, but "it feels like my best is an A," he explains, "and so if I get like a B or something like that, it's an ordeal." Like many kids who have a fear of failure, Carter doesn't believe he can mess up and come out the other side okay.

Recently, Carter took the SAT, which he knows can be important in college applications, and got a mediocre score. "Well, that's it. I guess I'm not going to college," he told us. His parents often try to help him by giving advice. Sometimes he wishes they would just let him fail on his own. But he hasn't tried that yet; he is worried about what would happen if he did. Kids like him who have a fear of failure don't believe they can recover from a fall, so they play it safe and don't take big risks.

School is what kids do a lot of the time. For those spending lots of time in Achiever mode, "you get so deeply tied up into seeing your achievements as your identity," says Amina. When things do not go well, a sense of hopelessness sets in.

Some signs your kid is in happy or unhappy Achiever mode:

HAPPY ACHIEVER MODE

- They have high standards for themselves and strive to perform excellently on the tasks given to them.
- They take the time to review their work to avoid errors.
- They express excitement or satisfaction when they perform well.
- They value organizing themselves to pursue their goals.
- When they experience a setback, they adjust and try again.
- They maintain a healthy balance of sleep, connection with family and friends, and downtime alongside pursuing their ambitions.

UNHAPPY ACHIEVER MODE

- They beat themselves up if they make a mistake, like not getting a top score on a test. They strive to be perfect in the tasks presented to them.
- They interpret less-than-excellent performance as a complete failure.
- They become overly discouraged and upset when faced with a setback or a performance below what they were striving for.
- They are excessively concerned with meeting other people's standards.
- They constantly sacrifice sleep, time with family, and other needed downtime to study or practice more.
- They exhibit signs of anxiety, depression, or some other mental health concern, all while maintaining a high level of performance.

Research shows that the way Carter and Amina respond to failure is common for perfectionists. Curran and a colleague ran experiments in which people came into a lab and filled out a survey of perfectionism.[16]

Then they were asked to compete against others on a stationary bicycle. Regardless of how well they did, they were told they had come in last. How would they respond to public defeat?

Everyone felt bad. They had lost. Who likes losing? They reported an increased sense of shame and guilt. But those scoring high on socially prescribed perfectionism were miserable on a whole different level. Their shame and guilt spiked far higher than those with low socially prescribed perfectionism.

In a separate study, participants were led to believe they were falling short of their goals. This time the goal was to see how perfectionism influences effort. Did the perfectionists get a boost from their desire to be the best? They did not. Researchers found that those with low perfectionism dug a little deeper and tried a little harder. Those with high socially prescribed perfectionism held back. They didn't want the misery again. Perfectionism doesn't improve effort (at least after failure). In this study it hurt it.[17] In the end, the perfectionists got a boatload of emotional pain with no performance benefit.

Curran has found that in recent years, perfectionism has been growing more common. It is also making kids sick. In 1989, 9 percent of college students ages eighteen to twenty-five felt the need to be perfect in response to perceived pressure from others, so much so that it required clinical treatment. By 2017, that figure had doubled.

Curran was stunned. He wondered why. Where was it coming from? Trying to understand the staggering rise in perfectionism, he spent two years digging into the causes.[18] What he found is not likely to make you happy: Parents, whether they mean to or not, seem to be making the pressure worse.

Curran found that young people's increasing fear of not being perfect was driven in large part by what they thought their parents wanted from them. Rising almost in tandem with socially prescribed perfectionism are increasing parental expectations and criticism, which include parents having standards that young people feel they are not able to meet (e.g., getting top grades or excelling in extracurricular activities) and making negative comments when students fail to meet these standards. This is one way students come to believe that their value as a person is tied to their performance in school.

Curran is very clear not to blame parents themselves. He argues that parents are simply distilling the values of a meritocratic, individualistic, neoliberal society. Parents feel they have to push their kids because the world is more competitive: There's another test around the corner, another expensive travel team that a kid needs to join to keep up. College admissions are looming and it's never been harder to get in or get a scholarship. There's no time for unconditional approval. Parents are not bad actors; they are rational actors responding to an increasingly unhinged environment. "Expectations are so far beyond young people's capacity," Curran says, visibly upset at the state of the world.[19]

Curran's conclusions can seem confusing when placed next to the zeitgeist of a moment when some parents, generally affluent ones, are more often accused not of criticizing but of hovering (helicoptering), of being snowplow parents who clear every imaginable obstacle on the way to success. How can we coddle and criticize *at the same time*?

Masterfully, if not intentionally.

Teens are razor sharp and pick up on subtleties like "Do your best," which, like Carter, they hear as "Get an A," says Richard Weissbourd, a psychologist and senior lecturer at Harvard's Graduate School of Education. "It can deplete or compromise the authenticity of the relationship," he tells us.[20] We say we care about happiness and not outcomes, but we let them stay up until midnight studying and run themselves ragged. We celebrate the As and the wins, but we wince just a little when the 70 percent rolls in. Some parents demand perfect grades and are willing to pay for them.

Teens pay attention less to what we say and more to what we do, including the many nonverbal cues we are likely not even aware we are giving.

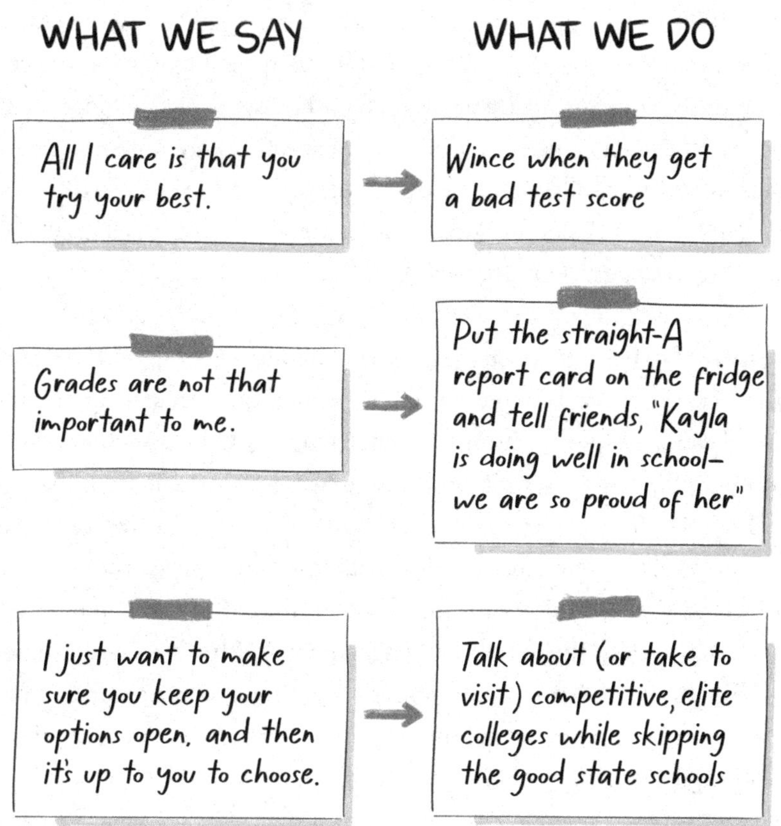

Achiever Mode and Sports

Most of us would love to wave a magic wand and have all the stress surrounding our kids disappear. Unrelenting pressure comes from literally everywhere, including hobbies that used to be a wonderful safe haven from the pressures of school: drama, music, chess club. For many kids in Achiever mode these are now chips in the poker game that is college admissions.[21]

Case in point: the world of youth sports. For many kids, sports are an energizing life force, a constructive, healthy, social way to find meaning by being part of a team and getting better at something. Athletes learn to win graciously, lose gracefully, make mistakes, recover from them, and help teammates do the same. They learn about their minds, their bodies, and how different humans really can be (there are, apparently, people who are happy to have hockey pucks pelted at them at high speeds as a goalie). For many kids, sports are an entry to engagement, a way to connect to peers, to coaches, to an entirely different kind of learning. For some kids, sports are their saving grace in school, the thing that gets them through.

But for way too many kids and families, the commitment has turned toxic. A massive U.S. sports-industrial complex demands early specialization and boatloads of money and too much time. Injuries are on the rise because of specialization. Kids don't get enough sleep. It becomes another platform on which they have to be perfect. College admissions and scholarships are on the line. One 2016 study found that the more money families pour into youth sports, the more pressure their kids feel—and the less they enjoy and feel committed to their sport.[22] Instead of a way to fuel emotional engagement with school, it becomes another drain on kids' limited resources, a time commitment that not only takes them away from family and friends but also prevents them from exploring something, anything, new.

Vanessa Rodriguez had never heard of field hockey when her adviser at a private school in West Hartford, Connecticut, told her she was going to be the goalie for the middle school field hockey team. She had just started sixth grade and had not expressed any interest in field hockey, but the team needed a goalie and none of the other girls wanted to do it. Shy and timid, Vanessa didn't even consider protesting. But when they put her in the goal that day and shot balls at her for hours, she remembers being in a state of panic.

She came home that evening shaken. Sitting on the brown couch in the family's small living room, she pulled up the legs of her pants and saw bruises. Her older brother, who also attended the school, was horrified. But neither considered talking to anyone. They both knew that as recent immigrants from Puerto Rico with limited financial means, they were lucky to be at the school in the first place. Their parents were involved and loving but didn't know if this was what normally happened in private schools. Maybe every kid goes through this? They also didn't feel they had any power to complain. Both their children were on scholarships at the school, and they had come to the mainland with the express purpose of giving their kids a better education. What if they lost their scholarships? Both Vanessa and her brother knew from experience that the public schools in Hartford, where they lived, were not good alternatives. So Vanessa did everything she could to fit in. Her brother immediately reached out to his friends to get intel and advice. "Have her wear football pads under her gym clothes," someone offered.

So that's what Vanessa did. "I decided right then and there that I was going to be the best field hockey goalie I could ever be," she tells us. If this was what the school said she had to do to be successful, then she was going to go all in. She did what many kids in Achiever mode do: She dug in and conformed. She replaced any doubt with drive and accelerated toward the goals set for her. She went to all the practices and gave 110 percent on each drill. The school asked her to jump, and she responded by saying: How high? She spent most of her time studying and playing field hockey. She also played softball and basketball and was in the debate, mock trial, and science clubs. "That was my whole life," she says.

She muscled through high school pursuing the list of tasks that had been given to her for how to be a good student, how to excel. She kept her head down, getting top grades, excelling at her extracurriculars. She didn't have many friends, she never went to parties, having no time and no invitations. She was too busy keeping quiet and excelling. "To get through school, I shut myself down," she recalls. She became president of the mock trial club and vice president of the debate club. And she continued to give hockey her all. She eventually became captain of the team. Then she made the state team, competing in tournaments across Connecticut. Everyone praised her for her accomplishments: teachers, coaches, parents. At no point did she complain.

Her senior year, multiple colleges offered Vanessa scholarships for field hockey. The only problem was she hated field hockey. She felt she was standing on the edge of a cliff, and all she could see below was darkness. She agonized over the decision of which college to go to. Could she take playing field hockey for four more years? She realized that she had been burying who she really was—what she enjoyed, what she wanted to do, the person she wanted to be—into a little box that was shut tightly within her. "I figured out that I had been just pushing through and not letting myself feel," she says. As the end of the school year approached, colleges were pressuring her for a decision, and she still couldn't figure out what she wanted to do. (Don't worry. We'll tell you what she decides in chapter 8.)

Achiever Mode and Agency

If the goal of adolescence is finding meaning and ways to matter, and discovering some of the clues to who you want to be, kids need to look around. Instead, young people who spend most of their time in Achiever mode are so focused on one outcome—achieving—they never look up to consider alternate possibilities. In economic terms, they crowd out the time and space to explore what they actually like or care about because they are playing too much field hockey or studying for too many AP tests.

Agency is the ability to identify a meaningful goal and marshal resources to meet it. This takes skills; it also takes the belief that you do have some power over your circumstances, and it frequently requires asking for help. Kids who spend too much time in Passenger mode struggle to do this because they are not that interested in identifying a goal, nor are they developing the skills to get there. Teens stuck in Achiever mode have a different problem: They have excellent task-oriented skills, but they don't believe they can change the circumstances they are in. They struggle to know what goals they care about outside of what is given to them. In high school, this can be easy: get into college (the more elite, or the bigger the scholarship, the better) or get a good job with potential for advancement. But when they get to college or start work in a role that doesn't have a clear-cut future, they often don't know what's next—like Amina.

Lisa Damour is a clinical psychologist and a bestselling author who writes and speaks extensively about supporting teens' emotional lives. One thing she's noticed is that kids who come into her clinical practice from modest circumstances tend to have more expansive views about their future: they believe they can live and work in any number of places. They also feel like they have more choices over where they want to go in their life. They can see a lot of pathways to adulthood, says Damour.[23] Multiple career pathways, a good college (versus a hyper-competitive one) that leads to jobs that allow people to support their families. These jobs range from healthcare to academia to the arts to staying home with kids.

But kids in New York City private schools and competitive high-performing Palo Alto public schools often see a narrower range of options: finance, tech, management consulting. "Kids of course want to replicate the lifestyle they had growing up," Damour says.[24] Many high-achieving students have been fed the myth that there is only one, narrow path to success—acceptance to a prestigious college—and they have internalized that message.

But that message is wrong. There are many fulfilling paths that allow you to learn on the job. Plus, what makes for a positive college experience is not a brand name or a well-worn path to Goldman Sachs. This is the secret that every Ivy League university wants to keep from you. It is easy to think of enrolling in an elite college as the equivalent of the golden ticket to Willy Wonka's chocolate factory. "I just feel like if I can get my son into a place like Stanford, he will be set for life," one upper-middle-class aspiring father in Oregon told us. Except that this isn't true. Research shows the only group of kids for whom getting admitted to an Ivy League school is a sure-fire way to change their life trajectory are those from the poorest families.[25] Widening the social network for children in poverty is a key ingredient for social mobility.[26] For the rest of the kids, it isn't the institution that makes a difference but rather how *engaged* they are while there.[27] Are they actively seeking out things that interest them? Are they finding people to help them when they need it? Are they building a community around them?[28]

Amina lacked the agency to figure out how to change her situation when she realized she didn't know who she was and what she wanted. She could feel it viscerally. She didn't have something she needed to succeed, which was weird considering her epic string of successes. It had never occurred to her that messing up might be a gift too, that the act of stumbling and toppling is needed to learn to get up and move on. Resilience is born from mucking through hard things, not being perfect in all that you do—even if the perfection come with lots of gold stars.

Deciding to take a year off was the brave first step she needed to take. After deciding to take a gap year from Yale and coming home, she was embarrassed to talk to her friends. She moped thinking, "I didn't want this for myself, this is the worst." Her mom took a different tack, telling her, "It'll be the worst if you let it be the worst. But if you make this into a chance and an opportunity for you to grow, then this can be actually a very good thing." (Amina loves this about her mom—after being wrecked by her daughter's decision to take a gap year, she dusted herself off and got behind her.)

Amina spent the semester doing an internship with a construction management company and working in a nonprofit start-up. For that job, she helped a family friend who had lost her husband to leukemia set up a charity. The friend was the CEO of an energy company and had no time. She handed to Amina the project of starting a 501(c)3, incorporating with the state, building a website, including hiring and managing web designers, writing the bylaws, and holding the first board meeting. The experience was scary—and thrilling. "It's really cool but also really frustrating," Amina says, "because there's a balance between freedom and guidelines." Achievers love guidelines. They don't love freedom. Amina was learning to navigate without explicit instructions—a useful life skill.

Amina struggled plenty because there was no road map. She was charting her course as she went. One does not develop agency overnight.

But through her navigating and diving into different experiences, Amina started to discover what she cared about. She gathered data on who she might want to be. She returned to Yale fired up and focused, fully engaged in her learning. She understands now that she does not need to graduate at the top of her class but can explore and make her time at Yale meaningful. (Work, she discovered, is lonely; she is so happy to be back among students who don't go home at 6 P.M.)

She's toying with ditching computer science for another degree. It's hard for her: She knows it's not an Achiever mode thing to do. But she suspects it's the thing she wants to do.

Takeaways

1. Kids in Achiever mode go beyond showing up and doing the bare minimum; they expend effort toward their learning, they are *cognitively engaged,* and some of them are enjoying the process and *emotionally engaged.*

2. But parents with kids who operate primarily in Achiever mode often face the Achiever Conundrum—they want their kids to push themselves and achieve, but they don't want them to break.

3. Many kids in Achiever mode are not enjoying school even though they are performing well. These students in unhappy Achiever mode are often plagued by perfectionism and haunted by a fear of failure. They have the worst mental health outcomes of all students, even those who are deeply disengaged.

4. A child operating in happy Passenger mode can be better off than a child stuck in unhappy Achiever mode.

5. All kids operating in Achiever mode are missing something: a level of self-awareness and proactivity that could help them be brave, take risks, and think about their own interests and goals in the education process, not just the goals that teachers and schools set for them.

4

Resister

Driving in Reverse

One of Samir's closest friends describes him as a golden retriever: super friendly, loyal, and easily distracted. He is warm and always animated, greeting us at a diner around the corner from his house with a big smile, flashing white teeth. Ten minutes into our conversation, the people at the table next to our booth lean over and ask us to keep our voices down. They are really talking to Samir, who has gotten louder and louder as he regales us with a story from his middle school experience. He nods and apologizes, then leans in toward us and says, self-knowingly, "Theater kid."

Samir grew up in northern Virginia, in the middle-class suburbs of Washington, D.C. He is the son of Indian immigrants, and education has always been highly valued in his family. He was in all the school plays—in seventh grade, he knocked it out of the park as an old British woman in *Spamalot.* By eighth grade, he was one of nine people cast in *Baskerville,* an adaptation of Agatha Christie in which the actors take on fifty-two roles. It was heaven. "I got to be this crazed desk clerk from Catalonia, a Scottish carriage man, and oh! I got to be the murderer. And I was British!" Samir told us, excited, talking fast, gesticulating as if he were a fifty-year-old politician making key points in a campaign speech and not a teenager recounting his glory days on stage. "I just love doing accents."

At eight, Samir was in the gifted and talented program. He had gotten the better end of the education stick. The program had better teachers, more field trips, and better projects, and he loved the hands-on learning. Plus, all his friends were in it with him. They would play together at recess, sit together at lunch, and ride the bus home. After school he and his two best friends, Anna and David, would play *Minecraft* together online after dinner, building elaborate worlds, including his favorite, a replica of the set from *The Hunger Games.* On the weekends they would hang out at Anna's house, playing hide-and-seek or baking cupcakes and decorating them to look like politicians. Obama's was a chocolate cupcake; Trump's was topped with orange icing.

One day at the end of sixth grade, teachers in his elementary school talked to students to prepare them for the big transition to seventh grade. As students filed out of his classroom, Samir held the door open for everyone. He was known for being kind and helpful. He was the last one to leave, and his teacher told him to attend the session in the school's theater. He entered the theater with various other kids and sat down on the carpeted gray steps. As the teachers at the front of the room began to talk, Samir looked around and noticed that he didn't see any of his friends. The room was filled with kids who were in the general education program and not the gifted and talented program. Samir's stomach dropped. "There is some mistake," he thought to himself, craning his head around to find Anna or David. He began to panic. His teacher had specifically told him to come here. But why wasn't he with all his other friends? "I wanted to cry, scream, and vomit all at the same time," he says. He didn't have the courage to say anything to his teacher after the session was over. But when his mom came to pick him up from school, he burst into tears and told her what had happened. She promised to call the school to sort it out, which she did. But no one ever called her back. She tried several times with the same results but wasn't sure what else she could do. Plus, she was a single mom, going through a bitter divorce that required her spending a lot of time in court on top of working six days a week as an on-call doctor running her own practice.

Years later, Samir would find out that there were several ways his school district identified children to be evaluated for the gifted and talented program. One way was a child scoring in the top 10 percent of kids in their school on an IQ test that was administered to students when they were seven. Those kids in both elementary and middle school automatically got sent for evaluation to see if they qualified for the program. Samir was not in the top 10 percent. But another way students were identified for evaluation was that a school principal or parent recommended them to be evaluated. Samir's mom hadn't asked for him to be considered in elementary school, so he assumed his principal had. His mom had no idea she was supposed to send an email to the middle school recommending he be reevaluated. Why would a school system consider a child gifted in sixth grade and ungifted in seventh?

When Samir entered middle school, he felt his world change overnight. He was the only one in his friend group not in the "smart kids" class. He tried to make new friends. He joined the drama club and found other peers he clicked with. But he missed his best friends. Kids in the gifted and talented program had a different schedule with different lunch periods, so he rarely saw them. "I sat alone at lunch every day," he said.

Life was very different out of the gifted program. He recalls an announcement on the PA system in seventh grade asking the students in the gifted and talented program to come to the gym for a school design tour across the district. Those kids would develop a vision for the school of the future. Meanwhile, Samir and his "less than gifted and talented" peers were left sitting at their desks, reading about algae in their science textbooks. He knew what he was missing because he had had it taken away: hands-on learning that fostered students' imagination and helped him to soar. "What I witnessed from my middle school's administration in particular was this treatment of the gifted kids as royalty, basically," Samir recalls. "I was in the outgroup. I felt this profound sense of social isolation."

Samir got the message that he was no longer special or smart. "There were so many times where I just felt like that label—*not* gifted and talented—defined me," he says. He began to develop test anxiety. When there was a test, he would fake being sick to avoid taking it. "I was so scared of failing," he told us. The evening before a test, he would try to study. But then he would become increasingly worried he didn't know enough and would fail. "For me getting a C was the end of the world," he says. He had always had straight As. He would feel his heart start to race, and all he could do was get up from his desk and pace back and forth, his bare feet padding rhythmically on his bedroom's bamboo floors, telling himself: "I can't do it. I can't do it. I can't do it." When his mom got home, which was often well past 10 P.M., he would tell her he was feeling sick and couldn't go to school the next day.

Losing faith in his own abilities, Samir didn't do the work, which resulted in bad grades that confirmed, in his mind, that he was dumb. This reinforced the negative feelings that made him not want to go to school and confront everything he was messing up: missed assignments, the fact that he was totally lost in most classes, the embarrassment and shame of his epic procrastination. He remembers thinking, "I can't believe that this one little failing of mine, when I was seven years old, has had such deep impact for my life."

He started to withdraw. He avoided school, teachers, classes, and his peers as much as possible. He refused to do homework. He sparred with his mom. He was depressed but didn't tell anyone because that's not what kids did in his school. "They perform," Samir says matter-of-factly, explaining the tears and stress and despair that came when kids in his school got anything less than an A.

"I was sad and anxious and figured, why come to school at all? I feel awful here," he explains.

So he didn't.

In seventh grade he missed fifteen days of school. At first his mom bought his excuses that he was sick. He really seemed like he was not doing well when he would come into her bedroom at 11 P.M. saying he felt awful and there was no way he could go to school the next day. But soon she caught on. She told him he had to go. End of story. When that happened Samir would go into "lawyer mode" and tell her all the reasons he couldn't go: He was going to fail the test, he wasn't prepared, he needed just a little more time to study to do well. She would insist. Sometimes she would win the battle and get him out the door to school. But a lot of the time she would admit defeat and go to work. "She cared about me, but you know, she couldn't be this overinvolved PTA parent. She was working all the time," he tells us.

In eighth grade he once missed school three weeks in a row. In the middle of the year, he had a particularly bad week. Deeply lonely and demoralized, he started getting strong, almost irresistible urges to cut himself. "It was really scary," he tells us. It became all he could think about. He told his theater friends, who told him, "Don't do it! We love you!" But the feeling persisted. One day after his last class, he was helping his Spanish teacher tidy up her room by pushing in the chairs and organizing the books. She was his favorite teacher and he could tell she cared about him. She asked him how his day had been, and he decided to tell her about his urge to self-harm. She took him straight down to a school counselor, who spent several hours listening to him and helping him probe why he was feeling this way. She also called his mother. "I felt heard in my feelings and affirmed," Samir says. "That was really what I needed." He never did cut himself, but for the rest of the year his mother's close attention to him felt like surveillance and monitoring. She was scared and constantly coming into his room to ask him how he felt, to ask him to come eat dinner. She pushed him less. Looking back, he says he knows his reaction wasn't helpful: "I was an eighth-grade boy. I'm like, get away from me, Mom. Go away!"

His transition to high school made everything worse. In ninth grade, he was absent eighty-seven days. When his school, which boasted of a culture of caring and compassion, offered a mental health screening, he lied and said he was fine. "We all lied," he said. "No one tells the truth on those things." One day when he was at school, he got called into the office of the school counselor, who asked him, "How do you plan to make up all this work?"—not "How are you?" or even "What is going on that you are not coming to school?"

Soon he stopped showering and brushing his teeth and rarely got out of bed. He considered suicide. At his lowest point, he remembers being enveloped in gray. His mom got increasingly desperate. She got him a therapist he hated, and after a few sessions he refused to go. She was juggling nonstop work, was worried sick about her son, and knew she had to get him to go to school. She would yell. She would scream. She would chase him around the house to try to drag him to school. He would hide in the shower and lock the bathroom door. She would pick the locks. One day, Samir stood in his room refusing to budge. His mom had chased him around the house and came in to try to physically get him to school. She grabbed his arm and pulled and accidentally tore his favorite green T-shirt at the neck. Of his six T-shirts, half ended up with rips in them from his mom trying to get him to go to school. "It was just a really dark and scary time for my entire household," he recalls.

Resister Mode: Driving in Reverse

Samir is one of the growing ranks of children with anxious school refusal, a state in which children won't go to school or stay there. This is not the same as missing the occasional day or ditching school to hang with friends. Rather, school refusal is driven by an intense fear and distress of going to school, staying in school, or taking part in particular classes.[1] Since COVID, incidents of school refusal have skyrocketed in the United States. Chronic absenteeism, where students miss 10 percent or more of the school year, jumped from 8 percent before the pandemic to 22 percent in 2021.[2] The problem hasn't gone away: one in four kids were chronically absent from school in the 2022–23 school year.[3]

Samir was deeply enmeshed in Resister mode: disengaged on all fronts and paralyzed by inaction. When students resist, they avoid learning. Unlike kids in Achiever mode, they are not cognitively engaged or emotionally engaged. They can't even muster the behavioral engagement of compliant Passengers, who coast along but are showing up and doing passable homework. Emotionally, Samir felt he did not belong in school. Cognitively, he was not invested in learning and so avoided anything related to it: reading, studying, doing homework, asking for help. Behaviorally, he had withdrawn completely, failing to go to school. He felt he had no ability to change his situation.

Some common signs that children are operating in Resister mode include behaviors Samir exhibited, such as repeatedly being late for school, missing school, or missing specific classes; chronically missing assignments; getting much lower grades; showing a noticeable change in social interactions and withdrawing into themselves. But there are plenty of signs that Samir did not have, including ongoing bursts of anger over and above the occasional adolescent outburst; repeated disruption of class or other activities; regular, extremely rude communication; and risky behavior such as alcohol use, drug use, or criminal activity.

Parenting a kid in Resister mode can be brutal. Somewhere between heart-wrenching worry and Incredible Hulk levels of frustration lies a sense that you have failed. It's easy to be embarrassed to have a child who refuses to try, who won't go to school, whose every fiber is committed to not doing what it seems every other kid is doing: *getting on with it.* You yearn for them to feel worthy but see how little they are doing to earn that worthiness. But too often when kids are resisting, adults see them as problem children rather than children with problems.*

---

* This is a shared perspective from experts working with children at risk, but we are especially grateful to Amy Berry for the wonderful turn of phrase to describe this conundrum in our interview with her on September 28, 2023.

Resistance is your kids' way of using what power they have to let you know things are *not* working. Since they are young, it often comes out in ways that seem strange to adults. Rarely do students give parents, teachers, or coaches a self-reflective soliloquy on the reasons they are resisting, their feelings and struggles. Instead, what you see is a pain-in-the-ass kid. For kids themselves, it is a cry for help. Instead of labeling children, parents need to listen.

There Is Agency in Resistance

Kids in Resister mode are desperately using what is under their control to make their voices heard. And they often are resisting for good reasons. Samir describes how shocked he was to learn that there was a class system in his school. Why, he wondered, would the active learning approaches so good for gifted students not be good for *every* student?* He was observing firsthand what scholars such as Edward Fergus of Rutgers University have studied for years: that students' effort is shaped by school policies and structures, which can actively hold certain children back rather than propel them forward.[4] Samir's impulse to opt out of the system that was making him feel terrible was not that of a compliant kid in Passenger mode. Instead, he was tapping into his internal urge to change things. He just didn't have the self-awareness or skills, yet, to channel this urge toward more constructive ends such as advocating for more hands-on projects or field trips for all students.

There is a silver lining to Resister mode: When kids resist, they show an urge to change their learning environment. Pedro Noguera, a University of Southern California Distinguished Professor and dean

* On this point, we 100 percent agree with Samir. Schools are not doing any favors to students who struggle academically by giving them less interesting, less applied, less relevant-to-the-real-world teaching and learning experiences.

of USC's School of Education, has spent decades researching how to help improve educational outcomes for *all* students. He worries that students who are struggling in school are often blamed for being lazy, suggesting the problem is solely with the student and not the context around them. He advocates for helping them to develop the ability to take action to change their circumstances, including critical thinking skills to observe the obstacles in their way, and strategies to work with others to try to remove those.[5] When kids resist they are asserting some control over their situation. Sometimes it's self-preservation. But it's often to the detriment of their learning. They are taking action to change their circumstances, but away from school not toward it.

Adults in families, schools, and communities can help kids build this agency and point it in a better direction. Every time a parent or teacher or coach sees a kid resisting and tries to understand what is driving their behavior before doling out consequences, they are helping children develop the self-reflection skills that are part of having agency. Agency takes time to develop; it is not a gift bestowed by Great-Aunt Wanda. When adults help young people not only self-reflect but also think critically about what they need and help them build strategies to move forward, they are helping them build agency. Ultimately, this agency empowers adolescents to leverage the resources and assistance they need to overcome barriers and pursue goals they have identified as important.

In this one crucial respect, kids in Resister mode have a leg up on kids in Passenger and Achiever modes. When kids are coasting or laser-focused on achievements, they take their learning environment as a given. They either do the bare minimum asked of them or strive to succeed within the framework they are offered. Unless a school is specifically designed to build students' agency, and most are not, kids in Passenger or Achiever mode prioritize compliance over self-reflection. They are going along with what the adults want and fitting themselves into the school's requirements. In their own, often counterproductive ways, kids in Resister mode are showing that they want to shake things up.

The challenge resisting kids face is that the impulse to change their learning environment is not the same as having the skills to *constructively* do so. Students who resist, avoid, and disrupt their learning by skipping class or acting out in school. Sometimes defiance is healthier than defeat. But if they don't get help to turn things around, they can slide from Resister mode into Resister identity. Their behavior cements adults' perceptions of them as problem children, fueling further resistance, which results in more negative consequences. It's like they are in reverse—and then accelerating.

Many resisting teens get noticed. When they disrupt classrooms, fight with peers, yell at principals and/or their parents, and get expelled, parents are called. School counselors are brought in. Game plans are drawn up. The kids who withdraw into themselves and avoid school, like Samir, are at a greater risk of falling through the cracks.

Being stuck in Resister mode in school is crushing for young people. Nothing seems to work. Their thoughts about school and their place in it become a poisonous loop. They think they are worthless, so they start acting worthless, which confirms their thoughts. The meaning they make of it all is that they are not capable and do not belong. Why try? They begin to develop a story about themselves: They are powerless and lack control to change anything.

"I had this lack of motivation, this feeling of emptiness," Samir recalls. "I don't want to take this test because I am going to fail. I don't want to do anything. I am just numb to all this. I can't move on."

Samir was a clear-cut case of a kid stuck deeply in Resister mode. His actions, feelings, and thoughts all screamed "No!" in the direction of school. But it's not always so obvious. Some young people sink quietly into Resisting—a tempest raging inside but they exude calm outside. These are a few common ways to recognize when children are in Resister mode. Note how often what you see looks similar but what they think and feel is quite different.

KIDS IN RESISTER MODE

THINK	FEEL	DO (AND SAY)
I hate this. I don't know how to succeed. I am just not going to try.	Set up for failure	Pretends to be sick a lot, avoids going to school
I don't belong here. People are so mean. I don't want to be here.	Isolation, sadness	Quietly not doing work in school, pretends to do homework, sits alone at lunch, misses assignments
What's the point? It's irrelevant.	Anger	Disrupts class; talks back to teacher, breaks school rules, skips class, gets in fights, doesn't come to school
I am stuck. I see no way to get unstuck. No one seems to care.	Powerless	Quiet, unresponsive when asked about school, doesn't bring friends home, withdraws into self or acts rebellious inside and outside of school, lashes out

How "Belonging Uncertainty" Fuels Resisting

Samir, like many students who resist, worries silently that he doesn't truly belong in school.[6] "My mom very much felt that it was just academics," Samir says, explaining his mother's view that his main problem was related to schoolwork. "But for me, it was really the environment where I felt so isolated, so profoundly sad."

He knew that others thought he was just evading work. "A part of it was having to do my work," he admits. "But a lot more of it was just facing my fears, coming to school dealing with an environment that made me feel awful." On the outside it seemed as if Samir was both overly anxious and lacking a strong work ethic. But internally, he was struggling to see where he belonged, where he added value, and whether he had worth that people could care about.

Belonging comes from feeling connected to others, and it is critical to human thriving.[7] People who have friends and support networks live longer, are happier, and have more meaningful careers. The reverse is also true. Being socially disconnected poses a risk comparable to smoking fifteen cigarettes a day. It is also "more predictive of early death than air pollution or physical inactivity."[8]

When we don't feel we belong, we tend to look for evidence to support it, collecting that which confirms our negative beliefs. Imagine you come late to a cocktail party where you don't know anyone. You see a group of five people near the bar chatting with drinks in their hands. If you are like most people, you assume the people know one another and wouldn't want you to interrupt. You scan the room for someone or somewhere you could more easily fit in. But the truth is, you don't know if the group by the bar are actually friends and wouldn't welcome an addition. Maybe they all met just now in the drinks line and would be happy to add a new person to the conversation. Students experience this too in school (minus the alcohol). "The teacher is a little bit too critical, a peer doesn't join your study group, some people roll their eyes at you, the homework assignment feels kind of pointless. Any negative thing seems like evidence that you don't belong because that's the lens you're applying to it," David Yeager, the psychology professor at the University of Texas at Austin, explained to us.[9]

This experience is known as **belonging uncertainty.** It sets in motion a process that prevents kids from taking the hundreds of small steps—asking for help with homework, talking to teachers when in doubt, reaching out to peers for advice, telling parents things are not going well—that make learning possible. Refusing to take steps to make learning work, they fail more. Resistance becomes the only option. Agency is deployed but in the wrong direction—away from learning and not toward it.

Samir could have talked to his friends more about how he felt. He could have told his mom that school made him feel awful. He could have reached out to the school counseling office rather than wait for his teacher to bring him. He could have asked a teacher to help him make a plan to catch up. But he didn't. It wasn't because he was weak-minded or had a character flaw. He was interpreting the many signals from school to mean *You don't belong here, you are not capable, you do not matter.*

When kids feel they don't belong, they can be touchy, be defiant, act out, seem closed off, and struggle with understanding and completing tasks because their minds are so consumed with scanning the environment to see if there are any threats (Is this kid going to make fun of me today?). This makes learning harder.[10]

"If kids are in a state of fear, they can't mobilize parts of their brain on behalf of concentrating, taking new information in, activating their working memory so that they can play with new ideas," says Pamela Cantor, a psychiatrist who has spent decades working with children affected by adversity. "When kids are in a state of fear, all of those processes are shut down."[11]

In 2011, Stanford researchers Greg Walton and Geoffrey Cohen found that reinforcing a sense of belonging for first-year Black college students at a predominantly white institution led to higher GPAs from sophomore through senior year, reducing the racial achievement gap by 52 percent.[12] They divided students in two groups. One, the "treatment group," read the results of a survey indicating that many students feel they do not belong at college at first but that these worries dissipate with time. They then wrote an essay and recorded a short speech to the next year's incoming freshmen about how their own worries had changed over time. The second group of students also read the results of a survey, but it focused on other topics, like how students got used to the physical environment of college. The results were staggering: In addition to earning higher GPAs, the Black students in the treatment group were more likely to be in the top 25 percent of their class compared to the nontreatment students. And perhaps most remarkably, three years later, they reported being happier and healthier.

When students are not actively questioning their belonging, they may find things annoying and frustrating but not paralyzing and painful. They are able to deploy a new strategy, find a new study partner, or remember that they got some positive comments from that same teacher on another assignment. They stay in rather than check out.

Resistance as Protection

While Stella invested in her learning in French and coasted in math and English, chemistry catapulted her straight into Resister mode. This was not preordained: She entered the class junior year having not thought much about the subject. But she had enjoyed science before so was not particularly worried.

That changed almost immediately. Mr. Jenkins, the teacher, had been teaching at the school for fifty years. He used a flipped classroom approach, in which you do readings and assignments at home and come to class ready to discuss them and ask questions. Stella was game for trying the method, and for the first couple of weeks she carefully did her assignments and prepared her questions. She quickly realized chemistry wasn't super intuitive to her—she didn't always get it. It was way harder than biology and less logical than physics. She asked questions in class, but Mr. Jenkins's answers made no sense to her. She asked follow-up questions to try to clarify. Mr. Jenkins would repeat the same answer but louder. Sometimes he even responded with "In college, no one will give you the answers." Stella found this grating. She wasn't in college. She was in high school *and asking for help.*

Stella bombed her first test. She went to Mr. Jenkins's student hours after school to ask for help. She told him she didn't understand the material. He would point to a question she got wrong and ask her, "What don't you understand about this?" She didn't understand *anything,* so she didn't know how to explain what she didn't understand. She was that lost. Mr. Jerkins repeated: "What don't you get about this?" She left the office fuming. It was unfair. She had to take the test again without him ever giving her back corrections to help her understand what she had done wrong. It was almost like he wanted her to fail.

Because of a scheduling snafu caused by the school, Mr. Jenkins decided to cancel labs, justifying his decision by saying, "There are no labs on the AP." This made Stella even more anxious. *Chemistry without labs?* It was already so abstract! To top it off, all her friends who were in her class seemed to be acing it. Stella was struggling and couldn't see a way out. She was trying. She wanted to do well and learn but felt she couldn't.

One day, she lost it. She had a panic attack. She doesn't remember how it came on, just that suddenly she could not see or breathe.

After that day, her parents got her a therapist and a chemistry tutor. The tutor helped a lot; he explained things until she got them. He convinced her she was panicking on tests and not confused. She got an 88 on her next test. But Stella decided chemistry was bad for her mental health. She would be in such a foul mood the period after chemistry that she would snap at her friends and have a terrible rest of the day. So she started to purposefully not listen or learn in class, shopping online and scrolling through TikTok—anything to distract herself from the lesson. "Listening to him only made me more confused anyways," she said. On Sundays, she would sit down and muscle through five hours of chemistry. She compartmentalized her misery, creating a force field to protect herself from Mr. Jenkins's negative energy.

Her resisting was a form of self-care. Mr. Jenkins was fired the next year.

When Resisting Becomes an Identity

A little resisting can be a good thing, a way to call attention to a problem: an undiagnosed learning condition maybe, or bullying or social isolation or racism. But when resisting expands from a class or a couple weeks to an identity, things can quickly spiral out of control, as they did with Samir. One risk is what the clinical psychologist Lisa Damour calls "costly coping."[13]

Those languishing in Resister mode often look for thrill and excitement elsewhere. In a study of more than ninety thousand U.S. high school students, teens who were disengaged in school were twice as likely to be engaged in risky behavior outside of class, including smoking cigarettes, using marijuana, drinking alcohol, binge drinking, fighting in school, skipping school, and joining gangs.[14]

Many years of research have found that the more disengaged students are, the more likely they are to report feeling sad, anxious, and depressed.[15] As we discussed previously, Resisters have poor mental health, like unhappy Achievers, those kids who appear to be nailing school but are actually suffering silently.[16]

When the story of a moment—*I failed my math test*—starts to become a narrative for a learner identity—*I am no good at school*—kids start numbing themselves with unhealthy pastimes, accelerating the downward spiral. Not trying at anything becomes an identity.

Identity formation is not a by-product of adolescence. It's the main goal. Sarah-Jayne Blakemore, a University of Cambridge London neuroscientist, wrote a book about the teenage brain called *Inventing Ourselves: The Secret Life of the Teenage Brain,* arguing that's how she thinks about adolescence—the time when we start to really become the person we end up being.[17] Of course we are never done, or fixed in a certain state. The beauty of being human is the ability to evolve, adapt, change, grow, learn. But the experiences and feelings and skills we build in adolescence become foundational. In this stage, teens grapple with questions of who they are, what they want to be, and where they fit into society. Erik Erikson, a seminal figure in the field of child development, called this stage of adolescent development "identity versus role confusion."[18] By testing many identities, teens start finding the one that feels right. Teens in Resister mode are often stuck in one that is not constructive for either learning or their mental health.

There is also a very real risk that kids in Resister mode, rather than leapfrogging to Explorer mode, slip into **learned helplessness,** extinguishing their agency. That's what happened to Samir, who felt powerless to change his circumstances. Demoted to the "dumb kids" class, lost without close friends, falling behind, he felt terrible and eventually sank into depression and began to give up.

Learned helplessness is not a place any parent wants their child to go. Research shows how it can alter our sense of possibility from "I can't do this" to "I can't do anything." In the late 1960s, a pair of psychologists named Martin Seligman and Steven Maier observed learned helplessness in two groups of dogs exposed to randomly administered electric shocks (we are thinking it too: the poor dogs!).[19] The first group could not control or avoid the shocks, but the second group could stop the shocks by pressing a lever. Next, they placed dogs from both groups in a chamber on an electrified floor. The random shocks resumed. But there was a trick. Part of the room did not have an electrified floor. There was no lever to turn off the shocks, but all the dogs could jump over a small barrier to get to safety.

The dogs that had learned to press the lever to turn off the shock immediately jumped to the other side the floor to escape the shocks. But the other dogs, the ones that had never had any control over their situation or any opportunity to change it in the first place, just sat there. They became lethargic and avoidant and lost general motivation. They felt helpless in the face of adversity and did not unlearn their helplessness even when the circumstances changed.

Students in Resister mode who develop learned helplessness have their brains working against them: Studies show an overall reduction in neuronal activity during states of learned helplessness.[20] Neuroscientists have identified that regions of the brain that typically fire up when people feel a sense of control show reduced activity in a state of learned helplessness.[21] Further, the level of coordination between different parts of the brain decreases with these feelings.[22] The prefrontal cortex, the air traffic controller, communicates less with other regions of the brain associated with motor control of the body, emotion, and memory. Command central is not able to manage flights coming in and those taking off. A brain experiencing learned helplessness will struggle to learn.

The good news is that with a little help, young people can learn to exert agency over their lives even when they find themselves, as they most certainly will at some point, in tough times. This is what the lever-pressing group of dogs learned. There are solutions. We can get out of this.

Looking back on fifty years of research, Seligman and his colleagues argue that this is the most important takeaway from their research. Hope can be cultivated. The skills to navigate obstacles to overcome problems can be practiced and learned.[23]

Brains develop the way they are used. When the lever-pressing dogs were figuring out how to escape the electrified floor, their prefrontal cortex was in full gear. This part of the brain is responsible for helping us address difficult problems. It evaluates the context or environment and finds solutions. It's expending a lot of energy in adolescence getting connected to other key brain networks—a process that continues into early adulthood. When adolescents struggle, their brains are building problem-solving capacities.

Young people in Resister mode often need help engaging their prefrontal cortex to reframe the situation they are in. They need to see that there are ways out, that they can be problem solvers for themselves. Often, they'll need our help getting there. We have to be critical problem solvers at first. Samir slipped far into Resister identity because he didn't initially have enough support. His mom was stretched between work and a messy divorce. Stella got help: from her parents, from a tutor, from a therapist. And then she was able to take over, figuring out her own way to make chemistry work (even if it ruined her Sundays).

Resisting kids need caring relationships to move forward and hopefully avoid slipping into Resister identity. Supportive relationships—from parents, mentors, teachers—create a safe space where disengaged children can begin to try, to challenge themselves, to find the help they need or to remove the barriers they face. In other words, the space to engage and learn.[24]

The Art of Clandestine Resistance

Sometimes kids are resisting silently and teachers don't notice. They comply with the rules in school, listen in class, do their homework. But internally they want out. Parents play a key role here.

On a wet weekday morning in the spring of 2013, Julia Black remembers coming into her kitchen in Somerset, England, to make breakfast and saw her daughter, Esme, curled up in the dog's bed. She recalls that her daughter, who is fair-skinned, looked very gray. Esme did not want to go to school.

"You might as well send me to prison," she told her mom. "Because that's what it feels like."

School felt one-dimensional to Esme, even though life didn't. She had started to read at an early age and loved to write her own stories. She loved music and dancing and playing. But school seemed to squash those interests. When she'd share what she put on paper, all the teacher noticed was spelling or punctuation errors. She enjoyed drawing pictures, but they wanted her to color inside the lines. She started to get the message that school didn't care about her, that her interests and creativity were not welcome.

Esme's teachers were not bad teachers and her school was not considered a bad school. She lived a comfortable middle-class life in a small town. It's just that school didn't work for her.

She had friends in school but did not feel any identity with school—in fact, she felt school trammeled her identity, trying to replace it with a uniform one that did not fit her at all. She got good grades because they came easily to her. She could whip through assignments with little effort, and she did. But she wasn't deeply engaged in her learning, and she didn't feel like there was anything she could do to make her classes more interesting to her. Quiet and deeply curious, she loved working toward things that meant something to her. But school was not one of those things.

Esme did not act out in class—she was too shy. She used what little power she felt she had to resist in her own way: She retreated, completely. In her English class, when the teacher would ask students to do ten minutes of quiet individual reading with their book, she would open her book, gaze down, and purposefully *not read.* She wouldn't turn the pages. She would just stare straight down at the same page seeing if anyone would notice. No one ever did.

She developed a story about school that made sense to her. "I knew I didn't matter to the system," she told us. She was a small cog in a machine when what she wanted was to be part of the engine, moving things, *doing things.* The two overriding emotions she remembers from that time in school: powerlessness in a system that did not care about her, and a mismatch between who she felt she was and what the system wanted her to be.

Esme doesn't remember the dog bed incident (she was nine at the time). But she remembers the boredom. "I remember every day feeling like sort of a sense of dread about going to school and then just really not enjoying it while I was there," she says from her college dorm room, her long light brown hair falling over her shoulders. "I felt like as a person I was on hold during the whole day. When I went home, I could relax and do things that I was interested in doing. It was almost like ticking a box—I had to go to school and just get through the day, and then when I got home I could be myself again."

Kids who are resisting are sometimes obvious like Samir, who stopped coming to school and doing his work. But they are also like Esme, pretending to read, silently avoiding learning, disengaged but not overtly disruptive. Parents, teachers, and coaches need to worry about both. Staying too long in Resister mode gets young people stuck, internalizing a sense of learned helplessness. No child is born a Resister. They develop an "I can't" narrative, of which there are many variations.

Esme's mom calls the Resister state "lights off." After the dog bed incident, she pulled her daughter and son out of school and homeschooled them for a bit. She had seen up close and personal how many kids struggled in school. A successful filmmaker when Esme started reception (pre-kindergarten), she changed gears after seeing how unhappy Esme was at the end of her school days. She joined the PTA and then the school board and launched events to try to make school more fun, winning an award for putting on a wildly popular circus. After a year and a half of homeschooling, the kids went back to school, and she launched a creative center in the village to try to draw out kids' passions. Young people from the top and the bottom of the achievement scale filtered in, bored, overwhelmed, acting out, all feeling powerless.

Over the years, Esme's mom worked on getting kids from "lights off" to "lights on," first outside school, then inside schools, and finally, in 2018, with parents. She firmly believes that every child has a passion, which too often gets buried or is stifled by the predominant focus on academics at school. "I was shocked by the level of disengagement in the students," she said. They would come to the center but have no idea what to do, where to start. They had no agency because they had never been asked, "What do you love?" and had never had any opportunities to explore the idea of who they were. She offered filmmaking, coding, engineering, technology, art, music, and anything else a child might want to explore. The kids enjoyed it. But the grown-ups—teachers and parents—often resisted, worried about the time it was taking away from the academics *that their kids were not engaged with.*

The experience was illuminating. "I just saw the stakes, the crisis in learning, really, really up close and personal," Black told us. She saw with alarming clarity that disengagement was pervasive, affecting high-, middle-, and low-income kids equally. And kids were suffering. Parents seemed unaware or too focused on grades to worry about disengagement. She wondered if they knew how unhappy their kids seemed.

Esme was lucky to have a mother able to see her daughter's resistance for what it was—a cry to change the environment she operated in—and to act on it in creative and connected ways. Esme's mom recognized her strengths and built on those, helping Esme avoid developing a Resister identity. Esme didn't just go back to school; she is now studying chemistry and biochemistry at a leading UK university. She's taking a year off to study science writing because she misses the creativity her mother helped to foster. She has a strong sense of who she is—a scientific and creative mind—and the confidence to find ways to combine those into a potential career.

Some signs your kid is in Resister mode:

- They often feel very discouraged and struggle to articulate why.
- They are convinced they are stupid/incapable, but others are not.
- They feel like an outsider; they are not part of a group of friends.
- They fight you on all offers of help.
- They have ongoing outbursts of anger.
- They feel a pervasive sense of helplessness.
- They believe their challenges are character defects and not areas for improvement or structural barriers to overcome.
- They make negative and degrading comments about themselves when they perform poorly.
- They stop doing schoolwork or going to school.
- They engage in in risky behavior.

Parenting kids in Resister mode can be stressful, anxiety producing, and at times heartbreaking. The natural instinct of adults, including parents, teachers, and social workers, is to respond to young people in Resister mode by trying to stop the negative behaviors. Get out of bed! Go to school! Do your homework! Behave in class!

Of course all children, including those resisting, need to know what is and isn't appropriate behavior and be held accountable for their actions. But addressing behavior without understanding why it is happening rarely works. Remember, veteran educators who specialize in helping Resisters get unstuck see behavior problems as a cry for help, not a character defect. You should too. After all, in the words of Elliot Washor and Charles Mojkowski, cofounders of Big Picture Learning, "Our greatest task is to buy students time to grow into themselves without giving up on them."[25]

Kids want to succeed, in learning and in life. Resisters show us through their actions that they don't care (Samir), can't do it (Stella), or are unhappy (Esme). When we see the actions, we should consider them a five-alarm fire signaling us to figure out what's holding them back. To get to the key questions of adolescence—*Who am I?* and *How do I fit into the world?*—teens in Resister mode need help getting out of reverse and into drive. When we respond from a place of love and connection, we can help channel the agency in resisting in the right direction, paving a clear way to Explorer mode.

Takeaways

1. Kids in Resister mode are taking initiative; sometimes in self-preserving ways, but it is directed away from their learning. At school they are disengaged emotionally, cognitively, and often behaviorally.
2. Some students have perfected the art of clandestine resistance. They look like they are participating in school, but internally they are actively disengaged.
3. Resisters are children with problems, not problem children. They need trusted adults to help them get unstuck and address the barriers they face.
4. When a student is unsure if they belong at school, it is hard to take the necessary actions to learn: asking for help, connecting with peers and teachers, digging in. This is called *belonging uncertainty.*
5. When kids move from Resister mode to a Resister identity, they are at risk of "costly coping"—numbing their frustration through things such as self-harm, drugs, or alcohol. They risk falling into learned helplessness.

5

Explorer

Productive and Happy

In elementary school, Tevin tried to do what teachers asked of him. He would come to school happy to learn and see his friends. He would look down at his worksheets and try to do them, but so many other things seemed more interesting: *Were the birds in the trees outside the window building a nest?* He found school boring and stifling—nothing but sitting at a desk all day, regurgitating facts. He would half listen to the teacher and answer the questions on his assignments in the shortest way possible. Little by little, he stopped doing his homework.

Teachers could see he was bright and curious. Though he was one of the few Black kids in his predominantly white neighborhood public school in Cedar Rapids, Iowa, he had many friends and asked lots of questions outside of class. But teachers struggled to help him comply with what was asked of him. He was constantly interrupting and off task in class. Midway through elementary school, out of desperation, the school gave Tevin an individualized education plan (IEP), in the hopes that the extra help would help with his misbehavior.

In middle school, Tevin continued to vacillate between Passenger mode and Resister mode. He would coast along, doing the bare minimum of what was needed, until he became so annoyed that he simply decided not to. He started skipping classes. More than once he got suspended. Sometimes his bottled-up frustration exploded, and he would disrupt his class, yelling at his teacher about how dumb everything was. All the teachers in his school, and even a few district leaders, knew Tevin as the "problem child." His family and friends worried he was tossing his life away.

Tevin's misbehaving came to a head his sophomore year of high school. One morning he was running late. When he arrived at school and checked in at the front desk, Ms. Lynch gave him an unexcused tardy, even though his mom had called ahead of time to alert the school he would be late. Tevin protested, but Ms. Lynch didn't budge. He started to argue with her. It was unfair. He didn't need another unexcused tardy. When the principal came out to settle him down, Tevin started shouting that he hated the school, they didn't understand him, they didn't support him, and classes were stupid.

The next day, the principal asked Tevin and his parents to meet at the school. Tevin went into the meeting prepared to apologize, even though he suspected he would still be suspended. Instead, the principal was kind and calm. He said he knew Tevin was a good kid at heart but that things couldn't go on this way. The school just wasn't working for Tevin, and his resistance was exhausting the school's staff. He wasn't suspending Tevin, but he didn't know if Tevin could continue to be a full-time student at the school.

This was more punishment than even Tevin had expected. However, the principal continued, he believed Tevin should try an innovative new high school program called Iowa Big. In this program, Tevin would spend half of each day at the high school; for the other half of the day, he would apply the knowledge he had learned to solving the community's problems, working on projects with local nonprofits, government agencies, and businesses.

Tevin's parents wanted more information—it didn't really *sound* like school. Plus, could Tevin really handle all that freedom? But in the end, they had very few options. They couldn't afford private school, and they knew Tevin needed something different. Several weeks later, Tevin enrolled in Iowa Big.

Through all the years of Tevin's acting out, his parents had never condoned his misbehavior. They met with the school when called, and they disciplined Tevin when necessary. But they also didn't see him as a problem child—just a kid with some problems. What they often told the school was that they never saw any of this disruptive behavior at home. He was inquisitive and able when digging into his personal interests. He was sociable and kind and had a real spark.

In 2007, when Tevin was seven and his parents were building a new house on the outskirts of town, he became fascinated with construction. He studied the blueprints as the foundation was being poured. He watched in amazement as the walls went up. He talked to the team building the house, peppering them with a million questions. He drew out floor plans for fun and asked his parents to help him learn how to do it on a computer. Then, using freely available computer-aided design (CAD) software, he began designing buildings on his computer after school and on weekends.

When Tevin's parents saw his curiosity about their architect's floor plans, they could have told him not to bother the construction crew—*they're busy, this is no place for a kid to explore.* Or they could have told him that he couldn't go visit the house because he hadn't done his homework. Instead, they got behind his interest and supported it. They let him talk with the construction crew and answered his additional questions during the car ride home afterward. They continued to bring him to see the house being built, even when he was acting out in school and lost other privileges as punishment. They were fanning the flame of his interest, helping it move from situational to individual.

It wasn't just his own house Tevin was curious about. On weekends, he pleaded with his parents to take him to open houses. So while Tevin's parents fielded regular calls from his teachers about missing assignments, they also piled into the car on Saturdays to check out different house configurations. Tevin would walk in and study the floor plan, envisioning how he might design things differently. On Sundays, he would sketch out new neighborhoods, and then his parents would inquire about where the park might be or how traffic would affect the layout.

Tevin was not in Passenger or Resister mode outside of school. He was an Explorer. His parents knew he needed something constructive to focus on—a place for him to develop his identity as capable and smart, rather than the "problem child." They helped to connect the dots between his interests and the real world, explaining what architects do and the kind of work Tevin would need to do to become one. They suggested he could even apply for an internship with a local architect, perhaps when he was in high school. Even as Tevin would come home feeling defeated by school, his parents saw that when he worked on his designs he perked up. He got more energy and was in a better mood. He became excited about what he was learning.

During his first week at Iowa Big, Tevin was in awe at how different things were: no rows of desks, no worksheets to complete in twenty minutes, no blackboard at the front of a classroom. Nothing looked closed and square, like he was used to; instead, everything seemed open and expansive. "It felt like I could finally breathe," Tevin said, "like I had been in an airtight container, and all of a sudden there was an abundance of air."

His first project was designing the school's all-school meeting space. His teachers knew about his interest in architecture. When they offered him the chance, he dived in, using all his CAD expertise. He was excited, nervous, and proud all at the same time. His teachers mentored him along the way: He learned the math behind the design process, and how to consult potential users of the space and incorporate their needs into his revisions. It turned out that more freedom over his learning was exactly what he needed.

One night, his mom came down at midnight to find him working on the project. "She's like, 'What are you still doing up?'" Tevin told us. "And I was, like, 'Just tracking this PowerPoint proposal.' I think that's when she and my dad really realized, *whoa,* we have never seen this excitement and love. For school, anyways."

Tevin had jumped from fluctuating between Passenger and Resister modes in school to Explorer mode. The meeting space redesign project was just the beginning. A flood washed out an important pedestrian bridge in town, and Tevin and his fellow students helped the city design a new one. He loved seeing his work have a tangible impact. With every project, his passion for serving his community grew.

His senior year, he decided he wanted to design his own project. Why didn't more schools use the Iowa Big approach? He suspected students didn't know there was even another way to learn. Over the next year, he became immersed in the question of school design. When he graduated from high school, he took a gap year—not to tour around Europe but to be a founding member of a new statewide organization spreading the word about education approaches like Iowa Big.

Tevin went on to enroll in Morningside University in Sioux City because he liked their focus on connecting academics to real-world problems and they offered him a merit scholarship. He graduated from college with a 3.9 GPA, a double major in business administration and public policy, and a double minor in law and sociology. He is now the youngest board member of the African American Museum of Iowa, has a job he loves as an innovation analyst for one of the country's leading clean energy companies, and is a frequent speaker at national conferences such as SXSW EDU (a popular education conference in Austin, Texas).

Few would have predicted this path for Tevin. He credits his enthusiasm outside the classroom for helping him avoid totally derailing himself *in* the classroom. He never internalized, like Samir, the idea that he was incapable. His parents made sure of that. He knew he was smart and could drive his own learning if only given the chance. His advice to parents of kids struggling in school? "What's in your backyard, or what's within your local community? Or what can you do on the weekends that's going to ignite that young person? To carry that passion with them—that may help them in *their* school and learning environment."

This is what Explorer mode looks like: when young people have agency and use it to boost their engagement in their learning.

The Explorer Advantage: Productive and Happy

Explorers have reached the peak of the engagement mountain. They are *behaviorally engaged,* showing up and participating; *emotionally engaged,* interested in the work and connected to the people around them; and *cognitively engaged,* putting in effort to deeply understand the content. But unlike kids who are in happy Achiever mode, who are also doing all these things, Explorers are activating something no other mode does: taking initiative in small and big ways to advance their learning. Exploring, in other words, requires the fourth dimension of engagement, *agentic engagement*—a critical ability all kids and adults need to navigate the massive technological and social changes happening around us.[1]

Unlike the other three dimensions of engagement, which are all about how students think, feel, and act in response to what they are asked to do in classrooms and schools, students with agentic engagement try to shape a more supportive learning environment for themselves. They connect their interests to what's being taught: *Can we calculate the potential growth of Beyonce's net worth using exponents?* They make suggestions about how to do the work they are asked to complete: *Can we work with a partner?* They seek help to investigate things they're interested in: *Can I install CAD software on my computer?* They express their preferences: *I want to focus on how President Truman grew the government bureaucracy for my history essay,* which is how Kia told us she "bent what is taught" to fit her interests. *Can I help you design a class on that topic?* That's the question that led Tevin to co-design a seminar on AI with one of his professors during his freshman year of college. Taking initiative is why Kia and Tevin both saw a boost in their grades once they were given opportunities to explore in school. They are not exceptions. Rigorous research across multiple countries shows that in classrooms where teachers support students' agentic engagement, kids get better grades and do better on tests. This is compared to classrooms *in the same schools* where teachers do not provide an environment that lets kids explore.[2]

In ways big and small, kids in Explorer mode influence the flow of their learning.[3] They sit at the opposite end of the spectrum from learned helplessness, exercising daily the muscle of actively questioning the world they are in. They ask simple questions of themselves: What do I care about? What are my interests, goals, and priorities? How can I constructively influence my environment to make something more interesting to me?

They are building skills not just to deliver a "product"—a 95 on the math test, an excellent argumentative essay in English—but also to take a creative journey of inquiry. This is exactly the skill they will need to live in a world where soon they will be collaborating with AI to create new solutions to problems: designing the ideas while technology generates the product.[4]

When schools don't provide an environment for exploring, it is up to us, families, coaches, and mentors, to find ways to practice exploring outside of school. Will good grades follow? Probably. But a child who maintains decent, if not perfect, grades in school—leaving open a range of future opportunities—and who is exercising explorer skills outside of school will develop critical mindsets and abilities: creating, questioning, thinking independently. These are skills the Age of Agency will reward.

Regardless of what they are learning or where they are learning it, students in Explorer mode take ownership over their learning. They pursue their interests, set goals, seek challenges, and don't collapse when the challenges get difficult or their goals change. When they face a serious obstacle, they ask for help. They look for ways to make their life meaningful. They reflect on their mistakes and grow from them. In this mode, they aren't know-it-alls but learn-it-alls, forever eager to deepen, expand, relearn, unlearn, and move forward.[5] They are not afraid of embarking on a task without clear instructions on how to do it "right," something kids in Achiever mode crave. When students are in Explorer mode, they gain energy from trying things and seek out people or resources in their environment to help them sate their curiosity. It isn't magic per se, but it's close.

Exploring can be hard work. But it is often "hard fun." It entails focusing, asking questions, seeking feedback, iterating, revising goals, and loving the challenges along the way, even if you don't love every minute of the journey. The result is that when kids are in Explorer mode, they are both productive and happy—an important middle ground between being mindlessly entertained and painfully grinding through homework.[6]

It doesn't matter when or how a child gets into Explorer mode. As long as they are not hurting themselves or others, the content of their exploration is only the canvas for their skill building. Some, like Kia, find a way to make government class super exciting by digging into the fascinating workings of bureaucracy. Many kids explore through sports or plumb the depths of the internet. Others connect dots between activities: If they love both cooking and international relations, they see an opportunity to host a cultural food event. They test their interest in medicine by volunteering in a vaccine clinic during a pandemic. They don't just attend a climate change protest—they start asking local businesses how they manage their waste.

Kids *don't* get into Explorer mode because teachers, coaches, or parents give them incentives: Rainbows, jellybeans, and sunshine will not an Explorer make. But neither does control, conflict, or pressure to perform at all costs, regardless of students' interests or well-being.[7] Explorers need an environment that encourages asking questions and taking risks. This is not all schools or classrooms, which is why it is so vital that parents try to create these conditions at home. By supporting this kind of agentic engagement, we offer a counterbalance to compliance culture—one that seeks to build a teen's identity through exploring, rather than to shoehorn it into conformity.

As we noted in chapter 4, Erik Erikson argued that the most important task of adolescence is developing a sense of personal identity. As teens attempt to construct a coherent sense of self, they try on identities the way they try on new outfits. This process requires asking questions: What do I care about? (Not just "What do my teachers and parents care about?") Who do I want to be? (Not just "Who does everyone around me want to be?") What do I value? (Not just "What do my teachers value?") You can influence this process. But you cannot determine it.

When kids are exploring, they develop the muscles to engage in this search for who they want to be: the curiosity to ask questions, the courage to put forward their own yearnings and hopes, the willingness to challenge norms that contradict a teen's sense of self. This is the opposite of the child who becomes a doctor only because she is told to, regardless of her interests or abilities. It means asking: What do *I* truly love about medicine? It's the flexibility to consider more than one path: Maybe I would be a better social worker than a doctor. As parents, we model this flexibility for our teenagers by leaning into the positive prosocial interests they develop and offering alternatives to the ones we like less.

"You want kids to imagine *some* future, not just one future," Daphna Oyserman, a leading academic studying identity in teens, told us. If they have just one imagined future, "you set them up for failure."[8]

We often get asked if every child can be in Explorer mode. Our emphatic answer is yes. Every child *can* be in Explorer mode. But that doesn't mean every child will be. Some kids naturally gravitate to exploring—diving deep and following their curiosity where it leads them. It can be hard, for instance, to convince kids with ADHD—who tend to focus for prolonged periods of time on things that fascinate them—to switch out of Explorer mode and help set the dinner table. Other kids need more support to get there, scaffolds to nudge them toward trying, and feedback to encourage the journey.

In order to get out of Resister mode, Samir, with support from caring adults around him, had to work his way through a host of challenges: belonging uncertainty, learned helplessness, depression, and suicidal ideation. These are profound challenges for any person, let alone an adolescent boy in high school. Children who face serious hurdles—from neglect to homelessness—will need help removing these obstacles. Others will need support ditching habits such as phone addiction to get unstuck (see Ending the Tech Wars: Boosting Real Engagement at the end of this book). But every kid can find ways to explore—online and off—like Mateo did with robotics, or Jimmy Donaldson did at 13 with his YouTube channel (aka MrBeast). Often young people who seem like they don't have any particular interests need little more than a nudge in the direction of exploring opportunities.

Some kids are in Explorer mode right in front of us and we just don't recognize it. Emily, a busy mom of two kids, remembers when it dawned on her that her son was super interested in weather. Ever since elementary school, he would grab her phone, check the weather, and tell her the details of the wind speed and humidity readings as she rushed to get herself ready for work and him ready for school. She found it annoying—he always wanted her phone—and didn't think much of it. Then one day when her son was in middle school, she was looking for her phone and found him sitting on the couch, toggling between the weather in various cities and comparing precipitation rates. She paused. "You know," she told him, "there's an entire job where all people do, all day every day, is study the weather. They're called meteorologists." Her son's eyes widened. "Wow!" he said. "I had no idea! That is *so* cool!"

It can be hard to spot kids' interests. They are chatty, busy, and prone to passing fancies. But if they return to something time and again without prompting, there may be a true interest there.

The chart opposite shows how young people in Explorer mode described how they think, feel, and act.

The Evidence That Agency and Engagement Matter

In 2002, Johnmarshall Reeve, a young professor at the University of Iowa, woke up on a cold February morning determined to prove he had a radical way to motivate kids in school: If teachers offered kids more autonomy in the classroom, students would take more responsibility over their learning and ultimately achieve more.[9]

This was not a popular view. Teachers like being in control, and plenty believe that with autonomy comes chaos. But Reeve had conviction. Early in his career, he had traveled to high schools all over the midwestern United States and observed classes for weeks on end,

KIDS IN EXPLORER MODE

THINK	FEEL	DO (AND SAY)
Black holes are really cool. I want to spend more time learning about them.	Interested, energized	I've been binge-watching science videos on them. I will ask my teacher if I can write about them.
Why are we spending so much time on Shakespeare?	Curious about why things are done the way they are	Shakespeare gets a ton of airtime. I will ask my teacher why and suggest we read a greater range of authors.
I guess I really messed up this essay. I don't get why the French were willing to sell Louisiana.	Frustrated, but motivated to learn why they got something wrong	Not sure why I got a B. I will talk to my teacher. Meanwhile, I will also read stuff and ask everyone, including my mom, ChatGPT, and my history-buff Grandpa, what's the deal with the Louisiana Purchase.
I can't believe my school sorts kids into "gifted" and "not gifted". That is so uncool.	Angry, wanting to find out how to change a barrier that is getting in the way of learning	Determine who has power and change it. Attend school board meetings regardless of whether one is invited. Run for office.

writing down everything the teachers said, as well as the way students reacted. He noticed a pattern. Students often asked a lot of questions or offered ideas and suggestions, trying to tie whatever was happening in class to their own experience. But teachers, for whatever reason—they were busy managing a disruptive student, or they needed to finish their lesson before the bell—didn't pick up on them.

Reeve hadn't yet coined a phrase for this pattern or realized how much students' participation in their own learning affected academic outcomes. But Reeve suspected students' motivation was directly related to whether their core needs were met, including the need for some autonomy and the ability to ask questions and assert their interest. He and his team of researchers saw that teachers were not responding to students' overtures: about 80 to 85 percent of the time, student questions and suggestions were missed by the teacher, left unanswered, dismissed, or ignored. Most were not treated seriously, if they were even addressed at all.[10]

"This is really tough on the students," Reeve told us. "I have a question, I have a suggestion, I'm interested in this. And I have the courage enough and initiative enough to speak up. And a teacher misses it, for one reason or another."

Reeve has great admiration for teachers. They are constantly juggling a huge number of often thankless and competing requirements. Still, it's not hard to see how quickly a natural interest in a subject, handled in this way, can turn to apathy. Reeve set out to find ways to convert that apathy back into engagement. In 2002, eleven years before Tevin's school, Iowa Big, was founded, Reeve started a ten-week controlled experiment at a high school in Cedar Rapids.

The teachers at the high school were divided into two groups. Half of the teachers (the experimental group) received an "intervention"—a workshop where they learned about student motivation theory and were shown empirical evidence proving that a new approach to instruction, called *autonomy-supportive teaching,* boosts children's motivation and engagement. The other half (the control group) received the intervention only after a ten-week delay.

When students said something like "This is dumb/boring/annoying," Reeve's team encouraged the teachers not to shut the students down but to take their perspective. *I hear you say you hate this. Why?* Teachers were also encouraged to invite students to pursue their personal interests within the lessons. *What do you want to learn about the solar system?* (Reeve found that initially teachers' biggest struggle was not dealing with an overwhelming flood of questions but getting students to have any questions or suggestions at all. They were so used to being told what to be interested in that they had become conditioned to be passive.) Reeve's team suggested that rather than tell students what they *have* to do, the teachers should use invitational language and give choices where possible. *Might you consider trying this?** Finally, they advised teachers to provide explanatory rationales for why they did things the way they did. *We don't assign homework to make you miserable. We assign it to help you consolidate knowledge independently.*[11]

It's worth noting these were not novice teachers: the average number of years of experience was fifteen, with an average class size of twenty-five.

The researchers returned to the school twice: after five weeks, and after ten. During each visit, observers sat quietly in the back of math, economics, English, and science classes in the experimental and control groups and took notes on everything the students and teachers were doing. The data collectors didn't know exactly what the study was about, which instructors were in which groups, or which items on their observation forms were relevant to the study.

What they found that school year—and over the next twenty years, through thirty-five randomized controlled trials in eighteen countries spanning the globe from Peru to China—was sobering and exciting. Students in the experimental settings were more motivated and

* Anyone noticing the influence of psychologists Richard Ryan and Edward Deci, gold star! Reeve's work comes out of the belief that humans need to have autonomy, feel competent, and be related to others to feel intrinsic motivation, the kind that makes you want to do something even if no one is demanding it.

engaged.* They were happier.** They were kinder.*** They achieved more.**** The effect sizes usually ranged from 0.7 to 0.9, which is a sophisticated way of saying Reeve's approach was a learning slam dunk.

This was true regardless of the subject—from math to English to PE—and whether the intervention lasted a semester or a whole academic year. It was also true regardless of the teacher targeted—it worked as well with strict instructors in Korea as it did with laissez-faire teachers in the United States. The students didn't displace the teachers' authority, and the subtle shift in how the teachers talked with the students made all the difference in how they received instructions and feedback. Students knew that their teachers cared about their interests, that their opinions mattered, and that they had choices in how they learned.

The students were building Explorer muscles through autonomy-supporting environments, and the results were clear. They were not pawns in their learning but authors of it.[12]

When Reeve and his team survey teachers, they identify four distinct teaching approaches—Structure, Control, Chaos, and Autonomy Support—and illustrate them with carefully worded examples, such as assigning homework.[13]

> STRUCTURE: Communicate what it involves to competently do the homework. Check that everyone understands what is required to successfully accomplish the homework.
>
> CONTROL: Make it clear that the homework has to be done well; if not, bad consequences will follow.
>
> CHAOS: Let the homework speak for itself rather than overexplaining everything.

---

* Increased engagement and increased agency and initiative.

** Increased positive self-concept and increased positive emotions and well-being.

*** Increased prosocial behavior and less problematic relationships.

**** Increased learning, increased skill development, and increased school achievement.

AUTONOMY SUPPORT: Offer a number of different homework exercises (e.g., three) and ask students to pick a few of them (e.g., two).[14]

Time and time again, Reeve and his colleagues have found that, more than all the others, the autonomy-supportive approach boosts students' agentic engagement dramatically. The power of choice is one of the key ingredients.[15] When young people are given a manageable choice (three options rather than twenty-five), it elicits introspection. They own their actions more, which makes them more invested in doing the tasks. Together with other subtle shifts, like using invitational rather than commanding language and listening to students' perspectives, giving students choices creates a virtuous cycle:

- The student puts more effort into their homework.
- The student does better.
- The student feels more competent.
- The teacher sees their effort and gives them more choice.
- The student feels recognized, their assignment becomes even more interesting, and they are more energized.
- The student is operating in Explorer mode.

Having some autonomy to make choices, students begin to ask themselves key questions like "What assignment do I want to do?" And when a teacher asks, "What did you like about the assignment?" it's a signal of respect but also an inquiry into interest.

The act of answering these questions builds decision-making abilities—*I can make a decision because I have been asked to do it so many times.* The autonomy that allows the questions in the first place elicits motivation and energy. Together they build the Explorer muscles that help kids not only perform better but also feel better: Students can take ownership because there is choice; can set goals because they have a say, and can seek and overcome a challenge because it's worthwhile—it's their goal, too. Without Explorer muscles, students are just responding. Who doesn't want some say in how they spend their days?

Parents can use these strategies too. We can give kids choices over their classes, their extracurriculars, even their chores. In *The Breakthrough Years: A New Scientific Framework for Raising Thriving Teens,* Ellen Galinsky argues that teens especially want parents to hear them and respect them. One good strategy for doing this is involving them in decision-making. Your middle school son relaxes after school by playing video games and then fights you when you tell him to get off and do his homework and chores? Galinsky suggests using the "shared solutions" strategy, which goes something like this: (1) Have a meeting with your son to describe the problem (not to lecture, blame or criticize), (2) brainstorm ideas together on how to solve the problem (parents have to take kids' ideas seriously), (3) talk through each idea and discuss why it works for you or your child or why not, and (4) pick one idea to try. Kids usually come up with the solutions that work, and when it is their idea the pushback is limited. Setting a timer to signal when to move from gaming to homework is one kid-driven solution to this video game problem that Galinsky has seen. Supporting their autonomy does not mean letting go of standards or expectations. It means including teens in the discussion around how to meet those, which conveys the respect they so dearly crave. Supporting their autonomy doesn't undermine your authority. It develops their agency.[16]

Often parents are afraid to give kids autonomy and choice around studying and school. What if my kid veers off course and it messes up their chance at college? Here's another question: What if by playing it safe and exercising limited choice or autonomy, they lose their motivation to learn or, worse, their will to care about their future? Tevin and Kia didn't need less autonomy and choice, they needed *more.* This is true for many young people today. Many adolescents we spoke to felt, as Tevin did in his traditional high school, that they are on hold. They yearn to see what they are made of and where they could fit in their community, but no one ever lets them out of the gate, so how can they? To find an identity, you actually have to look for it, you have to explore.

When schools are not able to help young people with this type of reflection, as most traditional schools are not, it's even more important for parents to step in.

Kids in Achiever mode often believe they are their GPA, college destination, or CV. Kids in Explorer mode have dug deeper. They may well want these things, but they've figured out why it matters to them.

Signs your kid may be in Explorer mode:

- They gain energy from engaging in an activity and learning about certain topics.
- They share with excitement what they are learning about with others, including parents, unprompted.
- They view failures and frustrations as opportunities to learn.
- They seek challenge in areas they are deeply interested in.
- They forge connections and supportive relationships that help them learn or master something they are deeply interested in.
- They get frustrated when they are overscheduled because it detracts from something they want to learn.
- They exhibit impatience or frustration because they want to learn or master something they care deeply about but cannot.
- They lose track of time because they are absorbed in learning more about or mastering something.

The Surprising Pivot from Resisting to Exploring

Samir hardly seemed a kid on the brink of Explorer mode. His freshman year was marked by not getting out of bed, not showering, fighting with his mom, and not going to school. He thought repeatedly about ways to take his own life.

After Samir failed ninth grade, the school assigned him a school student support officer named Helen, who, when she first met him, asked, "Why aren't you coming to school?" Compared to Samir's experience with his prior school counselor, whose first question had been "How are you going to make up all this work?" this was a subtle but profound shift. Someone finally understood that he was skipping school not because he was lazy but because he was suffering. The walls he had erected around himself began to lower. Because he was repeating ninth grade, he had to take another mental health screening—the school screened kids only in the ninth and eleventh grades. This time he answered honestly.

Yes, he had suicidal thoughts. He had even tried to take his own life.

He was quickly given an IEP related to anxiety and depression. He felt supported by Helen in a way he never had been. "She knew the barrier wasn't the ability to get through the work," he told us. "It was the motivation to get through." Helen began working with Samir, not just to halt his spiral of negative "I'm not enough" messages, but to help him develop the skills he needed to be successful. She suspected he had undiagnosed ADHD—one little noise was enough to distract him when he was studying or taking a test. She arranged for him to take tests in the assistant principal's office, where there were fewer distractions. If he started to feel anxious about his performance, she told him not to stay home but to come to school and sit in her office and study. She made sure he enrolled in a study skills class that supported students with ADHD even though he had not been formally diagnosed. "She put pressure on me, but also offered support on how to get organized," Samir said.

We've said it before, and we'll say it again: The magic place for learning lies between challenge *and* support. Over time, Samir's schoolwork started to make more sense. He began to feel more comfortable in school. He had people he felt connected to. The more work he completed, the more confidence he gained; he started to look outward, from what school offered to what he wanted to make of school.

When COVID hit and he had more free time, Samir thought more about how much that gifted and talented test had messed with his brain. He wondered how the district decided who got in and who didn't. He began watching school board meetings. Soon he was hooked.

He obsessed over districting maps. He dug into the underlying mechanics of gifted and talented programs. He started asking questions: How many kids got into the program? What were the criteria? How could it be fair that parent recommendations factored into screening for the gifted and talented program selections? What about kids whose parents didn't even know that the program existed? And what did all this mean for the millions of kids deemed *not* gifted?

Often students need this kind of unstructured and reflective thinking time to begin to operate in Explorer mode. It is an essential distinction between teens in happy Achiever mode—responding brilliantly to what others ask of them—and teens in Explorer mode, who are in touch with what they personally are interested in. Samir didn't know it at the time, but his self-reflection helped him tap into what he was passionate about. It activated the parts of his brain that help adolescents make meaning of their environments and develop goals they want to pursue.

In his journalism class sophomore year, the group watched the coverage of local school board candidates. Samir's hyperfixation with local politics was on full display in the class discussion. Afterward, a fellow classmate invited him to a photo shoot with a local school board candidate—the candidate needed pictures with students for her campaign materials. He went. He also stayed after to talk to the candidate herself. He told her that he loved going through the district's capital improvement plans and seeing which schools were overcrowded. The candidate was impressed. She told him he should run to be the student representative on the school board.

And Samir did. He put his hat in the ring alongside sixty other high school students from schools across the district. He was eliminated in the first round of Zoom voting.

But unlike other candidates, who signed off after they were eliminated, Samir stayed on. "I told myself, 'Why not? I am really excited for this election.'" He was the first one to congratulate the eventual winner. He offered to help in any way he could, and soon he was in close contact with the student school board representative, sharing his knowledge and ideas.

He eventually became the alternate on the superintendent's advisory council, a group of students who shared their advice with the school district leader. He was only supposed to attend when a student on the council was not able to make it. "But I said, 'Screw it,'" Samir told us. "I showed up to every single meeting." He loved it. Here was a place where he shone bright.

Samir was in full Explorer mode: exerting his agency to learn and do what he wanted. He was taking the opportunity to deeply engage in something he found fascinating. When he was studying school policy issues, he soaked up data and information, made connections, asked questions, and contributed his own ideas. He was productive. He was also happy. He loved learning more about school governance rules and increasingly felt competent. He felt like he had found "his thing."

At this point, everything that had been in a downward spiral in Samir's life had turned the other way. He began spending time with new friends. He was back at school and doing his work. His role on the school board gave him a greater sense of confidence, which gave him more motivation to try even harder in his classes.

His junior year, Samir ran again against 120 other students to be the student representative on the school board. He went all in. He studied the strategies of successful candidates in prior elections. The previous year's winning candidate had a website, so Samir made a website. He carefully prepared his responses to potential election questions. He had ambitious ideas he wanted to implement, such as putting a student support officer—like Helen—in every middle school and performing suicide risk screenings on students in each grade. (After all, kids don't become suicidal only in the ninth and eleventh grades.)

On a warm spring evening at 7 P.M., Samir sat in front of his computer and logged into the Zoom election. He was wearing basketball shorts and his only good shirt. He did not get eliminated the first round. He hadn't thought he would. But then he made it to the top ten. He was surprised. Then he was in the top five. His heart began to pound. Then he won.

"I never really thought I could take this obsession I had and put it to good use," he said. "That people would listen to me. It was like a door opened up for me."

Samir had envisioned a future self he wanted—school leader and social activist. The idea filled him with energy and excitement. It motivated him to reflect on how he could get there. He organized a plan and, with support, developed the skills he needed to make the goal a reality: socializing with peers, leading discussions, and understanding local politics. When his plan went off the rails, he adapted. Over the course of three years, he gained confidence that his work would pay off, especially if he bent it toward what he cared about. He was driving his own learning and charting his own path to pursue a goal. He was no longer afraid of challenges, because the goal was his—not the school's. He was operating in Explorer mode.

When we last spoke to Samir, it was a warm April day and we were sitting in a comfortable restaurant booth eating lunch. He had graduated from high school on time and then, finally, gotten diagnosed with ADHD. The medication was game-changing. He greeted us with a warm, wide smile and immediately began talking about his policy ideas around combating child labor. He mentioned four different Biden aides, a host of congressional representatives, and several state-level child rights advocates as if they were our next-door neighbors. He was a sophomore at a local community college, on the dean's list, and on track to transfer to the University of Virginia. He was happy to have a good relationship with his mom. Over weekly family meals, they talk about his career interests. In his freshman year, he co-founded a national organization to give students a greater voice in their school district's policies. Now he had his sights on attending law school to become a federal public defender. For fun, he had recently practiced what his oral arguments would have been if he had been the federal public defender in the U.S. Supreme Court gun control case *United States v. Rahimi*.

Samir's story is dramatic but not unusual. We spoke to many young people who were once stuck in Resister mode, struggling with their mental health and on a path to leaving school altogether, but who, with the right supports and opportunities, shifted to Explorer mode and transformed their learning journey. The reason kids who are resisting so often leapfrog to exploring is that they already are tapping into their own agency, their impulse to change the situation they are in. It's just that this impulse to take action is pointed away from their learning in school. But with the right support, either to learn better or to feel better or both, that agency gets pointed toward productive ends and Explorer mode is unlocked. Sometimes it takes a few weeks, as it did for Tevin, and sometimes it takes a couple years, as it did for Samir. It can often take longer for kids who spend a lot of time in Passenger or Achiever mode. They need help, not redirecting their agency, but trying to cultivate it.

Transcendent Thinking

When Samir learned he wasn't accepted into his middle school's gifted and talented program, he understood the facts of his situation. He was rejected. It sucked. He felt left out. But it wasn't until later that he began to reflect more deeply on what happened. Maybe it was not a personal failing but a problem with the very existence of a gifted and talented program? He began to wonder about school board policies and how he might take action to change them. He began to make sense of his experience, understanding himself against the broader picture of his school.

When he started to question things in this way, Samir was engaging in a process called **transcendent thinking**—when young people ask abstract, bigger-picture questions to make meaning of the world around them. Mary Helen Immordino-Yang, a professor at the University of Southern California who runs the Center for Affective Neuroscience, Development, Learning and Education, has spent nearly a decade trying to understand what this process does to teen brains. Since she was a kid, she's been fascinated with how we find meaning in the world. Her academic research is chock-full of articles trying to do just that.

"Schools spend all their time asking kids to do tasks but hardly any time asking them to reflect on the meaning they are making of their experiences," she says, noting that this task-driven approach undermines the type of thinking we want kids to develop.[17] Transcendent thinking, on the other hand, is a form of reflection that transcends one's current context. It goes beyond what we learn and requires thinking creatively with the information, imagining the perspectives of others, assessing the ethics of something, and uncovering possible implications for our lives and those of others. Transcendent thinking includes how kids feel about themselves and how they make sense of events around them.

When Immordino-Yang talks with teens for her studies, her team asks intentionally thought-provoking questions: how they choose their friends, think about their parents, and understand their ethnic identity; how they see their current schooling as contributing to their future; what academic subjects they enjoy most and why; why gang violence exists in their neighborhood and what could improve the situation. Teens who engage in transcendent thinking to answer these questions transcend the surface-level explanations to find deeper meaning. An example of a surface-level answer to the question about violence is, "Why does it happen? Because they take actions or do things that don't benefit them. They just get caught up in the moment." A transcendent answer is "[Violence] is a cycle. Like if you really look at it . . . it happens probably because their family is in a gang and they just follow it 'cause that's their role models, where they came from."[18]

By considering broader systems, forces, and processes that transcend surface-level information, teens are prompted to ask questions that go beyond what will be on their next math test. Samir engaged in transcendent thinking to figure out why he was rejected from the gifted and talented program. Tevin engaged in transcendent thinking when he began to wonder why more kids didn't have access to the learning experiences he was having in Iowa Big. Sometimes when students are engaged in transcendent thinking they look like they are "off task" in a classroom. They are not focused on the here and now of the assignment. But in fact they are doing the deep-thinking work of Explorer mode.

The first insight Immordino-Yang and her team uncovered in their research was that all young people in her diverse sample could engage in transcendent thinking. But not all kids do. At least, not all kids do that much. Some kids had two examples of transcendent thinking in a two-hour time period, while other kids had up to sixty-four. The level of transcendent thinking had nothing to do with IQ, income level, race or ethnic background, or gender. Demographics did not predict how much transcendent thinking kids would do.[19] Meaning making was an equal-opportunity experience.

When Immordino-Yang conducts her research she doesn't just talk to adolescents, she also scans their brains and compares their brain connectivity to the types of statements they made during interviews that included emotion-provoking videos (increased connectivity builds more efficient brains).[20] Immordino-Yang found that it was the kids who had more instances of transcendent thinking during mid-adolescence who, two years later, showed increased connectivity in different neural networks. These seem to enable a stronger sense of self. Transcendent thinking appears to help identity formation. These adolescents were more likely to answer, "I have developed my own viewpoint about what is best for me" and "I engage in self-exploration and discussion with others to figure out my views on life," and much less likely to answer, "I just hang with the crowd" or "I sometimes join activities when asked but I rarely try anything on my own." Additionally, it was these same young people with a stronger identity who were more satisfied with their lives: They reported better relationships with others and enjoyed school and college more.

Transcendent thinking is an important part of helping them do this. But young people need time and space to develop these skills. As Reeve and Immordino-Yang show, the more young people have opportunities to reflect, whether on what interests them most in a science lesson or on how gifted and talented programs work, the more they are able to do the exploring and questioning needed for their identity development. This is not about navel-gazing in one's bedroom alone; this thinking comes from relationships, discussions with others, feedback on their ideas, and engagement with other people's ideas. If adolescents only get to experience a conveyer belt of tasks that they must quickly respond to, they sacrifice this important reflection and meaning-making skill. They also may wake up in college, like Amina, and find out that they don't know who they are. Reflection is essential for helping kids figure out who they want to be and to build the agency to get there. It is also a critical ingredient for creativity, typically defined as the generation of ideas or products that are both meaningful and novel. If kids don't have time to reflect and feel safe to explore, how will they come up with novel or creative ideas?

Stella in Explorer Mode

Stella has traveled many modes so far: coasting in English and math, resisting in chemistry, and achieving in French. She's also had a good long stint in Explorer mode due to her dad, Dan.

Dan describes Stella as "a kid magnet"—she had always loved kids, and kids had always been drawn to her. At camp, or at family reunions, little kids were always around Stella, and she always loved playing with them. As a teen, she started to teach swim lessons to children ages four and five. The kids were excited, chatty, and not great at paying attention, and she found herself talking louder and louder to give instructions.

One day, instead of raising her voice to be heard over the din of the kids, she told them their instructions very softly, almost in a whisper. To her amazement, the kids all went quiet and leaned in to listen to her. She felt the rush of having solved a problem, helping her students focus and learn.

"Education is always something that has just been there for me," says Stella. It runs in the family: Originally a graphic designer, her dad, Dan, earned his certification to become a design technology teacher when Stella was in sixth grade. When she was a kid, she would teach a class of stuffed animals in her bedroom. But until high school it was a situational interest, something she thought about in passing but not in any rigorous way.

Then, in eleventh grade, Stella failed a test on *The Crucible*. "What's going on in English?" Dan asked her. She knew she didn't do well, but she also thought it was a poorly designed test. It was a list of quotes from the book that the students had to order chronologically, according to who said what. "That's trivia, not learning," Dan said. Soon after that, Stella sent Dan a text about how badly things were done in school, how much it made kids hate learning. Most parents probably would have told their kid to stop texting in class, pay attention, and get on with it. Dan took a different tack: The two decided to start a hypothetical school where kids would feel good about learning, whatever their level, and where they would love coming to school because they were learning about things they cared about. And grades, well, they would be different. Stella wasn't sure how. It was a spark moment.

> "I feel like one the goals for our hypothetical school needs to be having kids want to do the work without the need for a grade," Stella wrote.

"It's a key to self-directed learning," Dan responded. "I think there needs to be a balance between 'What do you want to learn' and also 'I bet you didn't know about this.'"

STELLA: "The 'I bet you didn't know about this' sounds more convincing than 'You need to learn this.'"

DAN: "We have to acknowledge how teachers do play a role introducing you to things you don't know that you don't know. You may not willingly want to learn about biotech because you don't even know that's a thing. Maybe you would love it?"

Stella began not just going to school and trying to make it through but using her daily experience as a student to develop her own educational philosophy. She would reflect on her experiences either as a student in English or French or chemistry, or as a teacher of small children learning to swim, and then talk about what they meant with her dad. After one particularly rough morning full of friendship drama, Stella was on the verge of tears in her English class when the teacher posed a question to the class. Stella didn't raise her hand—she was trying to hold herself together. But the teacher cold-called on her, and Stella could only stammer a response, her head down. In *her* school, Stella concluded, she wouldn't cold-call on students. If they were being quiet, it was probably for a reason, and putting them on the spot wouldn't help.

On another day, at the beginning of swim class, one of her students' parents got agitated and asked her why their child was still doing a Level 2 lesson when he had done a Level 2 lesson last week. Stella explained to the parent that their child hadn't mastered the strokes in Level 2 yet, so she wasn't going to move him up to Level 3 until they did. Learning wasn't a race. So, she wondered later, why was school structured like one, with one year for every child to learn the same skills, and grades to show who did best and who did worst? She began to think about the complicated role grades play in schooling, how she wanted her students to feel—excited, not despairingly bored—and what a school could do to unleash that.

Stella was engaging in the transcendent thinking that Mary Helen Immordino-Yang found to be so essential in building the connections in adolescents' brains—the iterative reflection and meaning making that kids in Explorer mode do. She wasn't just "in school." She was engaging in transcendent thinking about school. While she was in class, responding to assignments, she was reflecting on the nature of the assignments, how they could be constructed better to help children learn. She went totally meta. But it was fascinating to her. She was driving her own learning, initiating conversations with her father, asking questions, and looking for answers beyond her current context. She wasn't just reacting to what was asked of her but ultimately navigating the journey herself.

Stella's dad played a key part in creating the space to get her to Explorer mode. In response to Stella's ideas, Dan would prompt her to think about how hard it is to teach something. How would *she* teach English or French or chemistry? If not cold-calling, what strategies would she use to engage with the quiet students in her class? How would she know the silent students were learning? Dan saw what was inadequate about Stella's classes but also pushed her to think critically about how challenging teaching really is. Their ongoing conversation about a hypothetical school wasn't a blind defense in either direction, but rather a side-by-side inquiry. It honored Stella's interest, respected her voice and opinion, and pushed her to think harder.

This is agentic engagement: Stella chose what she wanted to think and learn about. She asked questions, found resources, and pushed back when she felt she was right. She was proactive, not waiting for her dad to ask her about it. In return, Dan offered authentic interest in her hypothetical school. He gave her constant feedback to improve her ideas and build them. He dropped some well-timed reminders that what she did in school was deeply connected to the goals she was developing for herself—becoming a teacher and starting her own school. He wasn't teaching her about school design as much as creating space for her natural interest in it. Once she cared about something, he didn't need to extract her efforts—they bubbled over.

Stella is developing more confidence in her ability to figure things out the more time she spends in Explorer mode. She offers up her own insights because she knows they are valuable. When Dan moved from training teachers to teaching kindergarten, he found he could not control a classroom of five- and six-year-olds. Stella suggested he whisper at the front of the room rather than yell.

"It worked like a charm," Dan reported.

Stella got into Explorer mode not because of what was on offer at school, but in spite of it. She felt anonymous, overlooked, and like no one cared about her goals through much of high school. Her interest grew out of her experiences: It developed from all she hated about school and wanted to change. It was then sparked outside of school by her father, who, by luck, had a teacher's ability to ask questions and have her think critically about something she cared about.

Dan himself would say this is something any parent can do. Notice. Ask. Play. Iterate. Do again.

Parents in particular can do this because they know their kids well and have more time and energy to invest in those sparks. No teacher can do that for thirty or one hundred kids—not with the demands the education system already puts on them. Many of those teachers, already at schools that aren't designed to harness students' agency, haven't benefited from Reeve-style training.

When it came time to apply to college, Stella created an Excel spreadsheet and researched over two dozen teaching programs in the United States, comparing the number of teaching hours each offered. She wasn't sure she had the grades to get into the one she wanted most; it was competitive, and her junior-year grades were not straight As.

She tried anyway. She made a plan, visited a bunch of universities, and applied to the ones she liked.

The day her acceptance letter was due to arrive, Stella was nervous. She had a swim meet after school and was "totally stressed out" for the duration of it. Meanwhile, Dan stopped at a party store on his way home to get confetti or streamers to celebrate. The store was closed. But he saw a box in the parking lot with packing materials. He loaded a carrier bag with handfuls of the small pieces of paper. When he got home, Stella opened the letter and found out she got in, and Dan threw the confetti all over her.

Will Stella build a school? We can't know for sure. We've spent enough time with her to hope she does. But what Stella does in five years is not what matters. What matters is that Stella stayed in the game, overcame the challenges she faced along the way, and learned to make meaning of her experiences in a way that helped her operate in Explorer mode. Stella learned to plan and adapt; to keep going when things got bad, as they always do; and to hope, even when it felt against all odds. She learned to get better at learning.

This is being an Explorer.

Takeaways

1. Kids in Explorer mode have *agentic engagement.* They take the initiative to shape a more supportive learning environment for themselves, which requires a degree of self-awareness about their own interests and desires.

2. To explore, kids need non-task-oriented time, time to engage in *transcendent thinking,* reflecting on the meaning of what they are learning and experiencing.

3. With the right supports, kids in Resister mode can often quickly pivot to Explorer mode.

4. Kids can build their Explorer muscles in small and big ways, from asking for more interesting work in the classroom to diving deep into an interest outside of school.

5. Parents play a vital role in supporting exploration outside of school, since many schools do not yet train teachers or design learning environments to support agentic engagement.

PART II

The Engagement Tool Kit

6

Navigating the Modes

Unlocking Constructive Conversations

Kids will have moments—hours, weeks, months, maybe years—in all of the modes throughout their long learning lives. Stella moved between modes depending on her sense of whether she could succeed, her teacher, her abilities in a particular class, and her mood that day. Her engagement cycled through resisting in chemistry, coasting in English and math, achieving in French, and exploring with her dad.

But sometimes moments in a mode last way longer than you want. Like Dan, Stella's dad, you can try to create the conditions for exploring to counterbalance whatever is making our kids coast, fight the system, or spin their wheels achieving. But importantly, you have to believe that the moment they are in can be just that: a phase. For them to be able to let go of the identity they may be clinging to, you have to think it's possible.

This can be hard to do. As parents, it can be tempting to label our kids, to decide that they are a particular kind of learner. But this oversimplification is dangerous. When we pigeonhole them, we risk limiting their potential and overlooking opportunities to nurture their growth. We are the most powerful force in their lives, even when they act like they'd rather eat nails than talk to us. If we don't believe they can switch modes, they will likely struggle to do so. We create the space for possibility.

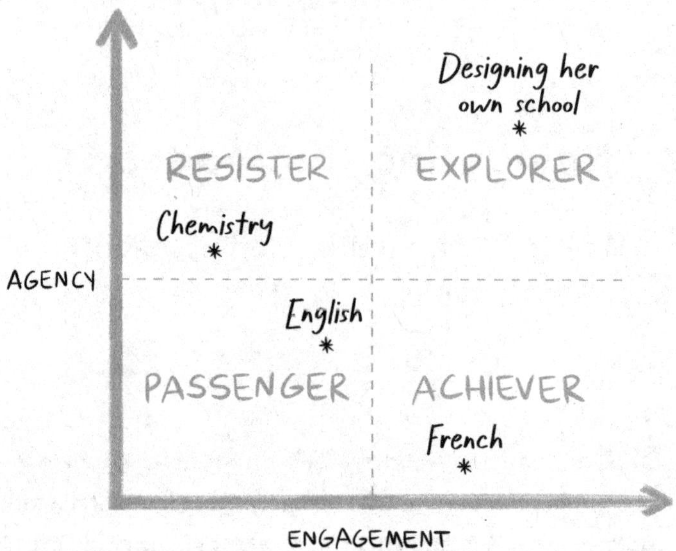

Remember Thomas? The Boston boy struggling in Latin at the Jesuit private school? He didn't end up there by accident. His mom, Maria, has an advanced degree, likes museums, and enjoys talking about serious things, and she wanted to give her son a chance to develop the same passion for learning. His elementary school had been easy and his peers not particularly studious. So she and her husband moved him, hoping if he was surrounded by motivated kids, he might want to step things up academically.

But instead of getting him excited about learning, it turned him off even more. Thomas and Maria also started fighting more. She would tell him to do his homework after dinner, and an hour later she'd walk by Thomas's bedroom. She locked his phone at 6 P.M. every evening so he could focus, but he would be pacing around his room, dribbling his soccer ball. "Have you done your homework? Have you studied for your test?" she would ask. He would look up from his intense focus on the ball, as if he was surprised to see her, and say, "What? Oh. No." She would come back and check on him half an hour later and he would be fast asleep with the school iPad resting on his chest.

To Maria and her husband, Thomas was not "a kid in Passenger mode." He was a Passenger. The evidence was overwhelming.

Meanwhile as his grades tanked, his interest in soccer grew. He asked to join a second, very expensive travel soccer team. Maria's instinct was to say no. He needed to get his grades up—not spend more time kicking a ball. "He just won't try," she told us, her voice laced with frustration.

Thomas hadn't always been a coaster. When he was younger, he was a confident, curious kid with a passion for current events and talking to adults. He'd stand in the corner at Christmas parties in his bow tie talking to adults about politics. When his dad, who worked in local media in Boston, took Thomas to the mayor's office for a take-your-kid-to-work day, the office staged a mock Q&A with the mayor. Thomas raised his hand and asked why Donald Trump had fired James Comey. It was such a sensation he made the local news.

Outside of his "nerdy" private school, Thomas didn't just show up: He gave it his all. In soccer, baseball, and basketball, coaches loved him. A few asked him to help manage the team, organizing schedules, tracking scores, and solving sports-team problems. Thomas paid attention to details and was a self-starter. He showed up early and never had to be reminded to do anything. His hunger to contribute went beyond the field: The same brain that could not bear Latin verbs seemed to have an endless capacity to remember every fact about every player—their history, country of origin, stats for hitting or goals scored, position vis-à-vis other players and other teams. With sports he wasn't just engaged; he was ravenous to learn and grow. Thomas no longer talked politics with adults but rather sports, bringing confidence to conversations about points, rebounds, player efficiency ratings, and true shooting percentages. In these moments, Maria saw a different child. "It lifts him up," she admits.

Maria began to see that Thomas was a Passenger in Latin (and math and English), but he also had a lot of Explorer moments. He would barely talk about his classes in school but bubbled over with insights about the history of a player or a pivotal moment in a game. He was always looking for ways to improve his times, his skills, and his knowledge. Even Maria admits he is dogged when dribbling a basketball or comparing obscure stats. She rethought her opposition to soccer. Taking it away from him—the thing he loved most—suddenly seemed nuts. "You can see that he feels terrible about himself at school," she said. "And so you want to give him something to feel good about, right?"

After some soul-searching (and some tough love from the nerdy school), Maria and her husband moved Thomas to a school renowned for its sports, with decent academics. He has a 3.2 GPA and does his homework. Maria still wishes he would study more for his tests, but he no longer feels like the dumbest kid in the class and he's comfortable asking friends for help. He's starting to understand his own habits, and what drives them. He has not become a star student overnight, but nor does he feel trapped. He wants better grades—an improvement from the resistance and apathy he felt at his last school. It will take work to get there, but resistance has been replaced with drive.

By making space for him to be an Explorer, Maria paved the way for Thomas to become the person he wants to become (for now at least). She also created the possibility that he get out of Passenger mode. The energy he derives through sports is something to be tapped. If they had taken that away from him, there would be no energy store to draw from. Maria sees the whole situation differently now.

"At some point, you let them take the lead on who they want to be," she says.

If you only saw Thomas in class or refusing to do his homework, it would be easy to label him a Passenger. Like many teenagers, he doesn't enjoy sitting and listening to adults drone on about mitochondria. But unlike Thomas's teachers, Maria and her husband have a broader view of their son—a kid who leads on the soccer field and by the coach's side in basketball, who digs in when learning about Steph Curry, and who loves to engage with adults when he feels smart and informed on a topic.

Thomas and Stella are like all young people (and all humans): They move dynamically among learning modes, thriving and wilting as their interests and emotions interact with their environment. When they get stuck, adults helped them get unstuck. For you, this requires noticing what's going on and responding in nonjudgmental ways (no matter how judge-y you are feeling). We show you how to do this in the following chapters, with specific advice for supporting learners in each of the modes.

The likelihood of this advice landing well will depend a lot on the ability you have, or are developing, to have constructive conversations with your teen. As we said before, discussion is to adolescent development what cuddles are to infants: foundational to building healthy brains. What follows are some approaches that apply to any kid in any mode at any moment.

The Power of Parental Discussions and Encouragement

If you doubt you have much influence, research suggests otherwise. In 1984 in the United States, Herbert Walberg, a pioneering professor of education at the University of Illinois at Chicago, published a major study about what drives student learning, including their engagement.[1] A key driver, he found, was something he termed the **alterable curriculum of the home,** namely, what parents talk about and do with their kids. Key to this magic "curriculum of the home" were parent-child conversations about everyday events; encouragement and discussion of books that parents or children were reading for fun; and monitoring and joint critical analysis of TV viewing. (Social media didn't exist in 1984, but it's just as easy to comment on Taylor Swift's outfit changes during the Eras tour as it was to comment on the Fonz's lack of outfit change, ever.) He also found that peer activities and expressions of affection, smiles, laughter, caprice, and serendipity had positive effects. He showed that the alterable curriculum of the home, often ignored in education, was two times more predictive of academic learning than socioeconomic status.

Thirty years later, this type of parent-child interaction has not lost its power. Findings from almost 450 studies have demonstrated U.S. parents' influence on student engagement, well-being, and learning.[2] When children are little, the most effective strategy is "cognitive-intellectual involvement." That's all the time you spent with your preschooler playing with blocks, singing songs, and reading bedtime stories; the millions of times you pointed to objects and named them "dog," "tree," and "plane"; and everything else that helped their tiny brains start to make sense of the world.

But when kids get older, the best thing parents can do to support their engagement and learning in school is "discussion and encouragement." Translation: Talk to them about what they learn at school and what is happening in their lives, cheer them on in their academic pursuits, and help them get through hard times. This, much more than direct homework help, helps teens grow.

The conversations you have with your children at home play a crucial role in shaping their relationship with learning. "Curiosity is contagious," writes author Ian Leslie. "So is incuriosity."[3] By engaging in meaningful discussions about kids' interests, experiences, and challenges, you create space for them to explore their thoughts and feelings and model what curiosity can unlock. These conversations serve as the foundation for the alterable curriculum of the home, the fertile ground that breeds exploring.

Regardless of what mode you might be working with, there are three key approaches that leverage the power of conversation. Many of the tips here come from expert teachers and child development specialists we interviewed who spontaneously shared their own frustrations with parenting children who were stuck. By implementing these approaches, you can foster a home environment that encourages exploration, nurtures curiosity, and helps your children develop the flexibility and resilience needed to thrive.

Tips to Avoid a Fixed Mindset

If you are going to avoid putting your kid in a box or condemning them to a single mode, the first thing you have to do is avoid *ever* saying to a child: "You are not a "math/history/art person." This is known as a fixed mindset—a belief that abilities are set and cannot be developed and improved.

You may sometimes model a fixed mindset without even knowing it. By recognizing what it sounds and looks like, you can try to avoid modeling or reinforcing it. For example, if your child starts talking about something you don't remember (highly likely) or never understood (it hurts, we know) or never learned (happens a lot), don't respond with incomprehension. Do not say, "I'm not a science person" or "I was never any good at science—go talk to your mom" or "You will never have to use quadratic equations in your life" (maybe true, but you will certainly use mathematical thinking). Instead try:

- Tell me more.
- I don't remember that from when I went to school. Can you explain it to me?
- I don't know the answer to that, but should we ask ChatGPT or Google?
- What does your teacher say?

AVOID LABELS

Tyra James, who has been teaching middle school math for more than twenty years, says that parents often announce at parent-teacher conferences that they are not a math/science/literature person. In doing so, they sometimes inadvertently limit their child's perception of what they can excel at. "The 'I'm not a poet' puts fear into their kids," she said. "If you say that, then the kids are like, oh, that's an option. It's an option for me not to be a poet. Right before they've even really been exposed to poetry." James believes deeply in the power of showing kids what's possible. She became a math teacher because she wanted young people to see a Black woman who was good at math, and not shut off their options—because of skin color or gender—to enter an exciting field.

Her subject choice makes her particularly sensitive to "I am not a math person." Math anxiety is real, documented in research from Mexico to Turkey and Denmark to the United States.[4] Clearly some people pick up on math faster, but often math anxiety comes from not having been taught well, sensing a fear of math in the adults around you, and eventually telling yourself you can't do it and then no longer trying. For parents and teachers, it's worth knowing that math anxiety is contagious, so try to avoid passing it on to your kids.[5] We don't often recommend being inauthentic, but this is an important exception. Being scarred by high school calculus doesn't mean you can't say, perfectly convincingly, "I am so glad you're learning algebra. Math is super helpful in life."

DON'T DISS SCHOOL

Another common way we model a fixed mindset is by dissing school categorically. A lot of what we hear in the mainstream media about schools today is in the form of complaints. It's too hard or too easy; too modern or too old-fashioned; too woke or not woke enough. Kids absorb this. And they get the hypocrisy of us trashing the system and then demanding that they do well in it. It's possible to acknowledge that the system is not perfect—few systems are—but it's also true that the more they put into it, the more they will likely get out of it. Treating school as monolithically bad can fuel their apathy.

Here's a true story: One London-based parent (whose uncanny resemblance to one of us, rest assured, is purely coincidental) who has done a lot of research on assessment and exams explained to her kids when they were in middle school why the assessment system they would face in high school was garbage. She explained that it was outdated, was hopelessly geared toward rote memorization, and would narrow not only what they would learn but also how they would feel about learning. Don't do this!

We are not saying you have to sugarcoat all that comes with middle school and high school (teens crave authenticity and deserve it). We are saying edit. As best you can, keep the complaints targeted and narrow. Avoid comments like "The system sucks," "Generative AI is making school obsolete," or "What you're learning in school is going to be totally outdated by the time you graduate." That doesn't mean you don't empathize with a test that felt unfair or a bad day. That's not a failed system but life: Some tests won't go well, not all teachers will be your cup of tea, and every day is not sunshine and flowers.

To create a positive culture of learning at home (or Wahlberg's "alterable curriculum of the home"), know that how you feel about learning will directly affect how your kids feel about it. Not having a high school diploma or its equivalent can have devastating consequences in the United States. So as best you can, make it seem worth their while—calling out what's wrong if you must, but also focusing on what's right and working, along with what can be improved.

Tips to Talk About the Content of Their Learning

Instead of putting your kid in a box—Passenger, Achiever, Resister—get them to open up about themselves as learners. Get curious about their learning through open-ended targeted questions rather than narrow achievement-oriented ones. Questions like "How did you do on the science test today?" "What did you get on your English essay?" and "What homework do you have?" tend to shut down the conversation, not expand it.

"My advice for parents whose kids are coasting is to dig into the content of what they are learning," says Mary Helen Immordino-Yang, the University of Southern California neuroscientist.[6] She did this consistently with her own kids, including her son.[7] When he was frustrated over an AP Literature assignment, she dug into the assignment with him. He wanted to compare Hamlet's sense of duty to that of the main character in Camus's *The Stranger.* She could see he was deeply interested in the connections between the two books and they talked through it. Then, when he said the teacher didn't like the idea of comparing two books—it wasn't really standard practice—she asked her son to think about why the teacher might be reluctant (rather than diss the teacher for his woeful lack of imagination). "I care how he learns to think, I care what kinds of dispositions of mind he develops," she says. "I don't care about his grade. It's not even my business—that's his grade."

To spur a conversation about the content of what your children are learning in school, try questions that open up the conversations:

- "What did you learn in science today?" If that yields a response like "Nothing," then try:
- "Were you still discussing cell division in science today?" If the response is simply "Yeah," don't give up. Try something like:
- "That is so interesting. . . . I learned the other day that the reason people lose their hair during chemotherapy is that hair grows so quickly because of rapid cell division that the drugs mistake hair for cancerous growth. Did your teacher talk about that?" If they (or you) have not one single memory related to cell division, take a "Teach me" approach, like:
- "Cell division. Interesting. I remember studying that. . . . That is when the cells divide in two or something? I forget. How does it work exactly?" Kids usually love demonstrating their superior knowledge to their parents, and getting them to "teach you" a concept often draws them out.

Talking about the content of school—be it causes of the Civil War or atomic structures in science—reassures kids that the content matters.

The key isn't having the answer but asking the questions. If they say ChatGPT knows everything, so they don't have to do the work, remind them of what calculators did for math. New generative AI tools are word calculators; they speed up "calculations" (finding and synthesizing information), but kids who use them will still have to practice thinking. Your job, as John Hattie, an education professor from the University of Melbourne, would say, is not to be a teacher but to be a learner—about your kid, about the content of their day, and about things you are curious about, modeling a love of learning for your child.[8]

GO DEEP, NOT BROAD, TO AVOID INTERROGATING THEM

Don't overwhelm your kid by trying to get a minute-by-minute rehash of every single class. You don't want to regurgitate all the boring stuff from work, and they won't want to re-create what was probably not a hugely memorable day. Get them engaged with what they are learning and to aim for depth, not breadth.

START WITH THEIR FAVORITE CLASSES AND THEN ASK ABOUT THE ONES THEY ARE STRUGGLING WITH

When kids are coasting or resisting, they are not always hitting it out of the park. And yet parents often start out by asking about the class or aspect of school they struggle with most. It would be like asking us about our most annoying work colleague or irritating project *every day.*

Expert teachers flip the script with their struggling kids. They ask first about things that their kids liked. Stella's father, Dan, always asks his daughter Alice, who has been struggling in school, about Model UN before bringing up math. She lights up while talking about the country she represents and what she's learning. "It's such a positive conversation," he told us. The discussion reveals to Alice as well as to Dan her excitement, and her interest creates positive associations with learning. Only after talking about Model UN does he ask about math, which is not a happy subject for her.

SPEND ONE MINUTE LOOKING AT THEIR SCHEDULE BEFORE DINNER

This will enable you to ask a few specific questions ("Did you dissect anything in science today?") rather than big unstructured ones ("How was your day?" which so often elicits the dreaded "Fine," because what are we really asking?). Every teacher we spoke to felt that parents should have a sense of what their children were doing in school, the classes they were taking, and the schedule they had. Glancing at their schedule before dinner should *not* be used as a micromanagement tool, but rather as prep for a better discussion. One school head we know calls this "parents getting ready for dinner table conversation." If we parents prepared one-tenth of the amount we prep for meetings at work or for a family barbecue, we might have higher-quality conversations.

DON'T FREAK OUT IF WHAT THEY ARE DOING LOOKS AND FEELS UNFAMILIAR

A lot of innovative pedagogies (ways of teaching) will look unfamiliar: Writing a comic strip about the Civil War. Creating videos to present an idea. Developing a game about atom structure. Learning a new way math is taught. Don't write them off because you didn't do them. Often teachers use these strategies as more engaging ways for students to access the content. Teachers' creativity is often stifled by our own fear of compromising rigorous instruction. But that comic strip about the Civil War for AP History may just be what your kid needs to get excited about postwar Reconstruction. Good teachers will typically balance that with learning how to write a good essay.

Avoid saying things like "Drawing comic strips is not going to get you a 5 on the AP." Instead try: "Who are the main characters in your comic strip and what are the challenges they are facing?"

TRY PROBING QUESTIONS TO MAKE LEARNING VISIBLE

If you try all of these strategies and still get monosyllabic responses, resist the urge to get angry. Staying nonjudgmental is crucial here.

Many educators we spoke to acknowledged how infuriating it is when their kids come home and say school was boring and nothing happened. One veteran educator told us her son came home and said school was "pointless"—and she was the head of the school. She (1) suppressed the urge to lose it, and (2) channeled her school know-how about how teachers can draw kids out, which includes "thinking routines" that researchers at Harvard University's Project Zero have spent years training teachers in. Luckily, parents can easily use them too.[9]

"Really try not to be judgmental," she told us. Instead, project curiosity. If they say something like "I didn't do anything in math," try some Project Zero–inspired questions to make learning visible to students, like:

- What makes you say that? Or . . .
- What was the unit about? Or . . .
- How do you think the teacher might have delivered that differently? Or . . .
- What would you like to see next time? Or . . .
- What are ways you might suggest that to your teacher? Or . . .
- What are the things you could do differently?

TALK ABOUT SKILLS THEY ARE DEVELOPING THROUGH SCHOOL AND SHOW HOW THEY TRANSFER

Another way to broaden the conversation is to talk not about the content, but about the skills they are developing that cut across subjects. If they bemoan a dreaded group project, mention that the World Economic Forum—a collection of very important people—surveys businesses and governments all the time on the most important skills employers need and that collaboration skills, the ones you build on group projects, are always high on the list. Teamwork is also used to save lives in hospitals, run restaurants, build fashion brands, and construct the James Webb telescope. When kids complain about multiple projects being due on the same day, highlight how this happens in the real world too and it's an opportunity to practice time management skills.

Here's how one veteran teacher used this strategy. Her son was deep into Passenger mode, uninterested in his classes, unwilling to do more than the bare minimum, and getting middling grades. But he was in Achiever mode outside of his core classes. He was a leader in extracurriculars, elected by his peers to be part of student government and a star athlete on two teams. When he complained about a group history project (there was a free rider who wouldn't engage and one kid who wanted to take control of everything), his mother pointed out the excellent leadership skills he was developing with student government and as an athlete. "Use those strengths" with the group, she suggested. She identified skills he had in one realm and showed how he could transfer them to another. She also set expectations—not trying was not an option—but her main focus was positive, on what he could bring to the group, not the deficits he appeared to be displaying.*

Tips to Model the Thrill of Learning

Remember John Hattie's observation that parents are their child's first model for learning? Parents need to model the "thrill of learning"—showing curiosity, engaging in the world, and making connections (to school or beyond).

Emily Brokaw, an experienced teacher and assistant principal of New Lake School in Dallas, Texas, has been experimenting with ways to boost student engagement. The main problem she sees is that schools

---

* Ultimately, her son put in more effort, graduated with decent but not great grades, and found his groove in college. He needed more freedom to pursue what he loved—engineering—and manage his own time, most of which he spends studying. He was what many educators call the slow burn: kids who take it all in as they go, not seeming all too excited along the way but saving it up for the future when they find a subject that really lights their fire.

have made kids tune in to compliance and tune out of their natural "thrill of learning." When a teacher is passionate about their subject, that passion is often contagious. The same goes for parents, who don't have to teach a subject but can model interest and enthusiasm for it. Just as we don't want to put kids in any boxes ("He's not a science kid"), we don't want to put a lid on how exciting learning can be by missing an invitation to be curious. (Kid: "Mom, we were learning about fusion today! It totally reminded me of *Oppenheimer*." Mom: When is your next test?")

Consider a dialogue we heard about between Diego; his father, Juan; and his little brother, Francisco. Diego's father is not a scientist, but he is a science buff. In his free time, he loves watching documentaries about Einstein and reading up on new discoveries from physics and biology. He also loves to share what he learns with his boys. One Saturday afternoon, Diego and his dad were hanging out in the living room of their Phoenix home. Juan asked Diego if he had studied Einstein's theory of relativity in his physics class. Diego said yes. "Listen to this," Juan said, and shared something he had just learned about gravitational time allocation. He told Diego that researchers used fancy atomic clocks (the most precise clock in the world, the kind NASA uses on GPS satellites) to figure out that time moves faster on the top of a tall mountain than down on the ground.

"What?!" Diego was wide-eyed. He sat for a minute, thinking. Francisco entered the room.

> DIEGO: Bro. Did you know time has matter. Time moves faster at the top of a mountain than it does on the ground. Seriously. Dad just told me about this study.
>
> FRANCISCO: Dude. Time doesn't have matter. No way.
>
> DIEGO: Yes it does. That is the only way that gravity would have an effect on it. Things have to have matter to be influenced by gravity. Being on the surface has more gravity than being way up in the air.

FRANCISCO: Are you crazy? Time is a *concept.* It's not an object. Only objects are affected by gravity.

DIEGO: I am serious, dude! Here, let's look it up.

The boys started pulling up YouTube videos, their heads pressed together, exploring the mysteries of gravitational time allocation.* They discovered they were both wrong in their discussion, but it didn't matter. The point wasn't getting the right answer. They were exploring something they were curious about and building their eleven-year-old and fourteen-year-old muscles to drive their own learning. This did not come from their physics homework or test scores, but from physics itself—and their dad's passion for it jump-started their learning. Juan opened a door, and the boys walked through.

Sometimes school can feel like a series of slammed doors. We need to keep opening them and expecting good things to be in those rooms and not decide early "That's not a room for you" (putting them in a box) or "That's a dumb room" (undermining a culture of learning).

Supporting More Explorer Moments

In the coming chapters, we will dive deeper into each of the four modes, offering practical strategies for supporting your child no matter where they are on the engagement spectrum. You'll learn how giving kids in Passenger mode more autonomy can help them discover their spark and ways to boost their learning strategies. You'll see how to help kids in Achiever mode balance their drive and take more risks by understanding that they matter regardless of their grades and using *productive struggle* to get comfortable with discomfort. And we'll show you how to get to the why with those resisting, including the work of constructing future possible selves as a way to get unstuck. Finally, we'll

---

* We had to look this up, and indeed it is true. Just try googling "time dilation" or "gravitational time allocation." It will blow your mind.

share what you can do to catalyze a love of learning that will help your child succeed in education in the Age of Agency.

If you are still doubting that you have enough influence to pull this off, we want to remind you that you do. Christina Bethell, the Johns Hopkins professor of public health you met at the start of the book, reminds us that good relational health is the number one predictor of what makes kids flourish. The key is prioritizing the relationship over whatever short-term goal you might be facing down: finals, college admissions, the SAT.

Maria had to stop fighting with Thomas about Latin, homework, and studying to figure out how to get him out of his Passenger mode funk. As she did, Maria started to see Thomas in a new light, as a kid with some Passenger tendencies who also has some Explorer moments. She's finding ways to change her mindset from fixed ("My kid is lazy") to growth ("My kid is an Explorer in sports who is building critical leadership, organizational, and initiative skills"). Maria may yet learn something about sports; Thomas may yet discover a love for math.

Takeaways

1. Modes are not identities. They are dynamic and fluid, and kids move among them. Our goal is to make sure they don't get stuck in one, moving from a moment in a mode to an identity.
2. Always see possibility and growth.
3. Help your children spend time in Explorer mode, ideally at least once a day.
4. Parents have tremendous influence over their children's approach to learning. Discussion and encouragement are powerful, free, and easy-to-use tools available to all parents.
5. Keep the channels of discussion open—to maintain relational health—because kids won't be able to hear the strategies we outline in the next chapters without it.

7

Finding the Spark

Supporting Your Kid Through Passenger Moments

In the 2010s, the developmental scientist Ron Dahl and Jennifer Silk, a psychology professor at the University of Pittsburgh, wondered what happened inside adolescents' brains when their parents nagged them. Because they are scientists, they actually wondered things like "What happens in the dorsolateral prefrontal cortex and caudal anterior cingulate cortex" when adolescents hear negative feedback from their mothers?[1] For our purposes, suffice it to say they were trying to unpack why kids are so averse to listening to our hard-earned wisdom and hanging up their damn coats.

They selected a group of adolescents and their parents, then separated the pairs to record the moms offering neutral statements, praise, and criticism. They then put the thirty-two boys and girls ages nine to seventeen into a functional magnetic resonance imaging (fMRI) machine to see which parts of their brains engaged and which tuned out. In the negative feedback condition, the trigger to activate the brain was a recording that started, "One thing that bothers me about you is . . ."

One mom (to whom we so relate) said this:

> One thing that bothers me about you is that you get upset over minor issues. I could tell you to take your shoes from downstairs.

> You'll get mad that you have to pick them up and actually walk upstairs and put them in your room. You'll get mad if I tell you that your room is a little dirty and it just needs sweeping and dusting. You get upset if your sisters want to do something that you don't agree on but three of them do, and you don't want to do it. You get upset too easily, and you just need to calm that down.

Not surprisingly, this bit of sage advice resulted in increased activity in the emotion networks of the kids' brains. It also resulted in *decreased* activation in the cognitive networks used to regulate their emotions and systems that help them see things from someone else's perspective (i.e., Could those children see where their parents were coming from?). Did the nagging prompt the adolescents to think about their frequent shortcomings and consider ways to improve their behavior? No. It basically pissed them off, shut them down, and set them up to check out of what was being said. The criticism increased their negative emotions, leaving them stewing, drawing attention away from solving the problem their parents were actually criticizing them about in the first place. While it probably doesn't take expensive brain-scanning studies to grasp this, it is worth reflecting on the fact that the study basically proved that nagging is counterproductive.

Other research confirms that nagging backfires. John Hattie, the professor from the University of Melbourne, examined the effects of parental involvement on student achievement across almost two thousand studies covering over two million students around the globe.[2] He found that one popular strategy parents use—nagging—does not make kids more productive and reflective but in fact results in them performing *worse* in school. "When parents see their role as surveillance, such as commanding that homework be completed, the effect size is negative," Hattie writes. Translation: When parents' "support" mainly consists of "Get this work done now!" kids' achievement goes down, not up.[3]

This might make us parents a bit defensive. We nag because we have asked two hundred times that they do their homework, wash the dishes, and get their shoes out of the hallway. We nag because procrastination is a feature as pervasive in adolescence as dirty clothes piled on floor. While we typically associate procrastination with Passenger mode behavior—Thomas refusing to study and Maria losing her marbles—all kids do it. (Adam Grant, a professor of organizational psychology at the Wharton School and perhaps one of the world's most productive people, admits that he procrastinates by working: When he's bored on a current project he procrastinates by working on another one.) When we face things that are cognitively or emotionally difficult—things that are unstructured, hard, lacking in personal meaning, or not intrinsically rewarding—we procrastinate. One study found that 80 to 95 percent of college students are procrastination pros.[4]

In our conversations with teens and their parents, young people complained to us that their parents nag them. Endlessly. Parents, on the other hand, say they nag because their kids aren't doing the work. They wait forever to start working or studying and then act surprised when a deadline suddenly *out of nowhere* hits them. For a parent, watching your child not do work and thus limit their future is bound to drive you crazy. Nagging, many parents explained to us, was the only tool they had to make sure kids got their work done.

The Counterproductive Effects of Nagging

But nagging doesn't really work. It doesn't work in romantic relationships,[5] and, as Hattie's study shows, it really doesn't work with teens. That's because nagging diminishes autonomy, which teens need to exercise to build important parts of their brain, and it elevates stress, which typically prolongs procrastination. That leads to more nagging and further diminishes autonomy.[6] Rather than helping them perform, nagging gives them the message that they are not competent, which deflates, not energizes, them. Their motivation goes down, not up.[7] Parents and teens get stuck in a **nagging-procrastination loop** from hell with seemingly no way out.

When we nag, or monitor our kids like drill sergeants, we solve for the problem in the moment—the test, the assignment, the paper, the project—but pitch the problem to the future. We won't be there to nag forever, and sometimes the negative consequences of not getting work done or failing an exam are exactly what a kid needs to feel motivated to study. By giving them some autonomy to fail a bit—a test, a quiz, some homework—we put them in control, which feels motivating (over time). Plus, without nagging, kids' energy is not absorbed by being annoyed, leaving at least some needed fuel to focus their attention on completing the task at hand.

Remember, a key goal of adolescence is for teens to develop an identity. School is one of the main playgrounds to figure this out. Since they have to do school, all day every day, one of the few ways they have to exercise autonomy is to choose how they do their homework and study for exams. It is their prime stomping ground for building their own internal drive. When we force them to study or get things done, from a place of love and often despair, we unknowingly impede their brains from wiring in a way that builds agency to learn to organize themselves effectively. To be able to eventually do homework on their own, they have to practice doing homework on their own.[8] No kid becomes skilled at dribbling a basketball by having a parent stand next to them and dribble it for them.

Counterintuitive as it may seem, parents need to stop and take a more nuanced approach. It might sound nuts, but when your teens sit on the brink of "failing," grossly miscalculating how much studying will be required, parents sometimes need to let them fail. We aren't telling you to let them bomb the SAT, or to let them do whatever they want. We're saying that kids in Passenger mode, or having Passenger moments, are testing the waters to see what they are capable of. When you don't nag, and instead let the assignment go, they own the decision and the consequences. They get an incomplete for their homework and gain insight into their own (poor) planning. Giving a kid who is not working more autonomy feels backward—we know. But think about it: Is your goal a kid who does their homework tonight or a kid who knows how to study, manage their time, and make decisions about their own learning?

This doesn't mean laissez-faire parenting. It also doesn't mean avoiding the helpful things parents can do to support homework: answering questions when they ask, creating quiet spaces to work, laying off the chores when there's a big test, and teaching the basic tools of *how* to study if they seem lost. Enabling them to work is different from forcing the work to get done. As Aliza Pressman, a developmental psychologist, says, "Let kids do for themselves what they can already do. Guide and encourage them to [do] things they can almost do. Teach and model for them the things that they can't do."[9] The level of scaffolding parents provide depends on the kid. Students who have learning differences, are neurodivergent, or are struggling with their mental health often need more direct support. Researchers have found this is also true of kids whose parents have limited financial means, largely because schools in low-income communities have fewer resources and are less likely to provide a high-quality education to their students.[10]

The trick is to find the right balance between expectations and support. Remember the magic nineteen motivation-boosting words that we showed you in chapter 1: "I'm giving you these comments because I have very high expectations and I know that you can reach them." Kids who heard these were twice as likely to take their teachers' comments and actually revise their essays.[11] The teachers are giving support (here's my feedback, use it to get a better grade) and setting high expectations. Embedded in both is respect for the student, and some freedom to make choices. Parents can use these principles too: Give kids choices around how they do their homework, convey respect when communicating that, and be crystal clear that your expectations are that homework gets done well.

Kids in Passenger mode need us—not breathing down their necks, but letting them know we believe they can do it. We are here to support them as they test different learning and time management strategies. You know the saying "Life's not a dress rehearsal"? For teens, it kind of is. They are trying different ways of doing things, including choosing TikTok over homework.

Replace Nagging with Autonomy-Supporting Strategies

Francisco was in fifth grade when he let his mom, Elena, know how he felt about her nagging. It was a warm spring day in Phoenix and she had just driven across their middle-class neighborhood to pick him up after school. The family had friends visiting from Colombia, along with Francisco's grandparents, who were in the car too. Everyone was happy and chatty until they got home and were walking across the backyard. "Francisco, sweetie, you need to finish your science project," Elena said, remembering the deadline as she balanced the groceries and thought about dinner. Francisco, who was walking up ahead, stopped dead in his tracks. A gentle, loving kid, he looked fierce for a moment. Even the visitors stopped.

"Mom!" he cried. "Why do you always do that?" He looked at her and then at the friends, as if they were all in it together. "Why do you do that?" he repeated before explaining, with remarkable precision, what it feels like to have autonomy (and have parents take it away). "You know, every time I do something on my own I feel *so responsible!* I just feel *so good!* But when you tell me to do things, I just feel like ugh, I have to do this, it's boring." He looked defeated.

Francisco needed autonomy, as do all kids. Loads of kids we spoke to backed this up, expressing a visceral need to make some of their own decisions. Cliff, a blond, blue-eyed ninth grader in New York who mainly coasts in Passenger mode in school, insisted that his parents wanting him to do things actively makes him not want to do them. He explained to us that not being asked to study for Spanish and getting an 87 on the test felt way better than being hounded to study and then getting a 92: "It makes me feel like I'm not even accomplishing anything when I get a good grade 'cause my mom made me study all night." Sam, a teen from Philadelphia, told us his mother texts him four times a day to remind him of things: "She texts me at like 11 A.M. when I am in class to remind me about homework that is due that night. She thinks I can't manage myself at all, but I think I can."

We are not naive—we have seen Passenger mode up close in our own homes. While these kids want the chance to show that they can do things on their own, parents know their track record and come to the reasonable conclusion that there is zero chance they will do the work without prodding. So, rather than giving them the chance to do it and mess it up, parents take charge. At dinner you ask, "What homework do you have to do?" versus "What are you learning about . . . ?" "How was your day?" becomes "How did your math test go?" From a place of love, you prevent the spontaneous moments of self-discovery (not studying and getting a C and feeling it sucks) and replace them with a never-ending 360-degree review.

We suggest a new approach: from **nag and control** to **autonomy supporting.** There is loads of evidence showing this shift can work.[12] To figure out if something supports autonomy, it's useful to ask yourselves an important question: *Will this help my child learn to do this on their own?* It is hard to learn to do something if you never get the chance to try. We are not suggesting you give them complete autonomy; they are young and still need your guidance and support. We are suggesting a subtle but powerful shift to strategies that help young people learn to do things on their own, a critical ingredient for developing agency. William Stixrud and Ned Johnson, authors of *The Self-Driven Child,* offer another piece of advice: Don't ever work harder to help a kid solve a problem than the kid does. It weakens them, and they come to believe the solution is in you—not them. The phrase they suggest parents use is "I love you too much to fight with you about your homework."[13] In our interviews, we found most kids want the opportunity to step up to the plate and show what they can do, though it sometimes takes a while. Think about the things you regularly say. Instead of "You should start your homework now," try "What's your plan for getting your homework done tonight?" We were inspired by an organization that trains educators in coaching skills.[14]

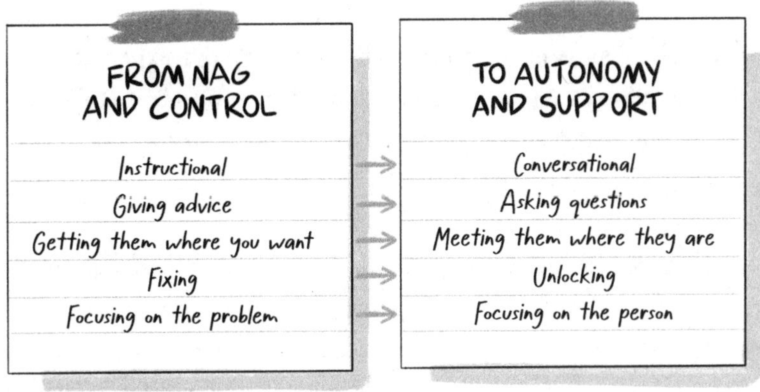

Source: Graydin Coaching.

In chapter 5 we learned about Johnmarshall Reeve's subtle yet highly effective autonomy-supportive teaching strategies that helped kids begin to operate in Explorer mode. The good news is that parents can use them, too.[15] And it doesn't matter if you have strict bedtimes and a long list of household chores or no curfew and no rules. The strategies are not about changing family values, discipline approaches, or your expectations for your kids. They can be used by parents with kids with learning differences, neurotypical and neurodivergent kids, and kids above and below their zone of proximal development.

An autonomy-supportive approach is fundamentally about style not form. And dialogue, as we've said, is essential to adolescent development.

Reeve has five strategies we particularly like. They may take a bit of practice. It takes teachers, who are practicing his approach eight hours a day five days a week, about a month to get fluid, he told us.[16] So give yourself and your kid some time to master it.

STEP 1: USE PERSPECTIVE TAKING TO LAY THE GROUNDWORK

Reeve's first tip is to listen without intent to fix. He calls this strategy the "go blank for a minute" method. He describes it this way:

> The first thing you need to do is temporarily put aside all the stuff that you want for your child, meaning your expectations, the desirable behaviors you want, and then concentrate fully on your child. Go blank in terms of what you want to impose on your child, and just listen to what they have to say.[17]

Reeve's idea is that instead of giving advice and wondering why your kids don't take it, you take their perspective first. Connect *before* you correct. He likens it to a *Star Trek* force field. When you don't use perspective taking, adolescents put up the invisible force field, guarding them from intruders. When they see an army of parental advice marching toward them, their natural instinct is to protect themselves from the onslaught. You might not be able to see the force field when it goes up, but you can certainly feel it.

Perspective taking lowers their force field. You are no longer an intruder. You are an ally asking about what is going on. You become a source of support.

The quickest way to understand someone's perspective is to ask. (Reeve likes to note that perspective taking is not the same as mind reading.) Try openers like these:

- How are you feeling about your homework tonight?
- What part of your homework is the most interesting to you?
- Do you see any connection between what you are studying and X job in the real world?

STEP 2: ACKNOWLEDGE

Next, really listen to your kids' answers. Remember, the goal is to try to understand their perspective, so you have to actually hear it. Kids have epic bullshit detectors, so do what you need to do to get in the place that you are actually asking and not accusing.

Whatever the answer is, validate it. Whether the response is "It's stupid, and I will never need to know about the Battle of Gettysburg in my life," or "It's boring, and I want to meet up with Leo tonight," explain that you get it. Kids have superpower senses for judgment, so you will have to suspend yours as best you can. Try something like: *I hear you saying it's really boring. My guess is that you would rather be with your friends. If I were you, I would probably feel the same way. In fact, I often wish I could blow off work.* This is not just getting them to lower their force field but disarm it altogether.

STEP 3: EXPLAIN

Next, offer what Reeve calls an explanatory rationale, which is just a fancy way of saying kids will be more motivated when they are given a specific reason for something. A specific reason is not "If you don't do your homework, you will get a bad grade" or "Do your homework because I said so."

Try:

> Just like Olympic athletes need a lot of practice on and off the court to master a sport, our brains need a lot of practice to master new material.

Or:

> Everyone faces things that they don't understand sometimes. Homework is an opportunity to dig in on your own time and learn.

Taking the time to explain the reasoning behind things (before, crucially, jumping in with any advice on the approach) helps students put things in context for themselves.

STEP 4: USE INVITATIONAL LANGUAGE

This is where you share some strategies your kids could use to tackle their not-done homework. The most important thing is to use what Reeve calls invitational instead of instructional language: *You might try doing twenty minutes and see where you get* is different from *Sit down at the dining room table and do twenty minutes right now before dinner.*

Try:

Have you thought about asking your friend for help?

Or:

Would you consider doing what you can now and asking your teacher for help when you get to school?

STEP 5: BE PATIENT

Reeve's final bit of advice is golden: Once you have done all that, and it doesn't do jack baloney, let it go. Remember, the long-term goal is to get kids in Passenger mode to care about school. Patience in this case is not only a virtue; it is the only path available.

"What I really want the child to do is not to do their homework today," Reeve told us. "What I really want them to do is build a value, a sense of importance in the activity of doing homework, or a work ethic. So I'm not going to blame or give up on you or be disappointed if you don't do your homework tonight. I'll try again tomorrow."[18]

This probably feels like a gamble. What if you change your mindset and change your strategy and your kid gets to procrastinate nag-free? In the end, we cannot force our children to learn. If they are uninterested and dragging their feet, it may be worth some short-term pain—a couple of missing assignments or bombing a test—to help them develop a sense of ownership. Without that ownership they will struggle to develop the drive and move toward Explorer mode.

Foster Interests Outside School

Jal Mehta and Sarah Fine, two researchers from Harvard University, spent six years studying what made a successful American high school. They visited respected high schools that were known not only for strong test scores but also for engaging learning experiences that sparked students' curiosity.[19] They spent days in the schools observing classes; interviewing teachers, students, and coaches; and triangulating data on student outcomes and school climate. They ultimately concluded that engagement in school—even the best ones—was poor. But outside of traditional academic classes, engagement abounded. Deeper learning happens, they found. It just happens more often outside or on the margins of school.

"Much of the most powerful learning seemed to occur not in core classes, but rather at the school's periphery—in electives, clubs, and extracurriculars," they wrote.[20] Students have more autonomy on the periphery; they are given space to choose which activities they want to join, so they already feel the benefits of getting to own their learning directions. Mehta and Fine also found that in these spaces students had the chance, without tests looming over them, to try things, fail, and try again. The stakes were low and the interests authentic. Kids had access to experts who weren't teachers lecturing them but guides supporting them. For the autonomy-loving teen, this is gold dust.

Mehta and Fine's conclusion is supported by over two decades of research on positive youth development. Fostering these types of experiences is important for all children but especially for the most marginalized kids, says Karen Pittman, a sociologist and cofounder of the Forum for Youth Investment. Too often the approach to helping low-income kids is to dish up intense academics and drug and crime prevention programming. These are important but not enough. To overcome the many obstacles they face, less advantaged kids also need the rich, varied, relevant, and exciting learning experiences Mehta and Fine describe. "Opportunities to earn a living, opportunities to learn, to explore, to contribute"—all autonomy-supporting endeavors—says Pittman, are essential for marginalized kids' healthy development right alongside tutoring and summer school.[21]

Parents can help their coasting kids by encouraging their interests and building their Explorer muscles, *somewhere.* For many teens in Passenger mode, this will happen outside the classroom, meaning out-of-school interests aren't a nice-to-have but a *must-have.* Clubs, sports, extracurriculars, community-based activities, and faith-based organizations are doorways through which kids walk and then practice exercising agency over their learning. It matters less *what* they are learning and more *how* they are learning. They light up because it feels good to have some say over it: What club or elective do they want to do? How do they want to tackle learning something? "Interest is the gateway," says Kelly Young, founder of Education Reimagined, a nonprofit based in Washington, D.C., and focused on learner-centered education. "It's not everything, but it turns you on to learning."[22]

When Brianna, a girl living with her mom and sister in the Bronx, saw *Watch Time: The Kalief Browder Story,* a series about a Black Bronx teen who spent three years in prison despite never having been convicted of a crime, she saw her family and community in the story: racism, the way Black men are treated by the law, the way her low-income community was always portrayed.[23] She felt angry and wanted to change things. But she was in middle school and too young to know what exactly she wanted to change or how to go about doing that.

Extracurriculars became her way. "What I love about extracurriculars is that they supplemented what was lost in the classroom," she tells us, now age eighteen. She describes her performing arts public school as drudgery—"a rule book," conformity, busywork, and testing, none of which felt meaningful to her. "I felt like I couldn't showcase myself in a way that I wanted to be showcased. . . . And so I felt so much anxiety around, they're gonna define me by this test score, and they don't know me. I just wish, I wish they would see me as an individual, you know?"

In school Brianna was mainly in Passenger mode ("Check the box" is how she described it to us), doing well enough in her classes to be able to focus on the things she really cared about, including getting out the vote, environmental activism, and leadership. Outside of classes, Brianna was curious, passionate, excited, motivated. "The things that really stuck with me—the real education as far as learning—came outside of school," she told us.

Like Brianna, many children will move through different interests as they grow. There is a fine line between letting your child's interests evolve and helping them stick to an interest enough so they can master and then fully enjoy it. A good rule of thumb is to encourage your kids to stick with something if it has been a clear passion that they have identified themselves and invested some time in. Otherwise parents can help by supporting their kids to evolve their interests and to catalyze new ones.

A range of things helped Brianna that you can tap into to help energize a kid spending a lot of time in Passenger mode.

NEVER TAKE AWAY AN INTEREST (SAVE FOR SOCIAL MEDIA) AS PUNISHMENT

Every kid needs to have a lot of Explorer moments, especially those who spend a lot of time coasting. So as tempting as it is to tie their good grades to participation in out-of-school activities or clubs, don't. Brianna's mother never took away the activities she loved because her grades dipped. Instead, she encouraged her to do the best she could in school and asked about her after-school work to get more people to vote. Maria was tempted to not let Thomas join the second soccer team, but she refrained, knowing soccer energized him.

SHARE YOUR PASSION

Parents who share their passions model the benefits of interests. They expose their kids to a range of new contexts, issues, and people. Some parents who work in service—school principals or teachers, rabbis or pastors or imams, nonprofit workers, municipal workers or mayors—do it by bringing their kids with them on trips, to school functions, and into reelection campaigns. The passions of Brianna's mom lay outside of work. The two would regularly go to poetry slams where justice, forgiveness, and social change were all common themes. Brianna knew her mom loved to write and would have loved to go to college to hone her craft. That hadn't happened, but she still composed poems for fun at home and shared her love of poetry with her girls. Brianna gained more confidence through her own writing, delving into poetry with her mother's encouragement. "I found writing so freeing," she told us, "because I can literally just write down all my thoughts and there are no restrictions at all."

ENCOURAGE ACTIVITIES THAT STRETCH THEM

Brianna's love of out-of-school activities started in seventh grade with STEP, a popular dance program her sister did. It was not a natural fit: Brianna was very timid, and the idea of being onstage scared her to death. But the coach reached out to her personally and encouraged her to give it a try. Brianna felt special, like someone knew her potential more than she did. "It was a confidence builder that I needed," she told us. She came to love the team atmosphere, the practices with all the other girls. She loved performing, with its feeling of everyone being in sync and the sense of accomplishment when the applause would break out after they finished the show. She became the team's captain in eighth grade.

FIND PEERS THAT INSPIRE THEM

When high school came around, a friend of Brianna's told her about Jeter's Leaders (named for famous New York Yankee Derek Jeter), a leadership program that awards a $5,000 scholarship for students.[24] She applied and got in, and suddenly her world opened in new ways. She was exposed to highly motivated kids at other schools—and big ideas. She recalls thinking: *Okay, I'm in this program for a reason. And if everyone else has these high goals academically, and they can be so well spoken and are so engaged within their communities and with their politics, I have the potential to do the same.*

Peers can have a big impact on how teens approach learning and school. Evidence shows what most parents already know: Friends who value school and are more motivated positively influence their kids' engagement just as friends who skip school have the opposite effect.[25] This is especially true for how students act and feel in school: *behavioral* and *emotional* engagement are powerfully shaped by students' friends and classmates, right alongside kids' relationships with their parents and teachers. Peers can be a negative, leading students to feel unsafe and to withdraw from their learning. Or, as in the case of Briana, they can inspire students to do more, lean in, and have higher ambitions. These positive peer interactions can make both school and after-school programs fun and welcoming places to pursue learning. This is why, since probably the dawn of time, parents have worried about their children falling into the "wrong" crowd.

Brianna's peers sparked new aspirations in her. So did trying lots of things as her interests grew and changed. She decided she wanted to become an engineer after she and her mom got caught in the terrible 2021 flood in which thirteen people died, trapped in their basements. She learned firsthand how climate change affected those with the least amount of resources the hardest. She wanted to be a person who did not just talk about problems but actually solved them. Brianna got a place at a top-five engineering program in the United States studying civil and environmental engineering. The lesson she took from all her extracurriculars? "I'm capable of doing things outside of my comfort zone."

HELP THEM FIND THEIR SPARK

Brianna found what excited and deeply engaged her. But plenty of kids need more help to find their spark.[26] "I just want him to find his thing," said one mother to us, concerned that her son had no clear interests or extracurriculars. She had tried various things—soccer, violin, coding—and nothing seemed to stick. She is not alone. In surveys of youth across the United States, one-third of kids say that they have not found their **spark.** They don't have a deep interest or passion that brings them energy and joy and is an important part of who they are.[27]

If you face this, sometimes the best place to start is with some keen observation. Your child might have an interest hiding in plain sight that you didn't even think was really an interest at all. We spoke to loving, involved parents who overlooked their child's interest for several years. In Beatrice's family, life revolved around sports. One day when she was ten years old, her teacher pointed out to her parents that she clearly loved art. They were baffled. They didn't do art. They never thought about art. They didn't know anything about art. They hadn't seen Beatrice do much art. And they had never talked about art beyond the occasional "love that picture" type of thing. They went home and asked Beatrice, who confirmed that she loved art, and she has been happily painting, sculpting, and 3D modeling ever since.

Observing closely what things kids naturally gravitate toward helps illuminate quirky, personal passions. Setting aside your personal preferences helps too. You may think sewing is a waste of time, but your kid may be a budding fashion designer (and sewing will come in handy). Not every kid will be a joiner, and not every kid will have a club they are interested in. But that doesn't mean you can't help them have more Explorer moments through supporting their interests.

Diego, Francisco's brother, whom you met earlier, is in Passenger mode at his Phoenix public charter school, choosing not to get caught up in the anxiety of his competitive high school peers. He proudly tells us he is a Passenger in school but an Explorer out of school. He cites his endless fascination with building airplanes to make his case. His parents confirm that he spends hours diving deep into online videos learning about all the different ways to maximize the flight distance of paper airplanes, trying and failing, and trying again. The house is littered with them. They give him the space to pursue his interests as he tries to test them from the top of the stairs or the couch or across the kitchen. They have never been interested in paper airplanes, but they muster curiosity because he cares. They ask about his models. How is he changing them? Why does he think the best ones work? They entertain endless competitions between airplanes. He lights up when he explains the different wing positions and how he is trying to fix the ones that really flop.

His parents aren't shutting him down or saying his interest is stupid. They are all in. As annoyed as they are with having to step around paper airplanes that are scattered across their living room floor, they are giving him space to explore. He has full autonomy over Operation Paper Airplane, unlike anything he experiences in his strict, academically oriented school. The airplanes are gateways to learning and developing talents. We don't measure them the same way we do academics, so sometimes we fail to treasure them as much, but they're just as crucial to helping kids develop the skills that underpin agency—identifying a goal that interests them, seeking to overcome obstacles, shifting course when things aren't working, applying themselves to figure things out. These Explorer moments will help him tap into Explorer mode.

Help Kids Optimize Their Learning

Some kids in Passenger mode need us off their backs. Others need the freedom that an out-of-school interest provides. But sometimes that's not enough to turn procrastination into proactivity. Some kids struggle to get out of Passenger mode not because they don't want to, but because they lack the learning strategies to digest and master new material. When we nag our kids because they procrastinate, they shut down.

We are leaning in the wrong way. If we help them develop study strategies so they know how to engage, autonomy will feel a far safer bet. It's our own take on the old maxim: We need to teach them to fish, not buy the bait, hook it, hover while they fish, and tell them when to reel it in (so not fun for either party). Autonomy support changes the tone and structure of the conversation: from directive to invitational; from solving for them to solving with them.

Much as we like to believe procrastination is about laziness, at its core it's a fairly treacherous combination of (1) a desire to feel good now and not worry too much about the future (a tendency teens have more than adults) and (2) poor emotional regulation.[28] Say your kid gets an assignment that kicks up some set of negative emotions: frustration that she has to leave TikTok (which is fun!) and study math (which is not fun!), confusion about the task, shame at not knowing what to do, distraction toward everything pleasurable, and disdain for anything that is hard. She *could* start on the assignment and reduce the tsunami of negative emotions. Or she could interpret the emotions as a powerful and indicative signal to avoid the task altogether. This is what Kia, in North Dakota, did when schoolwork started getting harder. Negative emotion problem solved!

Of course, avoiding the assignment leads to rumination, maladaptive coping (social media scrolling . . . browsing dark corners of the web), and low self-compassion. These *elevate* stress and lead to more avoidance.[29] You see where this is going: We procrastinate to avoid stress, thus creating more stress, which leads to more procrastination.[30] Kids (and all people) get caught in this downward loop we call the **Procrastination Cycle** (see the diagram opposite).

One of the reasons many teens get caught in this cycle is that they have never been taught how to study and learn well. They genuinely have no idea how to start. Like many children who spend a lot of time in Passenger mode, Thomas struggles to get into his zone of proximal development because he hasn't been taught the basic tactics of breaking things down into manageable chunks to effectively study. When Brianna started at her engineering program, she was stunned at how

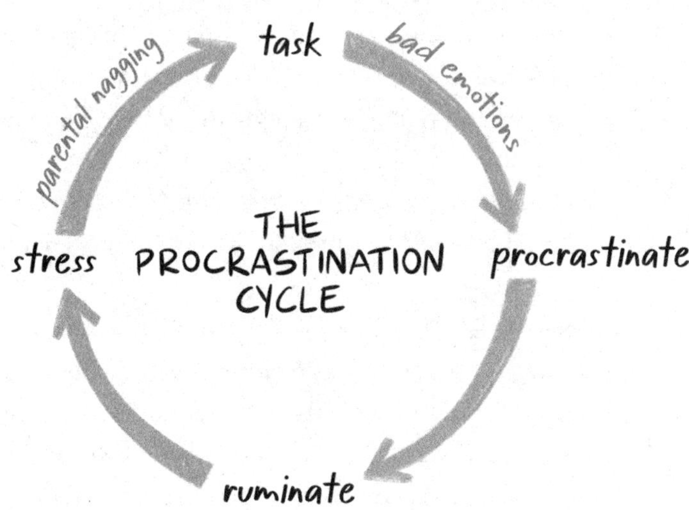

behind she was in terms of study skills. Her performing arts public school in the Bronx had not taught her how to take effective notes or study for tests. Amina knew how to learn to meet a goal set for her; she never learned to set her own goals and struggled at Yale.

How did so many kids in Passenger mode miss so many basic learning skills? Easily. Most schools spend way more time teaching kids content and less time teaching kids *how to learn.* Some students naturally pick these skills up and can organize their time, break down tasks, figure out when to ask for help, and reflect on how they are learning so they can improve. Thinking about your own learning process is called **metacognition** (a team at Harvard called it "coaching yourself as a thinker").[31] These are important mental skills that drive success in school and life. Developing them early often means children are seen as being good at school or any other activity they focus on. (So organized! On top of it! Such a good student!) They get positive feedback and try harder. It becomes a virtuous cycle. But other kids need those skills to be taught.

The way to help kids learn these skills is to replace the Procrastination Cycle with what we call the **Learning-to-Learn Cycle.**[32] The elements include:

- **Building awareness around learning.** Asking questions like: *What is my stress level? What are my mental resources?* This requires changing the narrative around stress from "must avoid" to "learn to manage."
- **Planning.** Asking: *What do I have to do?* This requires kids take inventory of what they have to do, and map out how they will do it.
- **Monitoring.** Asking: *Am I making progress or wasting time? Is this a good strategy?* This requires reflection on their studying in real time with the assistance of useful questions.
- **Evaluating.** Rehashing: *What did I do that worked for me? What didn't?* Reflecting on the learning process, not just the outcome, boosts learners' metacognitive skills and almost always boosts their performance too.

Helping kids with the Learning-to-Learn Cycle is scaffolding, not nagging. You don't make their plan. You show them how to plan. You support teens' planning without taking over—encouraging them to make a plan, checking on the plan, having them reflect on how the plan is going. Over time, you take away the supports as they develop the capacity to do more on their own.

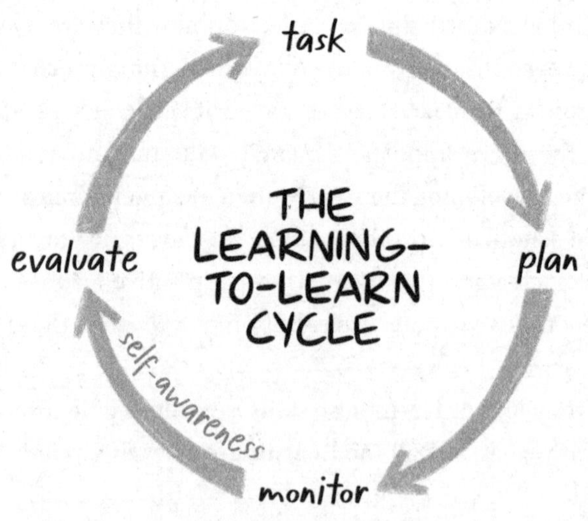

STRATEGY 1: BUILDING AWARENESS—HELPING KIDS MANAGE STRESS, NOT AVOID IT

Metacognition is not only about understanding your learning habits. It's also changing your thinking habits and the way you deal with stress, excitement, and distraction. Step one to building awareness around learning is to reframe stress as something to manage, not extinguish. Alia Joy Crum, a professor at Stanford who studies stress, showed just how powerful reframing stress can be when she ran an experiment with over 388 finance professionals whose lives were not exactly easy.[33] Crum found that the professionals who were told that stress can be enhancing and were shown the neurobiology behind stress—that stress is a signal from your brain to your body that you are preparing to do something important—had better health symptoms, perceptions of stress, and work performance than professionals who were told that stress is harmful and were shown negative impacts of stress.

But here's the real twist: *All* of the professionals in the study reported that their actual stress had not changed. They all worked in a stressful environment. What changed was how they interpreted that stress: (1) as bad for them and a sign that they were weak and underprepared and not capable, leading to more effects of stress, or (2) as useful, and as a sign of dedication to something valuable, which resulted in better health measures and better performance. It wasn't the stress itself that was most damaging; it was the mindset toward it.*

This works for kids too. In a rigorous set of studies with five thousand students across U.S. high schools, reframing how kids thought about stress and intelligence boosted their performance in core academic classes. In one of the studies, when kids were told that stress could enhance their performance, alongside the message that intelligence is not fixed but can be developed, they passed their math and

* Crum published later research emphasizing that a balanced message was more effective than a black-or-white one. Rather than paint stress as positive or negative, acknowledge that it can be both but that it's your response to it that determines the effects on you. In other words, agency matters.

science classes at higher rates, an increase in over 14 percentage points.[34] How kids thought about stress ended up changing how they reacted to it and, subsequently, how they did on tests.

Lisa Feldman Barrett, a psychology professor at Northeastern University and an expert on emotions, remembers her daughter preparing for her black belt in karate. The kid was tiny and her opponents were huge. Her coach walked over, looked at her, and instructed her to "get her butterflies in formation." He didn't say "Don't be stressed." Harness it. Use it. It's the brain's way of preparing you to expend a lot of energy. How you frame it in your brain determines what your body does.[35] Lisa Damour, the author and psychologist, puts it another way: Is the stress uncomfortable or unmanageable?[36] There are times in life when the stress is truly unmanageable, and that's when children need help. But most of the time the stress is just uncomfortable. That's okay. Life can be that way sometimes.

Start by helping your kids develop an awareness around their stress, looking for the source of it. Some questions you could try:

- Do you understand the assignment?
- Do you know how to do what's being asked of you?
- Is there something you might need some help with?
- Are you worried this will be hard/boring?

Then help reframe it with a "pragmatic, not positive," approach.[37] This framing is teen gold because, as we have said a few times, teens have epic bullshit detectors and don't want to hear how wonderful everything will be. Crum suggests three steps (the italicized language is ours): One, acknowledge it—*This is stressful because you care and you don't know how it will work out.* Two, welcome it—*Perhaps you are stressed because you care a lot about your exams, you care about grades and doing well. I admire that about you.* And three, utilize it—*Stress can be a powerful energizer and help drive you to get things done if you use it well.*

In other words, get your butterflies in formation.

STRATEGY 2: PLANNING—HELPING KIDS TO GET GOING

Once teens feel able to work and aware of their mental resources and stress levels, the question becomes *Do they know what to do?* A lot of kids in Passenger mode don't really know how to plan, prioritize, and persist with tasks, especially hard or boring ones. They aren't less able intellectually, but they haven't picked up these skills and habits yet.

We can help them develop these skills. Take the case of Luis, a mixed-race, middle-income kid. He spends a lot of his time in Passenger mode in his public high school in Denver. The school has a demanding schedule of academic classes. He spends all his days learning about the Napoleonic Wars and thermodynamics, but little time is devoted to learning *how to learn*. When he comes home from school, he likes to chill out. He plays guitar, plays video games, and spends a lot of time making "creative" snacks. He does not love homework and generally seems to slide by just fine with minimal effort.

One warm day in May he came home from school and plunked his oversized blue backpack on the dark wood kitchen table. He slumped in a chair, staring down at his hands. "I think I might fail history," he said. He was in AP U.S. History and had to get a 3 on the AP exam to pass the class. That day he had bombed the practice test getting a 1, the lowest score. The test was in two weeks. His mother, Susan, realized, for the first time, that he had made it this far with virtually no understanding of how to study. She internally panicked. Failing history freshman year would not look good on his transcript. But she remained externally calm, channeled her social worker training, and leaned into the moment autonomy-style.

SUSAN: Well, what are you going to do?

LUIS: I don't know.

SUSAN: Do you have a textbook? (*This was not rhetorical. Susan had never once the whole school year seen Luis with a history textbook.*)

LUIS: Umm . . . yeah, I guess.

SUSAN: Maybe you should read it?

LUIS: Oh! (*Luis actually seemed surprised at this.*) That's a good idea. I think it's under my bed. (*Luis headed to his room and returned five minutes later with a shiny, unopened textbook. He sat down at the kitchen table and opened it.*)

SUSAN: Do you have a notebook and pen? Maybe you should take notes while you read the book?

LUIS: Oh, good, yeah. I'll do that. (*Luis rummaged in his backpack for a notebook and pen.*)

LUIS: Mom, what am I supposed to do when I take notes?

SUSAN: You don't need to copy all the details of the textbook. But write down the main points after you read them. That will help you remember the major issues. (*She suggested he think about who the major players were, what was happening when and why.*)

Armed with the plan of reading the textbook and taking notes, Luis spent a solid seven days straight studying for his history exam. He asked his mom to let him stay home so he could study (it was review week and he wasn't going to miss any lessons). She agreed to do it, seeing how driven he was to try to catch up (she had never seen him so focused on anything related to school). He took the exam and got a 3. He was thrilled and felt pride in his accomplishment. With some very basic study skills and a good dose of motivating stress, he was able for at least one week to step it up to Achiever mode.

The world is full of executive function coaches who can help your child (and help you to help your child) work on planning skills, from charts to timetables to checklists.* We learned a lot from Ana Homayoun, a fast-talking academic adviser with two decades of experience. She takes a holistic approach to planning and emphasizes that students need to plan, not just for getting schoolwork done but also for movement and sleep. According to *Erasing the Finish Line: The New Blueprint for Success Beyond Grades and College Admissions,* her most recent book, developing higher-order executive function skills is usually ground zero for helping students. "Equipped with executive functioning skills, they gain agency over their daily happenings and the longer-term trajectory of their life," she writes.[38]

One example of what she does with students is to have them spend five minutes writing down on a single piece of blank paper all the homework, projects, tasks, commitments, upcoming activities, and due dates they can remember. Then they spend five minutes ordering them with a number 1 for those needing urgent attention and a number 2 for those where there's some time. The next five minutes is spent with the student identifying what they can control (video-game time, time in the park with friends) and what they can't (the due date of the essay). Fifteen minutes later, there is a plan.

Homayoun offers guidance on how to sustain the plan (transfer the plan to a planner, organize their binders and materials regularly). But the core of her advice is intention: Make a plan. Write it down. Keep track of it. Put everything on the plan: not just school tasks and studying but also downtime after school, sleep, sports, taking a walk with

---

* Experts say the explosion in executive function coaches has many origins. One is that we ask more of kids now than we did before, so they need more help to keep up. "We're asking kids to do things that they're not developmentally ready to do," says Ellen Braaten, associate professor of psychology at Harvard Medical School. That includes organizing their environment, thinking ahead, being flexible in their problem-solving skills, taking in information quickly, and coming up with a response in real time (which relies on processing speed)—and doing all those things simultaneously. The shift from a paper planner to learning digitally has meant kids need to manage multiple passwords and various learning platforms. The precipitous decline in unstructured free time means young kids fail to develop executive function skills the way they do best: through play.

the dog, hanging out with friends. Having a plan is not a punishment; it's freedom.

The key is taking that bit of time to make sure you plan before you start. And your role is to stick with them in the beginning when it's ugly, when math assignments are in English folders and apples are left deep in backpacks, rotting and likely inviting a rodent army. Don't try to do everything all at once (that has the same effect as sending your partner a four-part text on home improvement plans: cognitive overload, paralysis). Pick one thing. You can check their planners for two to three weeks until they get in the habit of tracking all their assignments and updating them. Remind them that a little planning up front saves a lot of video-game time later!

Remember we are training a developing brain and helping build new skills. With support, what is a chore can in time become a habit.

STRATEGIES 3 AND 4: MONITORING AND EVALUATING—LEARNING TO LEARN

When Gareth Southgate took over as coach for England's men's soccer team, few had much hope that the team would actually ever win anything significant. England's men had won the World Cup in 1966, but after that the team seemed cursed. Their Achilles' heel, aside from having a country full of pessimists as fans, was penalty kicks. Every single time a game was tied and went to penalty kicks, England choked.[39]

So Southgate focused on improving penalty kicks. His strategy was hardly rocket science. He had them visualize the kick but also factor in the environmental factors that would be present during a game. How would the player feel under pressure, with the fans booing and the feral British press waiting to mercilessly shame and skewer them? He encouraged them to pick one kick and stick to it, rather than waiting for the day and choosing it at a very high-stress moment. He had them practice penalty kicks so much they had to replace that part of the turf. They analyzed the kicks: Were they good? Could they be better?

In 2018, in the World Cup knockout round against Colombia, England won in a penalty shootout. The entire mood in England changed because Southgate had gotten metacognitive.

Southgate's strategy—a combination of practice, thinking, thinking about thinking, and analyzing—is not uncommon in sports.[40] It is, however, less common in school. How often did you, as a student, get a test back, look at the comments, and make notes about what you got wrong, reflect on what strategies worked or didn't, and strategize about what you might do differently next time? How often did you think about your performance under certain conditions (tired, hungry, stressed), and reflect on ways to change those? If you're like us, the answer is never. But the practice of doing this—thinking about thinking, or coaching your brain, is one of the most effective learning strategies. Increasingly, schools are recognizing the power of the metacognitive skills of monitoring and evaluating.

Harvard Westlake, an elite private school in Los Angeles, requires all kids take a class in seventh grade to teach them metacognitive habits.[41] Nord Anglia, a group of private schools around the world, has embarked on a multiyear project to develop metacognitive skills and measure them in a pilot program starting with twenty-seven schools.[42] But most schools, by dint of design, miss this. Luckily, they are not hard to teach. But like penalty kicks in the Premier League, they require time, dedicated practice, and a coach (that's you).

The main skill required for this coaching gig is asking good, nonjudgmental questions that help teens become aware of habits and strategies, reflect on their learning, and develop a bigger toolbox from which to improve learning. The following are some metacognitive questions.*

Monitoring Questions:

- How do you know what you think you know? How reliable is the information, and how comfortable are you that you know it?

* We especially appreciated the work of James Mannion and Kate McAllister in their book *Fear Is the Mind Killer* in helping us think about the right questions here.

- What do you already know, what needs clarifying, and what is completely confusing?
- What are the best ways for you to test your knowledge? Quizlet? Khanmigo? Mom? A friend? Inside your head? (Hint: This last one stinks.)
- How confident are you that you understand it? Did you check, because confidence is misleading?
- Are you still focused and on track?
- Is it time for a strategy shift?
- Might you need to ask for help?
- How good are you at managing distractions?

Evaluating Questions:

- You got an A on that essay. What did you do that worked? (You got a C on that essay. What did you do that didn't work? What could you do better?)
- You thought you were totally prepared for the test and you felt you bombed it. What do you think happened?
- What does it feel like when you finally understand something that you initially found challenging or confusing?
- How long did it take you to learn [fill in the topic]? Did it take more or less time than you anticipated?
- What is the difference between learning something and memorizing it? Which feels better?
- What tools or strategies can you use to remember things better? Taking notes, making flashcards, having a discussion, highlighting? (It's almost never this last one, FYI.)

Metacognition can be woven into daily life easily with a few strategically dropped questions to prompt thinking about thinking. If you deploy reflection techniques only when things go wrong, rather than all the time, your teen will see them coming a mile away and shut them down like French railway workers on strike. Use reflection daily, smartly, and especially when things go right. Then you have earned the right to ask, "What could I have done differently?" when the C or D comes rolling in. Always restrain the judgment and convey respect.

You might be suspicious that metacognition *looks like a lot more work.* And no teen (or adult), much less your happily coasting kid in Passenger mode, wants more work. It's not at all obvious that reflecting on something rather than doing more of it (math, rereading the English text) would be more productive. It feels better to jump into essay writing, tackle the word problem, or start the science experiment than to take two minutes to reflect on what you might need to know.

But research by strategy professor Giada Di Stefano found that a small dose of reflection—as little as fifteen minutes!—using the above metacognitive techniques can save a *lot* of study time.[43] In Di Stefano's research, employees who spent fifteen minutes reflecting through journal writing at the end of a day of job training performed significantly better on a trainee assessment than employees who didn't, and even had higher customer satisfaction ratings a month afterward.

Most of us equate hard work with more doing—a quintessentially American approach that the Italians and French like to laugh at. But when we fail to reflect, we miss the chance to notice that our strategies aren't working. Rather than adjust, we double down and work harder at something that doesn't work at all.

We are reminded of the saying "An ounce of prevention is worth a pound of cure." Helping your child optimize their learning is a small investment now that pays off hugely over time. If they study 5 percent better over time, imagine the compound returns this might yield! Once your kids figure out the basics of how to learn, they can apply them to any class and any learning situation. These learning-to-learn skills are an essential part of helping kids develop their Explorer muscles. Agency over their learning requires space to choose a goal, but it also requires the skills to get there. Armed with a toolbox of learning strategies, including a textbook and a to-do list, you won't need to nag them. Giving them autonomy won't feel risky; it will feel freeing.

Takeaways

1. Nagging doesn't work. It diminishes kids' autonomy, heightens their negative emotions, takes their attention away from the task at hand, often increases procrastination, and leads to worse performance in school.

2. As counterintuitive as it sounds, try giving kids in Passenger mode more, not less, autonomy. Autonomy-supportive parenting and teaching approaches boost teens' engagement in learning and achievement in school.

3. Help kids find their spark or foster the ones they have. The content of their interest does not matter (as long as they are not hurting themselves or others). Pursuing interests in or out of school helps to develop Explorer muscles.

4. Some kids can't get out of Passenger mode not because they lack motivation, but because they lack the skills. Help struggling kids develop *metacognitive* learning and study skills to be successful in school.

5. Help kids get their butterflies in formation. Reframe stress as your body preparing for something important, not a negative signal to run away.

8

Balancing the Drive

Supporting Your Kid Through Achiever Moments

At the end of her senior year, Vanessa, the field hockey goalie at the Hartford private school, was stuck. In a sense, the system had served her well. She had graduated with a 3.9 GPA, a list of awards, and multiple college offers. One was a full ride, and others had generous scholarship packages. All of them wanted her to play field hockey. But she had always hated field hockey. She didn't know what to do.

As she considered her college options, she began to reflect on who she had been in high school. She felt split in two. Over the years, she had drifted further and further from her neighborhood friends. Like Vanessa, many of them had come to the United States from Latin America, and when they were younger their shared experience had made them fast friends. Their parents cooked the same food and played the same music; they all made do with little money. But the minute Vanessa switched to the private school in tony West Hartford, they had begun to give her the cold shoulder. "They were like: Oh, you think you're better than us?' " she reflects. It stung. "I was like, no, I'm just me. I'm just trying to survive," she says. But the distance grew. She wasn't part of their circle and they didn't share day-to-day experiences.

She didn't fit in at school either. She was one of only a few students of color in a predominantly white institution. Every day she was reminded that she was different. She didn't have the nice clothes other girls had. After school breaks, she had nothing to say when kids talked about the cool places they had visited on vacation. Her family didn't have money to buy her a car, so unlike most of her peers, who drove to school once they turned sixteen, she got dropped off by her mom all through high school. She would make her mom turn off the salsa music one block away from the school. Vanessa didn't want to call more attention to how different she was. "It was always clear who the scholarship kids were," she said.

She rejected everything that could make her seem like the stereotypical Puerto Rican girl "because the stereotypes were negative," she explained. Sassy, loud, sexual. Her family home was full of Latin music—her father loved salsa and merengue and would sing passionately along to the songs of El Gran Combo. But she never felt safe to share that part of herself in school. She was experiencing *belonging uncertainty,* and she reacted by turning inward. She became quiet, dressed conservatively, and had few friends. She sensed that none of the relationships she developed in school would last.

She absorbed the message that she mattered at school only because of her accomplishments. Her coach and teammates cheered every time she saved a ball from going into the goal. Her teachers praised her for her diligence and hard work in classes. She was noticed and called out for her top grades through honor roll awards and gold stars. When she was the president of the mock trial club, her peers listened to her, and the club's coach spent extra time with her going over logistics and strategy. Her parents were so proud of her. Education was their number one priority for their children, and Vanessa was knocking it out of the park.

But facing college, she felt lost. Which Vanessa was she—the Puerto Rican girl or the prep school superstar? The one thing she did know was that she did not like field hockey. She called the only person she felt she could talk to: her brother. He was several years ahead of her and had gone to Tufts University. She shared everything she was feeling. She was confused and scared. She didn't think she could take playing another four years of a sport she had never liked. She didn't know what was wrong with her and felt like she was unraveling. "This was the first time I said any of this out loud," she says. She had always kept these feelings even from herself. She realized that throughout school, every time she felt unsettled, she had pushed her feelings aside to keep performing, to keep being the person she thought everyone else wanted her to be. Except now she wasn't sure who she was.

She had many long conversations with her brother, and she postponed her decision about which college to accept. She agonized. One weekend when her brother was home, they went out to the mall and walked around, looking at the stores and talking. He encouraged her to see college as a chance to reinvent herself—to bring her two identities together. What did she want? She wanted friends she could connect to, who would see her as both smart and Puerto Rican. She wanted to be part of a community and have people like her for who she was, not just what she did. She wanted to spend her time on activities that she really liked doing, not just the ones she was good at.

Finally, she knew what she wanted to do.

She turned down the college that offered her a full ride to play field hockey. She wasn't going to return to the sport. She would take out student loans instead. This was not the safe choice. But for the first time in her life she felt brave. She picked Boston College instead, because they had offered her a merit scholarship and because she could take part in the Asian, Hispanic, African, and Native American (AHANA) House programs, an intercultural center for students from diverse backgrounds.

In college, she was assigned an adviser in the AHANA House to help guide her through college. She frequently visited her adviser to talk about which courses she should take or how to process loan paperwork. Often, on these visits, she would find herself starting to cry. "Why am I crying?" she would ask herself. In high school, she had always held everything together. Now she was a mess. "I didn't realize the pain you hold trying to be something other people want you to be," she says now.

It took her several years to work through that pain. She spent a lot of time reflecting. She relied on her adviser. She made friends with other students who had had similar experiences at other prep schools. She went to therapy, mucking through the hard work of building a new identity—one that felt true to herself. She read widely about Puerto Rican history. She made several trips to Puerto Rico to visit her family and reconnect with her roots. She became active in student government, advocating for making the campus more welcoming to a diverse group of students. "I finally realized I could be both things," she recalled. "I can embrace both parts of who I am. I can love salsa music and be smart."

When Vanessa graduated, she decided she wanted to be a teacher. "I wanted to figure out how we build schools where young people feel loved and supported for who they are." She joined Teach for America, spending time in classrooms in New York and New Jersey. She then went on to serve in New York City's Department of Education, leading alternative programs. Today she is the CEO of New York City Outward Bound Schools, a nonprofit working with seventy schools across the city to design learning experiences that help students feel they belong and are deeply engaged in their learning. She knows she matters for who she is and what she is passionate about—at work, in her community, and at home.

Mattering Matters

Teens in Achiever mode have so much going for them that it's easy to overlook the support they need. They have incredible get-stuff-done skills and have mastered the learning cycle. They know how to study, and how to start their work and persist with it, and they earn grades that make them and us happy. But their success often masks their struggles. Like Vanessa, they've deeply internalized a version of success that the world values: grades, test scores, impressive college admissions. At some point, they have to decide if those are the goals they want. Plenty of kids in Achiever mode decide that they are, and continue happily achieving through college and high-octane careers. But many must confront the fact that the goals they have readily accepted from others may not be in line with their own values or the direction they want for their life. This can be both liberating and terrifying, as it was for Vanessa.

To nurture the good habits of Achiever mode without letting them slip into unhappy Achiever territory (the Achiever Conundrum), we need to help our kids gain balance and strengthen their Explorer muscles. For kids deep into Achiever mode, that means developing their own sense of identity, figuring out what matters to them, and building resilience. The key to providing this support is helping them feel they matter unconditionally, beyond their A+ performance; making sure they have time and space to reflect on what they really care about; and encouraging them to take on challenges despite the risks. Once Vanessa figured out what she loved—helping others, leaning into her Puerto Rican identity, drawing students out—she became unstoppable. Instead of being fragile and high-performing, she was focused and internally driven. When she combined this Explorer mode resilience with her Achiever mode work ethic, she started to soar. By unpacking the "why" beneath her drive, she could unleash the emotional engagement she was missing. All kids stuck in Achiever mode—or passing through Achiever moments—can do this.

The foundation of helping kids stuck in Achiever mode is making sure they know they matter for who they are, not just what they do in school (or on the field). This deep sense of **mattering** is essential for adolescents as they develop an authentic sense of identity.[1] In a hypercompetitive environment where success feels paramount, kids need to feel loved in all their three-dimensionality—not just for their grades. This doesn't mean giving participation trophies to every player, a strategy that might make sense in early childhood but that adolescents see through with X-ray vision. Rather, it means they need to feel:[2]

- Seen (People notice when I speak; I am not overlooked.)
- Supported (Others care about my successes and setbacks.)

- Valuable (My actions and contributions, small and large, are valued by others.)

If belonging is about feeling you are part of a larger group that values, respects, and cares for you, mattering is reciprocal: You have to contribute to others in meaningful ways to feel relied upon. It requires action.

The concept of mattering emerged in the 1970s, when Morris Rosenberg, a social psychologist, posed a simple (but bold for the time) question: Did children who felt they mattered to their parents fare better in life? He found they did; they were less depressed, less anxious, and had higher self-esteem. "Mattering really matters," he wrote in the 1979 paper with his original research.[3]

Infants feel they matter when caregivers hold them and attend to their needs. Toddlers feel it through those same bonds but also through play—exploring the world while staying firmly anchored to the safety of loving caregivers. In adolescence, mattering is about being loved unconditionally for the person one hopes to be—a student, sure, but also a sister or cousin or granddaughter, an athlete or entrepreneur, an active community member or school leader. To matter is to be seen in 3D, beauty and warts alike—not just as a 3.9 GPA who made the state field hockey team. The renowned developmental psychologist Urie Bronfenbrenner famously said, "Every child needs at least one adult who is irrationally crazy about him or her."[4] He meant the whole child, and not just the accolades.

Whereas kids in Passenger mode need us to support their autonomy—to give them space to make decisions and develop intrinsic motivation—supporting mattering for students in Achiever mode goes a step further. In a sense, mattering fosters a deeper form of autonomy: When kids are recognized as a whole person, not just for what they achieve, they feel free to follow their values and interests even when they lead away from traditional paths of success. The reason this is so hard for kids stuck in Achiever mode is that they get so much positive feedback for their performance, they never stop to ask, *What do I want or care about, and what would I do if I were not doing all the achieving stuff?* If kids in Passenger mode need to own their choices, kids in Achiever mode need the courage to ask what choices to make.

Achievers *do* a lot. But is it what they want to do? Too many kids are entering adulthood unsure of how to find a meaningful sense of direction. Nearly three in five young adults report lacking meaning or purpose in their lives.[5]

Parents of kids who spend most of their time coasting often want to change their level of engagement. Parents of teens who spend all their time achieving have a different challenge: They don't want anything to change. They love the performance—it reflects so well on them! It guarantees so much success! But this blinds them to the risks. In *Never Enough: When Achievement Culture Becomes Toxic—and What We Can Do About It,* Jennifer Breheny Wallace found that more than half of young adults in her research said their parents loved them more when they were successful, and a staggering one in four believed it was their achievement and not who they were as people that mattered most.[6]

Many of us think we show our kids they matter because we know we love them dearly. But in small and unintentional ways, we send the message that what really matters to us is what they can do, not who they are. If we can't help them feel that they matter to us now, in our homes, how will they possibly feel they matter out in the world? The answer for many is that they don't. In a nationally representative survey of young adults ages 18 to 25 in the United States, a whopping 44 percent said they did not feel they mattered to other people.[7]

FOCUS ON THE IMPORTANCE OF RELATIONSHIPS AND NOT JUST ACADEMIC, SPORTS, AND EXTRACURRICULAR OUTCOMES

A mind-bending amount of research shows that the best predictor of life satisfaction is the quality of the relationships we have. From Harvard's famous Grant Study, a seventy-five-year examination of what makes for a happy life, to loads of psychological research, we can say without reservation that encouraging teens to build strong friendships and good relationships with teachers, mentors, coaches, community members, and family is time well spent.[8] Caring relationships are especially important for kids who have experienced difficult life situations and trauma because they can restore a sense of safety and act as a buffer to external threats.*

Families lay the groundwork for nurturing and elevating relationships. Most of us spend too little time talking to our children about what makes for good relationships, including romantic ones. Articulate what it is to be a good friend: listening, empathizing, and being reliable. Acknowledge when they are a good friend, celebrate when they help others, and model the importance of taking care of yourself, your family, and community. Think of ways to build and strengthen relationships together: write thank-you cards for teachers who mean a lot to them, or bake brownies for the parent who always ends up with the extra carpool shift. Notice who people are, not just what they do.

Families can also try spending more time together, without any purpose besides enjoying each other's company. Academics have long shown significant benefits of what they call *positive childhood experiences,* including developing strong ties with family and community through cookouts or game nights or simply hanging out at the kitchen table chatting.[9] But many families spend more time on outcome-oriented activities (games, recitals, concerts, tutoring) than on simply being together. Without "social proof," or evidence of genuine mattering, kids are forced to rely on games and coaches and parents on the sidelines to validate their worth.[10] We're all for gaining confidence and forging relationships by being on a team. But too many kids stuck in Achiever mode over index on structured activities with tangible outcomes (CV-worthy pastimes) under index on friends and family time, community time—*just being* time.

* Trauma can also make it harder to build and sustain relationships, so often a lot of patience is needed.

ENCOURAGE AUTHENTIC CONTRIBUTION

William Damon, the author of *The Path of Purpose: How Young People Find Their Calling in Life* and director of Stanford's Center on Adolescence, defines purpose as "a stable and generalized intention to accomplish something that is at the same time meaningful to the self and consequential for the world beyond the self."[11] Key to that definition is that purpose is prosocial; it goes beyond the self. Going to the movies because it is fun is not purpose, but escapism. For kids, setting a goal of getting into college because it's meaningful for their future and finding a college that is a good fit for them (and not their parents' aspiration) is purpose. So is becoming the world's greatest skateboarder, a better potter, a financial support to your family, or a climate activist.

To help kids feel they matter, we must help them get beyond themselves and recognize needs beyond their own. This can happen through having a job, where people rely on you to show up and do work, or volunteering. The goal is for kids to contribute in authentic ways. Wiping down counters so someone else doesn't have to may seem small, but it's significant (if you don't, the grime builds and your co-worker has to do it, which they will not like). And volunteering, when done to meet real needs and not to just to check a box, can open kids' eyes to a much bigger world. In an era of unprecedented focus on the self, on social media and in the media, getting beyond the relentless drumbeat of "me" and into the lives of others can be a gift. According to the psychologist Martin E. P. Seligman, "The self . . . is a very poor site for meaning."[12] Thomas Insel, the former head of the National Institute of Mental Health in the United States, explains it differently: "In many ways helping others is more therapeutic than getting help from others."[13]

If you need a place to start, try the following:

- **Contribute at home.** Ask your kids to contribute, in real and meaningful ways, at home. Whether it's walking the dog, taking out the trash, setting the table for meals, doing laundry, mowing the lawn, helping a younger sibling with homework, or cooking meals for the family, household responsibilities offer opportunities that provide evidence to kids that they matter.

- **Help Others.** Encourage kids to help elderly relatives or neighbors, for pay if the neighbors can afford it, or for free if they can't. Raking leaves or bringing over a meal can really brighten people's day and show your child how valuable their effort is.
- **Get a Job.** Suggest they join the workforce. From scooping ice cream to waiting or busing tables, there's nothing like service to realize how rude people can be, how hard work is, and how lucky kids are to be able to spend time in school learning. From dog walking, to babysitting, to working at the local pizza place, teens will feel their efforts matter when people rely on them. (Additional benefit: more cash.)

Help Kids Reflect so They Can Grow

If mattering is being socially recognized, supported, and feeling valuable to others, young people will need to ask: *What do I want to contribute to the world? How do I want people to invest in me? What do I want to be relied on for?* While kids in Passenger mode need interests to expose them and spark their curiosity, kids in Achiever mode need to look up from their achieving and ask these questions about themselves and their priorities. For many who spend a lot of high school in Achiever mode, it's only when they go off to college or start work that they realize they have not asked themselves these most basic questions. *What do I like? How do I want to contribute? Who do I want to be?* Finding one's place in society requires some trial and error, and rooting around, sometimes inefficiently. To ask big questions like *What do I care about?* requires reflection, which means more downtime and introspection—things busy kids in Achiever mode typically don't do.

It took Vanessa years of reflecting on her experiences—where she had come from and where she was going—to unite her two separate selves into one coherent identity. Crucially, this reflection time was not outcome oriented. Her adviser was not telling her to reflect in order to pick a career and solve next summer's internship. Instead, she needed the time and space to engage in *transcendent thinking,* which we discussed in chapter 5. What did her experiences mean? Why did she play field hockey so long when she disliked it so much? What was it about her friends at college that made her feel seen? Why was it so important to her to learn more about her cultural heritage? Just as Samir questioned the criteria for selecting students for the gifted and talented program, Vanessa had to reflect on her own experiences and life choices. This kind of reflection not only builds more connections between different parts of the brain but also helps to build a stronger sense of self, or identity. And the clearer kids are about their own identity, the less likely they are to be buffeted around by everyone else's (becoming, in the words of William Deresiewicz, "excellent sheep").[14]

THE REFLECTION TANGO

Reflection can sound passive—it's anything but. When Tevin designed his own project, Samir got obsessed with the gifted and talented program criteria, or Stella started brainstorming better ways to teach, they were *doing* things and then thinking about them.

This transcendent thinking happens only when two different parts of the brain are working together: the taskmaster network and the imagining network. The taskmaster network, or executive control network (ECN), is used for "goal-directed thinking and focused attention" and is activated by emotionally and cognitively challenging activities in the external world—when we are moving, doing, executing.[15] Young people deploy it working on their homework, managing their day-to-day responsibilities, observing social situations, and understanding what's happening in front of them. And yes, when trying to manage the negative emotions generated by a nagging parent. When the ECN is engaged during conversation, young people typically speak faster, demonstrate high energy, and maintain direct eye contact.[16] This brain region works overtime for always-on-the-go kids in Achiever mode.

The imagining network, or default mode network (DMN), meanwhile, is the reflective, meaning-making area of the brain. It can pull us away from our current context or perspective and pushes our consciousness into imagined realities, pasts, and futures, and into the perspectives of others. The DMN lights up when our minds wander or when we daydream, and it helps us contemplate the bigger picture of a situation, connect the dots of the world at large, and generate novel solutions to problems. Kids need to engage the DMN to think creatively.[17] While the taskmaster network is used to *play* soccer—picking who to pass to, keeping track of the score—the imagining network is used to reflect on soccer's place in society: as an activity that brings joy or might land us a scholarship, or as an occasion to wonder why female athletes are paid so much less than their male counterparts. When engaged in this type of abstract thought, young people and adults speak more slowly, move less, and avoid direct eye contact.[18] When kids are in Achiever mode, their taskmaster network is firing on all cylinders, but their imagining network may not be. Vanessa did just this when she pushed herself through years of field hockey without stopping to let herself reflect on whether she truly wanted to be playing it.

But for kids to build their Explorer muscles, the two networks need to work together. Think of them as being like a pair of professional dancers. Each needs to know the steps of the tango, and each needs to be fit. But each knowing their individual part won't win them any awards on *Dancing with the Stars*. It's the way they dance *together*. The ECN and the DMN need to work together to make that connectivity stronger and more efficient.[19] The goal is not two networks, each individually strong; it's two networks that work together, enabling them to communicate more efficiently.

When the networks work together more, essential skills are developed: metacognitive abilities, creativity, and curiosity. For curiosity to be piqued, we need to notice a gap in knowledge (Why is it raining so much more this year?) and imagine different possibilities (Is it climate change? Is it the natural variability of precipitation? Is it the Gulf Stream?) using the imagining network. We then need to activate the taskmaster network to analyze and interrogate, to reason and evaluate. That toggling is also essential for creativity, typically defined as the ability to produce novel and useful ideas.[20] That definition goes way beyond the classroom conception of creativity—often associated with art or drama—to key skills for innovation and everyday problem solving. Consider some of the component parts of creative thinking: generating new ideas, evaluating and improving on ideas, expressing one's own ideas through various media (words, video, art), and answering open-ended questions.[21] Creativity is key to not just inventing new things but finding different ways of doing old things. Rethinking energy uses; tackling disinformation in AI; and scaling eco-friendly housing to meet the demands of mass urbanization require chemistry, engineering, design, computer science, and bold new ways of thinking. Creativity is more than a future-ready skill; it's also considered by many to be essential to happiness. Some great philosophical and psychological thinkers even considered it to be the pinnacle of self-actualization.

Adolescence is *a key* moment when the brain is learning the steps to that tango—steps that help teens understand themselves. It is the act of both exploring and doing that helps the brain forge connections. Brains develop as they are used: A brain that explores, imagines, wonders, and evaluates will become better networked than one that does not. With no time to practice the imagining as well as the doing, teens won't learn to dance well. And they need those tango skills to be an Explorer.

When schools don't create any space for powerful reflection, they undervalue the imagining network and the developmental need for adolescents to begin to make meaning of what they are doing. This happens too often, according to Mary Helen Immordino-Yang, who is leading research on *transcendent thinking:* "We do not want our young people to think outside the box, to try different ways of understanding things, to engage in deep emotional poignant debate with each other about very hairy problems. We just want them to get the right answer by the day we want."[22]

To be sure, we want kids who can get to the right answer. But we also want kids who know why it is the best answer among a sea of possibilities. We want kids who are adaptable and can explore hard questions in complex environments. They need reflection if things are to feel meaningful and joyful, leading to emotional engagement, which so many in Achiever mode lack, busy as they are completing tasks. Kids operating primarily in Achiever mode can do a lot—but do they care only about the outcome or also the ideas? To support Achievers in their quest for balance, to help them engage in powerful reflection, and to foster their creativity we need to make time for **mindfulness, daydreaming,** and transcendent thinking.

DESTRESS WITH MINDFULNESS

Mindfulness practices can help stressed-out students in Achiever mode walk themselves back from the edge of unhappiness. Research shows that regular reflective practice can lower stress.[23] While not a replacement for doing the hard work of therapy, it is a small way to work toward finding calm in what can feel like a chaotic world.

Olivia, a white seventeen-year-old who spends a great deal of the day in Achiever mode in Los Angeles is, on paper, privileged in many ways: She's got wealthy parents; lives in a beautiful house; and attends a top private school with plenty of resources to support her development in music, leadership, and sports. But internally, she feels like she is walking a tightrope. Like most kids zooming ahead in constant Achiever mode, she pursues a dizzying array of activities, many of which are done with an eye to getting into a top college.

During COVID, at the encouragement of her mom and cousin, Olivia took up meditation and has kept it up ever since. She has devised her own reflective practice. At the end of each day (or days when she thinks of it), she spends ten minutes reflecting on three things:

- **Daily stress inventory.** She asks herself: *How stressed do I feel, especially with midterms coming up?*
- **Assessing four realms.** She assesses four things: social dynamics, academics, physical health, and self-image. *I feel a lot of tension with my best friend. Why?*
- **Taking action.** When she notices a pattern, she addresses it. If it's academic, she talks to a teacher. If it's self-image, she talks to her mom. If it's social dynamics, she might suggest to a friend that they meet at a coffee shop to hang out.

The practice doesn't change the extraordinary number of things she's doing, but it does change her sense of control over her life. She feels calmer when she goes through her day. She feels it sustains her through tough periods. She is more self-aware about what she needs and uses this to ask for the help she needs.

Every child can benefit from mindfulness. But kids in Achiever mode have many fewer opportunities to have the downtime needed to practice it. They are simply too busy rushing from one thing to the next and often miss out on the stress-reducing benefits that mindfulness can bring. Plus it helps make the space for the type of reflection needed for daydreaming and transcendent thinking.

FOSTER CREATIVITY WITH DAYDREAMING

Kids' daydreaming is not a character flaw. It doesn't lead directly to a fate of laziness or a lifetime of living at home in your basement. Too often, adults see only absentmindedness and a failure to pay attention; they don't see relaxing, pondering, or activating the imagining network of the brain.

Peter, a white sixth grader, remembers perfectly the bright posters of the deep ocean and outer space on his third-grade classroom walls.

He would stare at them and think about how the world worked. "I was trying to figure out why stuff happens," he recalls, "like, why don't we just fly off with the centrifugal force of the Earth spinning?" But in his top-rated public school in well-to-do Long Beach, California, he felt stupid. School wanted him to do everything quickly—just "[get it] done, done, done," he says. While he was pondering the mysteries of the universe, he failed to complete his work on time. As punishment, he would lose recess. He would sit alone at his desk to finish the assignment while all his classmates went outside to play.

Jerome L. Singer, a clinical psychologist and professor emeritus at Yale, was known as the "father of daydreaming," which he described as spontaneous, self-generated thought not directly related to the task at hand.[24] Singer was an advocate for understanding why people daydreamed and the benefits it brought to creativity and innovation. He was a lonely voice sixty years ago, when he started his work. Many researchers, psychologists, and educators saw daydreaming as a bad thing. Many still do today: When studying daydreaming, researchers often use terms like *task-irrelevant thoughts, zoning out,* and *absent-mindedness.* Daydreaming is seen as hampering learning outcomes like literacy and numeracy, which is why so many studies try to figure out how to get students to do it less.[25]

But Singer and his colleagues saw the benefits of what they called **positive constructive daydreaming**—a type of daydreaming that "reflects curiosity, sensitivity, exploration of ideas, feelings, and sensations" and is associated with openness to new experiences.* Positive constructive daydreaming is associated with a range of important processes and outcomes: "self-awareness, creative incubation, improvisa-

---

* Singer, together with his colleagues John Antrobus and Tang Zhiyan, recognized that not all daydreaming is created equal. Some daydreaming slips into rumination (called guilty dysphoria daydreaming), where people obsessively imagine things going wrong and begin to feel guilty and anxious. Other times, people daydream because they struggle mightily with focusing their attention on either the task at hand or their own thought process, which limits their ability to get things done in the world.

tion and evaluation, memory consolidation, autobiographical planning, goal driven thought, future planning," and many others.[26] All these things help young people navigate the world. Daydreaming fosters creativity and can help enable more Explorer moments.

Parents and teachers can't force young people to daydream, but they certainly can help them have the *opportunity* to do so. Daydreaming really only happens when young people are not responding to external input or stimulation. That means parents need to refrain from encouraging kids to fill every free moment with a purposeful activity (studying, doing the dishes, prepping for the SAT). Here are some ways to support positive daydreaming:

- **When you see your kids staring out the window or otherwise spacing out, resist the urge to interrupt them right away.** Who knows—they could be the next Einstein, who famously developed the theory of relativity while loafing about Bern and staring at clocks for hours on end. (Of course, they might also just be thinking about what's for dinner.)

- **Talk to them about the importance of radical downtime.** Remind them that downtime is *not* scrolling on their phone or binge-watching their favorite Netflix series. William Stixrud and Ned Johnson, the authors of *The Self-Driven Child,* define radical downtime as "doing nothing purposeful, nothing that requires highly focused thought." Kids need this to have space for daydreaming.[27]

- **Model taking time for reflection.** If our children don't see us carving out time for reflection, they may feel it is not something worth doing. "I don't rest very easily," says one stressed-out high school junior at a competitive high school. "Partly it's because my dad is never, ever still. He doesn't sit."

TRY A TRANSCENDENT THINKING APPROACH TO ASKING ABOUT SCHOOL

In addition to making sure our kids have time for mindfulness and daydreaming, we can actively prompt them to engage in transcendent thinking. The key is *not* to ask broad, vague questions *about meaning* itself. We have tried this on our own kids, with epic failure. "What was meaningful in school today?" or "What meaning do you make of that movie we saw last night?" We find that such questions result in blank stares, eye-rolling, and soft mutterings of "Your book is so annoying, Mom." Broad questions don't feel authentic—they sound contrived.

Instead, be curious about specific things already happening around them—less *What role do you want to play in the world?* and more *Why is the world hating on Travis Kelce just because Taylor Swift is flying back from Japan to see him?* This also works to help start a dialogue about what they are learning in school. For a list of questions to try, we turned to our colleague and friend Dave Hamilton, a Boston design technology teacher who has spent much of his life working with teachers to foster creativity and inspire transcendent thinking through asking good questions. Your goal is not to give them answers, but to plant the seeds of curiosity so that they want to find the answers themselves (if you state a connection between things, they *don't have to find it*). Some questions he suggests parents try:

- **How did this get here?** Point at anything and ask, "How did this get here?" Your kid might say, "Mom put it there." Explain you want the full story, from the object's origin to this moment. For example, Dave's daughters love avocados. More than half the world's avocados come from Mexico and Central America, which he knows his older daughter is studying in geography class. So, "How did these avocados get here?" Is this a good thing or a bad thing that avocados travel the world? Every step of the explanation can intersect with traditional school disciplines and spark engaging questions. Accuracy is less important than finding connections to subjects they are studying and questioning the underlying meaning of things.

- **What problem does this solve?** Try assuming that if humans made something, they did it to solve a problem.* Posing this question helps kids think about cause and effect. For example, your child has to write their history paper on the Gutenberg press. It is the night before the deadline, and they "don't even know what to write about." What problem did the Gutenberg press solve? (Books could only be written by hand.) And what problem did *that* solve? (Only a few people had access to knowledge.) What are some of the possible downsides from solving this problem? Each solution unveils a new problem to explore and unintended consequences to consider.
- **How else could we have solved the same problem?** This question allows for speculation and extrapolation. Besides Gutenberg, who else was trying to solve the problem in 1440? What other solutions were possible?

Transcendent discussion evokes strong reactions in teens because it asks them to consider deeper questions and explore complex moral dilemmas. This helps with emotional engagement, something key for all learners but especially those in Achiever mode. It also engages both the imagining and reasoning brain networks, the DMN and the ECN. By putting the two together, kids deep in Achiever mode can start to tango and experience the joys of exploring.

However, to do this, they will also have to take some risks.

---

* It doesn't matter if you don't believe this.

Overcome the Fear of Failure: Embracing Productive Struggle

Kids in Achiever mode are giving all they've got. For many, that means success—high marks, top of the class, standout in extracurriculars. That's all good, except when being at the top becomes the goal at the expense of everything else. When you are at the top, there is nowhere to go but down, so why risk trying new things and, gasp, failing at them? Why risk pushing yourself out of your comfort zone and then struggling? To figure out how you matter requires a lot of trial and error, which requires risk and reflection. Am I a party girl or a serious student? Maybe both? Engaging in transcendent thinking requires being comfortable spending time in the realm of uncertainty, where there are rarely clear-cut right and wrong answers.

Fear of failure gets in the way of kids in Achiever mode building Explorer muscles and rising to their full potential. Playing it safe doesn't encourage exploring; it hinders it. Take Sadie, a fifteen-year-old who spends all her time achieving. Sadie attends a progressive private school in Portland, where small class sizes and encouragement of teachers to put less emphasis on grades should, in theory, help with her fear of failure. But they don't. If Sadie is confused or lost, she will definitely *not* raise her hand to ask a question in class. She does not want to risk looking dumb, or not having the answer, something every kid in Achiever mode told us they hate. This is a fragile kind of intelligence that can easily crumble. What we want instead is resilient intelligence, which comes from being comfortable not knowing something.

The goal is not to force these kids to fail. The goal is to expose them to risk so they get used to being uncomfortable and operating in uncertainty. When Amina got to Yale she wished she had experienced more failure in high school so she would have known what to do when she stumbled in college. In exposure therapy, the therapist does not expose a patient who is afraid of spiders to a tarantula on day one. Instead, the arachnophobe may start by looking at pictures of the spider and talking about her fears. Next, the therapist might produce a small spider in a cage. The act of confronting this fear, even in a small form, is what builds bravery. We can't think our way to being brave; we have to feel it. That's the evidence that will eventually allow the arachnophobe to confront the spider outside of the cage.

Productive struggle—getting comfortable with being uncomfortable in learning—for students stuck in Achiever mode is a little bit like exposure therapy for the arachnophobe. Since kids in Achiever mode don't like to fail, they avoid it. They need exposure to the idea of doing something they might not be good at to realize the planets don't stop orbiting the sun.

In a sense, productive struggle for achieving kids is about pushing the boundaries of the learning-to-learn cycle. Whereas coasting kids often need help mastering basic learning tools—planning, monitoring progress, and evaluating strategies—to engage in their learning, students in Achiever mode need help embracing challenge, risk, and growth. These are advanced learning tools for deepening engagement. By building resilience—through productive struggle—we get comfortable with discomfort. This is perhaps one of life's greatest skills, and it has deep applications for learning. Learning is hard, and effort requires courage. We get stronger through tough training; we get better at math from toiling a bit in the confusion; we have a better friendship after a hard discussion. Pushing through hard things is how we learn. Achievers don't need to master a lot of learning skills; rather, they need to explore where their learning might take them.

On a bone-cold winter evening, Kate, a forty-eight-year-old, white upper-middle-class mother, sat in her daughter's private school gym in London with one hundred other parents. Their children were preparing to take an exam to get into middle school. The teachers were there to explain the process and how they might support their kids. The exams were high stakes, and the parents in the audience were an ambitious lot. Everyone knew that with each passing year the competition got stiffer. More kids took the exams, fewer got in, and parents went a little loonier. The children were ten.

In the gym, an English teacher put on the Smartboard a picture of

James Nottingham's Learning Pit. He smiled, then started to explain the diagram.

In the early 2000s, Nottingham taught in an ex-mining town in the North of England and found that when it came to the classroom, the kids liked to play it safe.[28] Like Sadie, they didn't raise their hand if they didn't know the answer. When given some choices about topics to explore, they stuck to things they knew. He drew a diagram of what actual learning looks like: the spark of a new idea, the false belief that you understand it, the descent into not knowing, and the figuring it out. One child said it looked like a pit (it was a mining town, remember). The idea of the Learning Pit was born.

An idea starts off easy because you aren't thinking about it very hard. Let's say, for example, that you have memorized the definition of photosynthesis, the process by which green plants and some organisms use sunlight to synthesize foods with the help of chlorophyll, sunlight, and water. But then your teacher asks you to talk about a component—say light-dependent reactions and the role of chlorophyll, or the overall purpose of photosynthesis. You realize you are lost—you can recite the definition, but you don't know why it matters. This is the moment you fall into the pit. Once you're in the pit, you need to *find a way to get out:* asking a teacher or a peer, watching a video on YouTube. Slowly, you start to piece it together. As you master the topic, you come out on the other side at a higher level, both more knowledgeable and more resilient. You did something hard, and that's evidence that you can do hard things. That's productive struggle.

As Kate listened, the English teacher explained that over the course of the coming term, the kids would all fall into that pit—the school would be sending homework that was way ahead of their ability. The kids would struggle mightily. They would not like it. And you parents, he said with a knowing smile, will not like it either.

Do not help them, he said. Encourage them to struggle, to try. Let them know the goal is not reciting the answer but grappling with the problem. As the kids wrestled with the work, they would get more comfortable with struggle, and then, with help from their teachers,

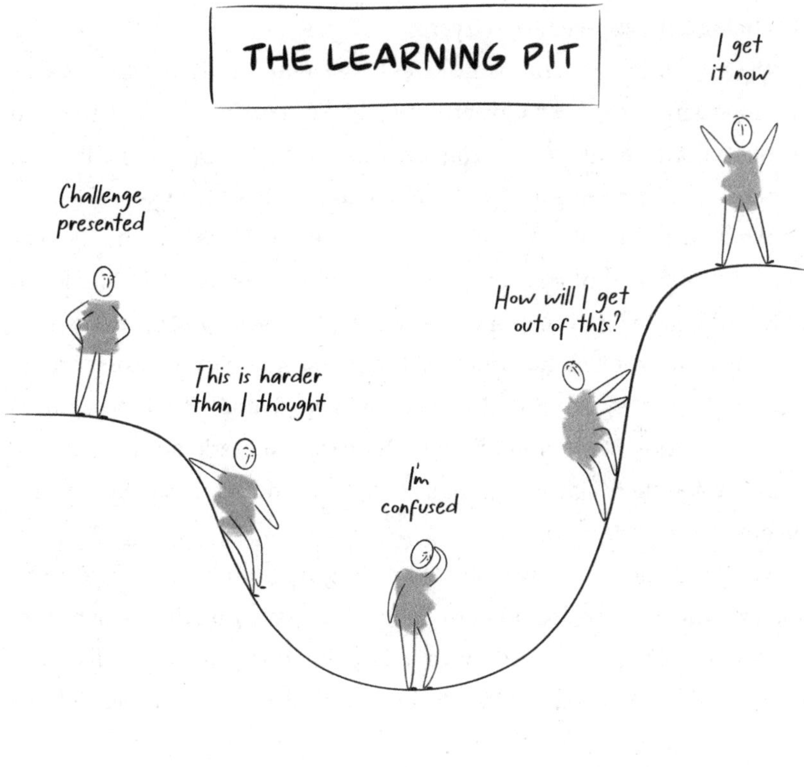

Source: The Learning Pit from James Nottingham, LearningPit.org.

and from their friends, they would *climb out of the pit.* Allowing them to flail a bit would have two outcomes. The students would have the memory of climbing out of the pit, an important reference they could return to the next time they learned a new idea and got confused. And they would know *how* to get out of the pit, a lesson that would serve them well not only on the exam but also in life. It would cultivate not just confidence that they could meet hard goals but also the skills and experiences of doing so. This was what Amina was missing when she enrolled in Yale.

"This will hurt my daughter's confidence," insisted one father. "We can help them, right?" asked one mother, who seemed to have missed the entire point of the presentation. The teacher had of course heard all this before. It happened every year.

In spite of the general panic sweeping the room, Kate thought this sounded smart. She was an athlete and knew that you had to push through hard things to get stronger. This seemed to be the intellectual equivalent. She resolved to let her daughter, Isabel, struggle.

And yet the next few weeks proved to be harder than she had expected. Isabel had more than a few perfectionist tendencies: She loved to do things well and reap the praise of adults, who since she was very small had marveled at her work ethic and her maturity. Pleasing others had become a way of being. As Isabel slogged through English passages she barely understood and toiled with math that made no sense to her, Kate heeded the English teacher's advice, reminding her daughter, "It's meant to be hard."

But then the test scores started rolling in: 30 percent, 40 percent. Isabel seemed to be losing confidence. She gave up when her homework got hard. She seemed more irritable and less willing to listen to Kate's advice. Kate started to get uncomfortable. It didn't feel right to let her daughter flounder.

After a night of tears and frustration (first Isabel's, then Kate's), Kate went to the school to talk to the teacher. She wanted to ask him why he was so intent on destroying the souls of such small children. The teacher assured her that Isabel was making progress in school. She was more resilient than Kate realized. He asked her to trust him. Reluctantly, Kate backed down.

Soon after Kate's visit, Isabel's scores started climbing: 40 percent, 50 percent. They plateaued at about 60 percent. Isabel's mood improved, and the storm appeared to be over. At a regularly scheduled parent-teacher meeting, Isabel's teacher raved about her progress. She was clocking 60 percent on problems that were a full academic year ahead. She was getting better at dealing with frustration and setbacks. She was gaining confidence—not just in math and English, but in asking for help when she was confused and learning to check if she really understood something. She was learning to solve problems, including in her own learning. She was coming out of the pit.

THE POWER OF LEARNING TO ASK FOR HELP

What the parents never saw—because they were not in the classroom—was that the teachers were in the pit with the kids. They didn't toss them over the edge, peer over the side, and cackle. They knew that the kids were struggling, and they offered them support without lowering the bar. Work in pairs. Ask me if you have a question (but think first before you ask). Write down the thing you are most confused about right now. The kids were meant to feel stuck, but not alone. The teachers showed the kids they had a team behind them, supporters who cheered on their victories, whether small or large. The students were learning to ask for help when things got hard, a key Explorer skill.

Once she saw Isabel's scores improve, Kate realized her desire to rescue her daughter from hardship was born from love but ultimately counterproductive. Isabel would struggle with a million things in her life, from math and English to heartbreak and career setbacks. She needed to know that she was capable of problem-solving. She could always rely on Kate for support, but for Isabel to build that capability, Kate had to step back.

We parents have all been in Kate's position. Watching your own kid suffer is a special form of hell. But a kid who struggles—and sometimes fails—will end up more prepared for challenge than a kid who breezes through their work without breaking a sweat. Isabel had demonstrated the textbook definition of resilience—and Kate had almost prevented her from developing it. Isabel is still a perfectionist kid. She loves to excel. But she does not wilt at challenges, and she asks an endless array of questions to make sure she is learning.

Isabel and Sadie and their like-minded peers operating in Achiever mode are not outliers. Many kids in Achiever mode are used to working hard but not used to failing. In fact, they spend most of their time making sure it never happens. The American cultural aversion to failure seeps into many of our classrooms, the very places that should be encouraging intellectual risk-taking. Even the U.S. Department of Education is concerned about it. Several years ago, it released a detailed study comparing how teachers teach eighth-grade math across three countries, including Japan and the United States.[29]

In Japan, teachers spent 44 percent of their time giving students material they didn't know and asking them to figure it out; in the United States, teachers took this approach 1 percent of the time. In Japan, a student would sometimes stand at the board for over half an hour trying to figure out how to do a problem—no one was concerned or embarrassed. In the United States, teachers offered steps to solutions before students tried the problems, to *prevent* them from struggling. Not surprisingly, the United States consistently performs well below its high-income peers in international tests of math, whereas Japan is a consistent top performer.[30]

As parents, we need to get comfortable with discomfort—ours and our kids'. This does not mean refusing to help your child when they have a total meltdown or ignoring them when they are deeply anxious. When we taught our kids to ride a bike, if they fell off, skidding along the concrete and cutting their hand, we picked them up, dusted them off, and gave them a Band-Aid. But if they pushed off and began to wobble, we squashed our instincts to rescue them before they fell and mustered every ounce of encouragement we could: *You've got this! Look ahead! Keep going!* How could they *not* wobble before they coasted along on two wheels? Nottingham says there are three mental states kids occupy when they are learning: relatively comfortable, relatively uncomfortable, and panicked. Panic deserves a hug from us and checking what they need. But too many parents step in at relatively uncomfortable.* "It's counterproductive," he told us. "Struggle is where we learn."[31]

---

* George Davison, former head of Grace Church School in New York City, moved science projects into school because of the ridiculous amount of "help" parents were offering at home.

American culture in particular celebrates hard-won, solitary success. But no great things in life were achieved without obstacles and challenge. Most entrepreneurs are seasoned failures. A big data study of forty-six years of venture capital investments—investments in start-up companies, most of which fail, while a select few become Google—found prior failure to be "the essential prerequisite for success."[32] The key is learning from each mistake. James Dyson of vacuum cleaner fame loves to tell students that it took him 5,127 prototypes to develop the first bagless vacuum cleaner. "To be an inventor, you have to believe that there is always a better way of doing something," he said. "And, you can't expect to get it exactly right the first time. Every iteration can be improved upon, and each of these failures teaches you something that you can apply to the next iteration. . . . It's highly frustrating, of course, but worth it."[33] This kind of creativity combines transcendent thinking (the ability to imagine "a better way of doing something") with the hard-won lessons of repeated failure. When reflection and productive struggle come together, great things can happen.

SUPPORTING PRODUCTIVE STRUGGLE AT HOME

Here are a few tips to help kids when they start to stumble. If a child is struggling mightily with English and gets low marks on her essay, try not to say, "Great effort. I know you tried hard." Praising effort alone can send the mixed message that their effort indicates the extent of their abilities. Without realizing it, you have subtly told them you don't expect they can write a good essay. Instead, praise the *strategies* that worked well—effective studying, help received from a teacher, designing flashcards, recording notes and listening to them while walking the dog—and then brainstorm different ways to approach the essay next time around.

Many kids who operate most of the time in Achiever mode are at their core fragile. They've never flirted with getting bad grades, or not making a team, or not being seen as upstanding. They are terrified of what would happen if the facade cracked. Overcoming their fear of

WHAT WE SAY	WHAT WE SHOULD SAY*
Grade A: You are so smart!	You must have worked so hard to do that well. What strategies do you think worked?
Grade B: What happened?	I noticed you studied hard for that. Do you feel you covered the material you needed to?
Grade C: Are you kidding?	That must be frustrating. What strategies might help better next time?

* If you say these but dont mean them, your kids will 100 percent know and it will backfire.

failure and venturing beyond the expected path does not mean ditching hard work or the love of achieving. It starts by taking small risks to build up confidence: taking a class you might not be good at because it interests you; writing a paper on a topic that you know little about but that piques your curiosity; quitting field hockey to try climbing because it seems cool, even if it might not look as good on a college application.

Kids need productive struggle to learn to become brave, take risks, and drive their own learning—just as they need the time and space to reflect, and the support to know they matter for who they are not just what they do. Helping kids in Achiever mode build Explorer muscles can be hard because no parent wants to mess with a good thing. But maybe it's time for a better definition of a good thing.

Takeaways

1. Kids in Achiever mode need to feel they matter unconditionally, beyond their A+ performance.
2. Kids in Achiever mode *do* a lot. We can help them make time and space to reflect on what they really care about. A first step is helping them carve out downtime, which includes destressing with mindfulness techniques.
3. Real downtime is also needed to foster creativity and imagination. If kids seem like they are daydreaming, let them! This is how new ideas are born.
4. We can encourage transcendent thinking by asking open, big-picture questions about school or life. Remember the goal is the dialogue this spurs, not getting the right answer to the question.
5. Kids in Achiever mode don't like to fail, so they avoid it. Encourage productive struggle and small risk-taking to build bravery.

9

From Pushback to Progress

Supporting Your Kid Through Resister Moments

At the end of year 10 (which is what Brits call ninth grade), Eddie announced he wasn't going to school anymore. We've seen this story before with Samir; it is classic resisting behavior. Eddie's parents were stunned. He was only fifteen. He had his GCSEs the next year, a set of very important exams in England, and Eddie needed to buckle down, not check out.

His father, Chris, an educator with thirty years of experience teaching and running schools, had been on the other side of the table for this conversation hundreds of times. He usually advised parents that "if you give it enough time, and put the right interventions in place, it will solve itself." Now he found himself trying to apply his own advice. "None of that really prepared me," he admitted. "It's a real shock to the system," he said, when it's your own kid struggling.

There had been a few signs that things were amiss—Eddie would say he was ill, and Chris suspected he was fine. But his son's announcement that he was not going back to school *ever* was a bombshell. Eddie, who is white, lives a comfortable middle-class life, and his parents never questioned the idea that he would finish school like the majority of his peers. Chris and his wife leaped into action: For two weeks, they did not leave Eddie alone in the house, juggling work schedules to make sure one of them was always home. "You have to figure out the cause," Chris told us, which in his experience ranged from bullying, to being bored, to being in an abusive relationship with another child or, worse, an adult. "You've got to slowly, over a period of time, discount those things. . . . You don't know. You just don't know."

Chris called the school and made sure someone came to visit Eddie. It was important to have many people investigating the source, and for the school to convey to Eddie that whatever the problem, it could be sorted out. "Always give a child a way out of a situation," Chris often tells new teachers. "Because if you don't, the guarantee is that child will find a way out of a situation, and it won't be pleasant."

Then Chris spent as much time as he could with Eddie—walking the dog, mountain biking, getting a burger at McDonald's. He mainly just spent time with him without prodding. But there were moments when he would encourage Eddie, ask questions, listen to him, and offer guidance in small doses. Slowly, Chris learned that Eddie felt like he didn't have any friends at school anymore. He felt distant from everyone else. Eddie had always been shy, and making friends had never come easily. Then, when the school reversed their decision to let him take several classes he had been looking forward to, classes related to entrepreneurship, he decided he was done. There was nothing drawing him to school. He was out. Why go back?

Chris encouraged him to go back to school and finish off the year, which was almost done, knowing how much harder it would be if he waited until fall. "There's a light at the end of the tunnel," he said; summer was right around the corner. They discussed what Eddie wanted to do—be an entrepreneur—and what skills that might take. Chris found a friend of a friend who was an entrepreneur who spoke to Eddie and told him he probably wouldn't be able to achieve his goals without finishing school.

Chris emphasized that he did not go into Eddie's bedroom, sit on his bed, and ask him what his plan was. "It would set off his fight or flight," he said. He looked for nonthreatening, nonconfrontational ways to connect. It wasn't always successful. "You get knocked back fifty times," he told us, but each conversation "was an inch further forward." The conversations got longer and longer, and eventually it was Eddie who finally said, "Well, yeah, I've got to do this."

After two weeks, Eddie agreed to go back to school. But when the day came, he refused again. At this point, Chris and his wife doled out some firm parenting. Eddie had to go to school. This was not easy; Chris knew his son would be happier at home. But Chris explained that he and Eddie's mom had to work to earn a living. Plenty of expletives ensued.

Eddie finally relented. He finished the year off, and over the summer break Chris continued talking about Eddie's future—and connecting it to Eddie's present. They got a license plate (called a number plate in Britain) for a car that Eddie would get when he was seventeen. They put it on Eddie's bedroom wall as a reminder of the person he was hoping to become after he got through his exams. Chris helped him secure an apprenticeship for after GCSEs. The school said it would let Eddie tie some of his coursework to mountain biking, something he loved. Chris checked in with the school about Eddie's social struggles. It turned out that several other students had asked if Eddie was okay. "It wasn't as black as he painted it to be," said Chris. The school gently helped reconnect Eddie with some of his peers.

Chris didn't just help Eddie imagine a future self—an entrepreneur who had his own car—he helped him identify the steps to get there, including taking his exams. "So he starts seeing a future for himself. That gets him through the present," he told us. Chris didn't issue ultimatums and threats but drew Eddie out, letting him frame his choices so that he'd ultimately feel they were his. Sure, Chris made him go to school—but only after he'd given Eddie time to work through what was going on.

Chris had an unfair advantage over the rest of us. As a veteran educator and teacher, he had experience and context for what Eddie was going through. For most of us, our experience comes from the one or two kids we have, and we don't have a great sense of what is going on inside schools.

Children with Problems, Not Problem Children

Parenting kids in Resister mode is not easy work, no matter what experience you have. Parents often feel judged: by teachers and school administrators, by other parents, by friends and family. You may feel afraid, which typically comes out as frustration, desperation, or resignation. This is only natural—none of the success stories we heard in our research were simple fixes or one-and-done strategies. Parenting and development don't work that way, especially when it comes to kids who are resisting. We are all figuring it out as we go. So start by setting aside the fear, as best you can, giving yourself some grace and self-forgiveness, and try to read the signals your teen is sending.

Kids in Passenger mode take little initiative, so they need to build it, delving into genuine interests and learning to learn. Kids in Achiever mode are investing in their learning but are afraid of failure and often have not developed the self-awareness to know what they care about or the resilience to drive their own learning accordingly. They have to move beyond their identity as defined by grades and achievements and be willing to risk trying things they might not be good at (right away). That's when they develop Explorer muscles to drive their own learning.

Resisters have agency, but it's pointed away from their learning. There may be times when this is self-protective and positive, especially in physically or psychologically unsafe contexts. But kids in Resister mode often need a more serious intervention to remove practical barriers to engagement and make way for building a different identity. To get them to take initiative in a direction that advances their learning, we need to help them change their circumstances, showing them that they have some choice over their learning.

The goal is to prevent kids in Resister mode from checking out completely. If students spend too much time going in reverse, using their agency and impulse in ways that get in the way of their learning, they risk developing a Resister learner identity—*School isn't for me, I think it's dumb, I have better things to do.* Some may tip into learned helplessness—*I can't do anything to change my situation.* If they feel powerless to change their situation, they will resign themselves to an identity that is defined by avoiding learning and becoming smaller or by disrupting their learning and becoming larger—in a not-so-constructive way. Parents and teachers have an important role to play to make sure resistance doesn't cross this line.

The secret Chris used was not some great insight from teaching, but one from being human. It was connecting with his son and building trust. It was taking his emotions seriously, not dismissing them or condemning them. It was helping his son remove the obstacles Eddie saw as immovable, allowing him to believe he could move forward. Finally, it was helping Eddie imagine a future possible self that had promise—an exit ramp.

Rather than criticism and control, which can erode agency and keep engagement in reverse, this approach validates Resisters' experiences. It allows you to partner with them on solutions, and focus on their potential. It's about recognizing the person buried beneath the behavior, the reason behind the resistance. By leading with empathy, tackling obstacles side by side, and inspiring a motivating vision of their future, parents can help reignite resisting kids' engagement and unleash their innate agency—empowering them to shift into Explorer mode.

Take Resisters' Emotions Seriously

It's hard not to see Resister mode behavior as disrespectful, inappropriate, or mean. But kids in Resister mode are often using the only tools they have to show us that they are hurting and something is not working for them. This does not remove the need for consequences for bad behavior. Chris set plenty of boundaries. Eddie had to come to meals, he had to be respectful to his parents, and eventually, after Eddie backtracked about going back to school, Chris made him. But instead of dismissing children's emotions, parents like Chris see them as signals that help is needed. These parents become coaches, not hall monitors. Someone has to see possibility in kids who are resisting, because they are not able to see it for themselves.

But to help a kid who is in Resister mode, you have to get in the door. That means your kid will have to let you in, which means they have to want to let you in. Coercion and control may work in the moment, but the only way to help a kid deep in Resister mode is through trust and connection. When kids are having Resister moments, it is easy, in a million little and unintentional ways, to sever that connection—especially when we are busy and quick to judge.

Take the case of Francisco, the autonomy-loving eleven-year-old from Phoenix. On a warm April day, his mom Elena was at work when she got a call that she needed to pick him up from his public middle school. Her ex-husband had (another) "last-minute, very important, totally urgent" meeting. Annoyed, between her own meetings, she drove to school quickly.

Francisco climbed in the front seat. "How was your day?" she asked, an eye on the clock. "It was okay," Francisco replied. "Did you learn anything interesting?" she asked. "No." She glanced over at him. This was not his typical demeanor—perky, making jokes, hanging his hand out the window. He was withdrawn and still. A jolt of panic went through her body—Francisco had been bullied earlier that year. When it happened, her cheerful child had disappeared. He had gone quiet, not telling her about what he was experiencing. One night she found him crying at 3 A.M. in the corner of his room. His body language in the car suggested something had gone off the rails again. She feared the worst.

What followed was something Elena later told us she wished she could do over:

Elena: Is something wrong?

Francisco: Well, yeah. Elliot was really mean to me today.

Elena: Oh, no. What happened?

Francisco: Well, I was in the bathroom and Elliot comes in. And one of the stall doors was jammed, and he said I did it, but I didn't.

ELENA: Oh. That doesn't seem so bad (*relieved he didn't get beat up or have his stuff stolen*). Did you tell him you didn't do it?

FRANCISCO: Yes. But he didn't believe me! (*Tears well up in his eyes.*)

ELENA: Well, that hardly seems to be something to be upset about.

FRANCISCO: You don't understand! I didn't do it! He accused me of it and I told him I didn't, and he *still* said I did (*voice rising and visibly upset*).

ELENA: That's not a big deal.

FRANCISCO: He is *lying*, Mom! I talked with Ms. Cho about it afterwards.

ELENA: You skipped class to go talk to the school counselor about that? Class is important, Francisco. You have to learn to let things roll off your back. (*Looks at the clock, calculates that she has three minutes to get to her desk for her meeting.*)

FRANCISCO: You don't get it. (*Turns away, crosses his arms, looks out the window. Proceeds to give her the silent treatment until long past dinner.*)

For the rest of the day, Elena vacillated between relief, frustration, and concern. Relief that the incident wasn't a return to the bullying earlier in the year. Frustration that Francisco was taking such a small thing so seriously and being so dramatic. Concern, because he had let what she perceived as a little incident get to him enough that he missed valuable instruction time.

Francisco had sent a clear signal that he was not happy. He directly told Elena he was upset and what it was about. Not every child is going to be so forthcoming with their emotions. Not every family welcomes conversations about feelings, and kids in Resister mode who have been struggling for prolonged periods of time often express their emotions in inappropriate ways. One student who spent years in Resister mode described it to us this way: "I was trying to advocate for what I knew I needed, but I didn't have the words—so it often came out in anger."

Taking your child's emotions seriously can be hard. But remember, teen brains crave respect, not judgment. Their emotions are often big, and don't always make sense to us, or may seem trivial. Sometimes whatever advice you offer is rebuffed. The key is to keep trying, and keep the following advice in mind.

AVOID THE POSITIVITY PARADOX

"Never say to a child, 'You shouldn't feel that way,'" says Christina Bethell from Johns Hopkins University.[1] This is true for minor incidents like Francisco experienced and more severe events as well. It is the lived experience and the meaning children make about incidents and traumas themselves that influence how those events show up in our bodies, minds, and nervous systems. It is our emotional experiences that can turn on or off negative epigenetic pathways.

This means that what *actually* happened (Elliot accused Francisco of jamming the bathroom door) is less important than your teen's *experience* of what happened (Francisco feels the injustice of being wrongly accused). In other words, the meaning teens make about something, rational or not, matters a lot. Dismissing children's emotions is, in essence, dismissing their experience.

This is important for avoiding what Bethell calls the **positivity paradox.** By refusing to acknowledge your teen's negative feelings in an attempt to make them feel better, you actually make them feel worse. Recognition and acceptance are important first steps in helping kids in Resister mode. "When pain is acknowledged, it lowers negative emotions and stress," explains Bethell.

With recognition and validation comes empathy. Lots of studies show that when children and adolescents have empathetic parents, they are better able to regulate their emotions and are physically healthier, with lower levels of inflammation in their bodies.[2] When you don't know where to start, try some of these phrases:

- That sounds hard.
- That must feel terrible.
- I can see that you are really mad.

HARNESS THE POWER OF EMOTION COACHING

One of the most important parts of taking our children's emotions seriously is getting in touch with our own feelings about feelings. Lynn Fainsilber Katz, a psychology professor at the University of Washington, studied how conflict such as divorce affected children's development. Katz classified parents' approach to emotions with two categories: those who believe emotions are useful and instructive and worth exploring, and those who think emotions should be dismissed because they are dangerous, annoying, or inappropriate. She found that parents' own feelings about feelings predicted not just children's grades but also their behavior with others.[3]

The emotion-dismissing parents do not love their kids any less. They dismiss negative feelings because they think those emotions are painful for their children and their role is to protect them to help them feel better. But doing so can lead children to believe that their emotions are not important or valid, sowing self-doubt and insecurity. Further, these kids do not learn to recognize or manage their emotions because they have internalized the idea that when they feel strong negative emotions, they should avoid them or distract themselves.

Distracting at age four, when ice cream solves everything, is one thing. But even then, kids miss a chance to learn about handling hard emotions (disappointment, frustration, anger). Studies show kids who don't learn to regulate their emotions are more likely either to become self-destructive through sadness, anxiety, worry, depression, and guilt, or to be aggressive toward others, with angry outbursts, bullying, and defiance.

Conversely, emotion-coaching parents (as Katz calls them) see it as their role to acknowledge children's emotions and help them develop strategies to cope. Researchers like Katz have found that when parents use an emotion-coaching approach, children develop the ability to better self-regulate, a skill that serves them well not just in school but also in life. Popular parenting experts today such as Dr. Becky Kennedy, author of *Good Inside,* embrace and articulate this message beautifully. This results in children who are more emotionally competent, in and out of school. They are less angry, misbehave less, and are more optimistic. Further, kids who struggle with friends at school and get emotion coaching at home are better able to move past social struggles. Parents can help inoculate kids against the class queen bees and jerks.[4]

This is particularly important for kids with marginalized identities, including Black and brown kids and kids who are neurodivergent. Simon, a seventh-grade boy with dyslexia, gets taunted in his class because he struggles with spelling. Simon's parents took his emotions seriously as he was struggling with school and helped him work through them. They also reinforced the idea that dyslexia makes some things harder but others easier. "I can't spell," he told us, "but I am really creative. I don't care what the other kids say." **Emotion coaching** is a type of social buffering, providing a force field around your kids when they leave home and face the harsh winds of the outside world.

What was most surprising in Katz's research was that these effects held regardless of parents' overall warmth or harshness with their children. You could be strict and make a kid practice hours of piano every day but still attend to their emotions and get all the good effects. You could also hug and fuss over them all day long and not recognize or help them understand their own emotions and miss those effects.

MODEL HOW TO MANAGE BIG EMOTIONS

What's the last big emotion you had, and how did you handle it in front of your kids? Did you yell? Sulk? Cry? Pretend nothing happened? Or did you show them that big emotions happen and you handled it?

Modeling healthy emotional coping is yet another sweet-spot parenting challenge. Teens need to feel safe and understand from you that things will be okay. But sharing your feelings—your disappointments, your frustrations, your worry—instructs them that life delivers plenty of challenges and that part of being human, and living a good life, is figuring out how to muck through difficult things.

Studies of families undergoing divorce highlight the benefits of modeling healthy emotion coaching. Researchers found that parents who didn't talk about the divorce with their teens (in an effort to shield them) had children with worse mental health outcomes from the divorce than parents who shared their feelings. The divorcing parents who talked about the sadness and frustration but also assured teens that they would make it through had children who were more emotionally well adjusted one year later.[5]

Share your mistakes and slip-ups with your kids. Show them how it made you feel (embarrassed, inadequate), and what you learned from it. Jenny once told her kids that about a mistake she'd made in a story she wrote in *The New York Times*. Her kids were horrified. She told them mistakes happen and you own them. She acknowledged the error and apologized to the person affected, and the paper printed a correction. It was uncomfortable, but the sun rose the next day, and Jenny was even more careful with her fact-checking in the future. Her kids learned that even if you feel like the world is ending, it usually isn't.

If someone hurts your feelings, model how you handled it (if you happened to handle it well): *It really hurt my feelings when Mel didn't invite me to the coffee morning. So I waited a while to respond, because I thought I might not handle it well. Later, I told her I was bummed not to be asked, and hoped she would include me next time.*

This is a far better strategy than zipping off a scathing email to Mel and then spending the evening wondering why she didn't write back.

HELP KIDS DEVELOP THEIR OWN STRATEGIES

Strategizing with kids—not for them—can help. Lots of studies show that the most powerful impact of emotion coaching comes when parents teach their kids how to identify and come up with their own strategies. Some prompts include asking questions like:

- What do you think can be changed in this situation and what can't?
- Could you try seeing this from a different perspective?
- Who else might be able to help you right now?

Learning to identify sources of support and allies in any situation is a critical life skill. Many of us wait too long to develop it, perhaps because of America's affection for rugged individualism and the inaccurate view that asking for help denotes weakness. We can model looking for support to show how it's done: asking a boss for help, announcing you are confused and need someone to clarify. As the old saying goes, a problem shared is a problem halved.

Chris encouraged Eddie to get an internship. Eddie needed help doing this because it was totally unfamiliar and he found the process intimidating. So Chris showed him how. He identified someone in their community to whom Eddie could talk. He made the initial introduction. He brainstormed with Eddie about how to prepare for the meeting. And then Eddie took it from there.

Get to, and Address, the Why

A lot of parents are busy people, and it can be hard to take the time to try to get to the bottom of your kids' behaviors. But to forge trust and connection, you sometimes need to pause and ask, not react. The answers you get might surprise you—and prove invaluable in finding a solution.

Serene is one such example. She has a round face, light black skin, impeccably done hair, and large, curious eyes. She was a bubbly, precocious child who soaked up learning—after third grade, the school suggested she skip a grade because she was so advanced. Her mom, Shamariah, did everything she could to support Serene's success. She checked out stacks of books from the library, baked with her and her sister, and always taught the two how to behave well (she calls it "home training," which includes sayings like "Be classy, not trashy"). She enveloped her girls in a deep family and church community.

In fourth grade, things took a turn. One January day, right after the break, Serene came home and pulled out a yellow piece of paper. It was a disciplinary note that Shamariah needed to sign. Serene had hit a boy with her lunchbox, and she was in trouble. Shamariah was taken aback. Her heart was beating fast, and she could feel her hackles rising as she looked at the yellow paper in disbelief. Serene was a model student. This was not the norm for her—and definitely not an example of being "classy, not trashy." But Shamariah took a deep breath and resisted the urge to judge. Instead, she asked Serene a simple question: "Why did you do this?"

Serene launched into an explanation of the bad day she had had at school. A boy threw a carrot at the back of her head at lunch and told her she needed to go on a diet. After lunch, on the playground, he kept up the taunts, making fun of Serene for being fat, calling her a bitch. She told him to leave her alone, but he didn't. So she hit him with her lunchbox and got in trouble.

Shamariah was furious. Why had no one gotten Serene's side of the story? She told Serene that hitting was absolutely not okay. "Do not fight evil with evil, fight it with good," Shamariah told her. But she also told her that what the boy had said to her was not okay, that she loved her, and that she was beautiful. "I felt it was important for her to understand that she was perfect," Shamariah said. "She's beautifully and wonderfully made." Shamariah did not sign the paper; instead, she took time off work and talked with the school principal.

But the bullying didn't stop. Over the next several years, the cycle of bullying and violent outbursts recurred. There were taunts about Serene's weight, and racial attacks, including once being called the

N-word. Serene would get angry and fight back. Resisting was a form of self-preservation. To parents of Black and brown students, this might sound familiar. Too often, when incidents occur between children, especially between white kids and kids of color, schools disproportionately discipline the Black or brown student. Black boys are two times more likely than white boys to be suspended or expelled from school.[6]

As time went on, Serene's anger grew and her confidence plummeted. In a world in which she felt she had no control, disruption was what she could hold on to. "I would trip people on purpose and pinch people who made the comments; then I would lie and say my day was good, when really I was hurting the people who were hurting me," she said. "I would have done anything to change."

Switching schools or even staying home some days wasn't an option: Shamariah was a single working mom, and she needed everyone to work together to figure out another solution. But asking a kid in Resister mode to change without changing the environment they are in can be unfair and is often unlikely to work.

So Shamariah studied up on school bullying. The lunch buddy strategy had good evidence behind it, so Shamariah had Serene's father join her at lunch once a week. In a similar vein, Shamariah assisted in school events to be there while it was in session, allowing her to see the dynamics of what was happening with the kids so she could better talk through things at home. Shamariah forged a close partnership with the school staff who found where and when the bullying was taking place—in unsupervised areas in times like recess, lunch, and transitions between classes—and the school ensured that Serene spent time in those places only with adult supervision. Most crucially, Shamariah advocated for the school to connect Serene to in-school support: A school counselor became Serene's "go-to person" in tough moments for a shoulder to cry on and a nudge in the right direction. The bullying did not disappear, but the incidents decreased dramatically.

Serene was in Resister mode because a lot of kids made life hell for her. She knew acting out wasn't the solution, but at the time it was the only way she knew how to respond. Her mother stayed by her side, listened, and worked closely with the school's principal and staff to get her the support she deserved. This meant Serene didn't slip into learned helplessness like Samir and many others in Resister mode. Because of this, the school saw Serene as a smart and capable girl with problems. Her potential was never dismissed. "If I had let it ride, that would have happened," Shamariah said. School administrators searched for ways to engage her and give her positive experiences. When the school offered Serene an opportunity to be a leader, she grabbed it, and she has been active in school leadership ever since.

When we last caught up with Serene, she was a junior and flourishing. During COVID, she started her own baking company—a customer favorite is her Black Santa cookies. During her sophomore year, she got a job in a local bakery to fulfill the internship requirement for her innovative high school, Bostonia Global. That internship turned into a job. She is intrigued by the idea of being an entrepreneur but has lots of other things she is also interested in.

For Serene, having a voice and using it mattered. It helped her grow up and turn things around. Serene recounts an incident when she was walking home from high school and a kid started making fun of her for being fat. She heard it but blew it off. "You do what you want to do. Say what you want to say, it won't bother me. I just didn't really care," she said.

If step one is taking the emotions of kids in Resister mode seriously, step two is understanding the root cause of their resistance. Shamariah got to the root cause of Serene's resistance by asking her to explain why she hit the kid with the lunchbox rather than punishing her.

Countless root causes and barriers keep teens in Resister mode from engaging in their learning, and many aren't clear-cut. It's our job to identify them and then work to overcome them. By helping kids identify and solve the problems—showing that they *are* solvable—you help build their agency. Once they stop feeling powerless, and once the real barriers they may be facing are removed, they can turn their agency from heading in reverse back into drive.

Serene needed a lot of support, from her mom and then the school, to start to feel her own power. But when she did, she became fearless. She stood up twice in front of a TEDx auditorium crowd and talked about what it was like being mocked for being fat. She explained what it was like to feel like a target, and how to learn to brush it off. That's agency. To help kids in Resister mode, parents and teachers need to know what is fueling the avoiding or disrupting. Without an accurate understanding and adequate context, adult advice is useless, and you will almost certainly drive your kid further away with threats and consequences.

This takes serious listening skills, which most adults are not great at in general, especially when it comes to their own teens. The number one message we heard from kids, hundreds of interviews and reams of published research, from pediatricians and dozens of educators to child development experts, was that teens have things to say and too often adults dismiss them or try to fix them in weird ways. We need to be curious, to ask open questions, and then really, actually listen. In nationally representative surveys from 2022, when teens were asked what they needed from adults, the number one answer—40 percent of respondents chose it—was for their parents to "reach out more to ask how [they're] really doing and to really listen."[7] One teen put it best: "Don't only look at me through the keyhole. Open the door."

One reason we're not so good at listening is that we've been around awhile and we've been through a lot and we have some hard-earned wisdom to dish out. Michael Bungay Stanier, a coaching expert whose book *The Coaching Habit* has sold over a million copies, says the main reason we fail to listen is that we are champing at the bit to give advice.[8] For the last two decades he has worked with thousands of managers from virtually every industry to help them use everyday coaching skills to promote their teams' learning and development. Without fail, people everywhere get in their own way. Instead of listening, we become "advice monsters." We do this because we want to (1) have all the answers (to look smart), (2) rescue others from bad things happening (parents do this a lot), and (3) look in control (because "successful" people and parents are always in control).

Parents are guilty of all of these. Parents of kids in Resister mode told us epic tales of how they had tried to force their kids to work, or go back to school, or try harder, by explaining how their actions were destroying their chance at college or ruining their future. They threatened, cajoled, bribed, and pleaded. Rarely did we hear parents say, "I set aside my fears, my anger, and my concerns and simply asked why my child was resisting."

Daren Dickson from Valor Collegiate Academies told us we should try to think less about our own experiences and more about our kids' experiences. Less teaching and directing, more listening and processing. He borrows some wisdom from narrative therapy, where therapists are trained to take a **decentered and influential stance** in conversations.

"You have influence, but you need to de-center your own experience and you need to center the young person's experience," he tells us. That means really listening to their experiences without thinking about how things were for us as kids or what goals we have for our children. So many kids he talks to, he explains, "feel like their parents don't listen to them or are telling them what they need to do with their life in a way that doesn't feel aligned with who the kid feels they really are."[9]

Amy Berry, senior research fellow at the Australian Council for Educational Research, calls this "putting on our detective hats," some-

thing she says both teachers and parents should do when they see students avoiding or disrupting their learning.[10] Every child will have their own reasons for disengaging from school. But we came across three common ones that we describe below.

BULLYING

Bullying, including cyberbullying, is a common reason why many kids end up in Resister mode. Sadly, it's way more common than most parents realize: Twenty percent of children ages twelve to eighteen report being victims of bullying in school in the United States.[11] Most schools, and many U.S. states, have antibullying policies that require public schools to investigate bullying in a timely manner, take actions to stop it, and provide support to the victim. But school staff are often overwhelmed. They often don't witness the incidents directly: As with Serene, harassment may take place in "between spaces" like hallways, bathrooms, and playgrounds. When it happens online, it can be impossible to know about. Kids do not always share what they are going through with their families because of shame, fear, or not wanting to worry their parents, which is why keeping the channels of communication open is critical.

MENTAL HEALTH ISSUES

Another common reason for resisting is mental health struggles. It's hardly news that too many kids are suffering. Annie is a creative and strong-willed teen. She liked school, but in eighth grade her grades tanked. She was spending a lot of time alone, not doing her work, and making a lot of not-so-plausible excuses for why. Her parents tried everything, from supporting to punishing, to no avail. She began cutting herself—always on her thighs, so she could hide it from her parents. It made her feel human—seeing the blood—and it was a punishment for the consequences of her behavior, she told us.

One summer day, just before school let out, Annie's parents got a call from her progressive private school that no parent ever wants to get. They believed Annie had plans to seriously harm herself. Her classmates had reported disturbing messages posted on Annie's social media. Her parents immediately enrolled her in an in-patient program. When they went to the school to clean out her locker, they found something deeply disturbing: an old essay she had written for English class among her papers. It described her desire to commit suicide. The teacher, in a clear violation of her duties to report mental health concerns, had given her a C+ and failed to inform anyone.

Eventually, after many diagnoses and doctors, her parents learned she had social pragmatic communication disorder, which made interacting with peers very difficult for Annie. This was at the core of why Annie had become deeply depressed. Once they realized the root cause behind Annie's resisting, her parents jumped in to do everything they could. They changed schools multiple times until they found the right fit. Even after the crisis passed, they made sure she went to therapy weekly to develop coping skills to help her throughout her life (her mom believes in being as diligent toward mental health as physical health). They instituted a full transparency policy, with her teachers and parents having access to her assignments and due dates. By tracking her work and sitting beside her at home, Annie's parents helped her build study habits, organize her work, and advocate for herself by asking for help. They take it day by day and give themselves a lot of grace. Her parents have rethought their definition of success. Doing well in school had always been a top priority, especially for Annie's father, who has high expectations of himself. Now what they want most for Annie is for her to be happy, not get straight As or play a certain sport. "I realized that when I was trying to help her perform, in school and out, she was just trying to survive," her father says. His priority now is helping her develop and grow.

Annie's not out of the woods. But at her graduation from one of her schools she gave a speech about her mental health struggles and her journey toward self-acceptance and happiness. "It was the proudest moment of my life," her dad said.

OVERWHELM

Another major cause of kids slipping into Resister mode is falling behind. Sometimes kids in Resister mode are simply overwhelmed. They miss some work, it piles up, they skip classes, and suddenly they feel like there is no way to get on top of it. They start to feel bad about themselves, which only makes things worse. Eventually, without help from family or school, they decide they've blown it. They are never going to graduate, so they give up.

This was the case for Antonio, a Latino boy from a resource-strapped family. In elementary school in Tennessee, Antonio operated mostly in Achiever mode, on the honor roll, thrilled to get As and bring them home to his family. But in middle school and the start of high school, his priorities switched. His social life became way more important, and he switched to Passenger mode, getting Cs and Bs. When the COVID pandemic came, Antonio slipped from Passenger to Resister mode. He was scared about catching the virus but found studying alone, at home, lonely. "It's so unmotivating to have to push yourself without any friends," he told us. He stayed in his room. He rarely did his homework and stopped logging in to class. He felt bad about himself for missing assignments. So he slept a lot, often staying in bed all day. He became depressed. His parents were busy all day trying to make ends meet. His father worked long hours in construction six days a week as his mother juggled the needs of his multiple younger siblings. They didn't notice that when students were allowed back to school in a hybrid approach, Antonio was reluctant to go. He had failed a lot of classes. "I felt like I had kind of messed up my chance," he told us. We heard this same thing from many kids in Resister mode—their feeling that there was no way to catch up and they had permanently blown it.

Luckily, Antonio's high school, Valor College Prep, a tuition-free charter school, had designed a community outreach team to help support students like Antonio, whose poor grades and variable attendance made him eligible. Gustavo, a loving and compassionate former pastor, was assigned to be Antonio's mentor. Gustavo helped

Antonio navigate a path back from academic failure. He assured Antonio that he was not a lost cause. Gustavo, Antonio, and Antonio's parents worked as a team. Some of the things they did to help get him caught up and less overwhelmed were to develop a catch-up plan that laid out how he could make up his work and to connect him to teachers in the school for support and office hours visits; equally important, his father spent regular quality time with him. Gustavo gave Antonio's busy father golden suggestions for how to reconnect with his teen: "Don't give advice. Don't talk about construction. He isn't interested in the type of wood to use or drywall. He loves music, ask him about his favorite band. He loves poetry, ask him about that. Ask him how he feels in school. Ask him about a specific class he has like geometry." Knowing his parents cared and were there for him was an essential support in Antonio overcoming his feelings of overwhelm and failure. With everyone's help, he made up his schoolwork and was able to pass his junior year and get back on track. He sailed through senior year, digging into his classes and becoming a school leader. He got into college in Chicago and in Nashville, opting to stay closer to home. He has decided he wants to be an architect.

GET IN THE TRENCHES

Once we've developed a base of trust and found the root cause behind our teens' resistance, we're ready to take the first step toward solving the problems. In order to do this, we have to show them we are not fighting them but helping them. Chris really dug into Eddie's "why," Shamariah stuck by Serene, and Samir had his support officer and eventually his mom. What these stories have in common is that adults showed they cared and helped the kids stuck in Resister mode see that their obstacles were manageable; they weren't stuck forever. In other words, the grown-ups got in the trenches with them.

We didn't make this term up: trauma-informed psychologists use it. Sue Johnson, a pioneer in emotionally focused therapy, explains it this way: "You back the hell up and you join them where they are. You have to join the resistance. The person is saying I can't take one step forward."[12] So don't make them step forward. Get down where they are, sit alongside them. Eventually, when they feel you there, *really there,* the two of you can start to envision ways to make the threat of the first step smaller.

Resistance, to someone in Resister mode, feels safer. They have a pattern that feels predictable. Change feels risky. By honoring how they feel and being curious about it, you might be able, in time, to help them see that a way of doing things isn't working for them anymore. Neuroplasticity is the brain's brilliant ability to reconstruct and lay new wiring (growth mindset is both psychology and neurobiology). You see what they are fighting and then let them know new circuits can be laid. "I know you feel you are keeping yourself safe by staying home. Are you happy with being home all day alone? Could we envision going to school for an hour, or maybe a morning?"

As we have said before, adolescence is a period of big emotions. This can be exciting and, simultaneously, terrifying. Many students in Resister mode react to big feelings by shutting them down. At that point, crawling into the trenches with them may be your best bet.

You can signal to your child that you are here, by their side, by reaching out and not giving advice and guidance from a distance but offering deep empathy, allyship, and support. To do this, try some of the following approaches.

- **Be nonjudgmental.** "I've noticed you've been feeling really down lately. I'm here for you if you need me."
- **Acknowledge struggle.** "I see things are hard for you. I want you to know you can share anything with me."
- **Express a desire to understand.** "I can't imagine how hard this must be for you, but I want to understand and help you in any way I can."
- **Validate feelings.** "I see you are upset. Remember, you're not alone in this. What's one thing I can do right now to support you?"

- **Share personal experience.** "I remember a time when I felt overwhelmed and struggled to find my way out. I know our experiences are not the same, but I'm happy to tell you about it if it would be helpful to you."
- **Offer alternative ways of connecting.** "If talking feels like too much, we can go for a walk, or do something you enjoy. Just being together can help too."
- **Give unconditional support.** "It's okay to feel not okay. Sadness is as much a part of life as joy. But you are not alone."

Whereas kids in Achiever mode need to lean into struggle to build resilience, students in Resister mode need the opposite: They need support to help them overcome their struggle. When you're fighting next to them, resisting kids can slowly build confidence in themselves to solve problems. Samir not only overcame his learned helplessness, he became a leader. Eddie went back to school but also got on a path to being an entrepreneur. Serene worked hard to accept who she is, and is helping others through student government. Resisting kids need goals but also deep assurance that they will have support in the intimidating early stages.

Focus on the Future, Tie It to the Present

Too frequently, resisting in one class or for a period of time results in young people not just being in Resister mode but assuming a Resister identity. What starts small quickly engulfs everything. Research on student engagement, including our survey of students, shows that the most disengaged students are often checked out across the board.[13] The misery spills over.

When kids get stuck in this identity, they have a hard time imagining what their future place in the world could look like. Like kids in Achiever mode—though for opposite reasons—they struggle to answer some important questions: *What do I care about? Where can I see myself in the world? What can I contribute?* Achieving students struggle with these questions because they've internalized other people's goals for themselves, lacking the agency to dig into their own passions; resisting students, because they have their agency pointed away from their learning and are often acting out from emotion, not because they have a clear alternative vision for their life.

After establishing trust and getting to the bottom of why kids are resisting, the final step is nurturing a vision of a possible future self that excites them. This means helping them to see there is a way out, and many pathways to better places. They will not always be stuck—no matter how stuck they feel. Just as kids deep in Achiever mode need to reflect and ask themselves critical questions to take on challenges, kids in Resister mode need some help imagining a brighter path ahead (the evidence they have so far is not great).

As parents, you cannot do the deep work of identity development for them. Becoming oneself cannot be outsourced; it can only be supported. But you can help guide them toward interests, values, and ways of being in the world that are constructive. You have lived more than your children and can help them see which interests help rather than harm, nourish rather than deplete, edify rather than tear down. As they journey in and out of identities, we encourage those that help them learn and grow, and point out when people or platforms diminish them. Even if we see clear as day that things look bad, we have to remember we are their best bet at coming out the other side in one piece. Cynicism and doomsaying are not helpful, regardless of whether we feel them in our core.

Along with millions of hours of carpools, endless cooked meals, thousands of Saturday art projects, and a whole lot of laundry, helping your teen build an identity rooted in values from your family but constructed from materials of their choosing can be seriously exciting stuff. We can show our kids having Resister moments that the idea of adapting and growing may be daunting but might also be thrilling. Identities, like brains, are malleable. We can be and do many things. And we can discard identities that are not serving us well.

This idea is the life's work of Daphna Oyserman, a professor of psychology at USC Dornsife. Oyserman has found that helping kids construct an image of a future possible self and identify actions and obstacles to getting there improves both academic outcomes and their sense of purpose. In 2006, Oyserman co-conducted a study with 264 low-income eighth graders in Detroit, Michigan.[14] To start, researchers asked the middle schoolers to imagine themselves one year in the future: "Next year, I expect to be . . ."; "Next year I want to avoid being . . ." Then students completed a series of activities, including interviewing a peer and sharing that peer's academic strengths with the class, choosing a role model and investigating what obstacles they faced, and developing strategies to reach their own goals.[15] All along the way, the kids shared what they were doing with one another, because peer influence in middle and high school is profound. It wasn't just imagining a future possible self; it was doing guided work to identify role models, think about challenges they faced, and actively try to understand how their role models got around those.

Oyserman witnessed remarkable improvements in standardized test scores, grades, and overall academic performance after these future-oriented interventions. Simultaneously, she observed a decline in depression levels, absences, and in-school misbehavior. The research has been replicated by many over the past nearly two decades. These are remarkable outcomes for kids who faced tremendous obstacles.[16] "The future can be made to feel relevant and part of one's current self," Oyserman writes. "Crucially, once activated, this malleable sense of the future can produce changes in behavior both immediately and over time."[17] Oyserman's research proves the power of unleashing what she calls "identity-congruent" imagining and planning for the future. We wish it would take place at school for everyone, but we know it can exist at home.

One of the most important things Chris did to support Eddie was to help him reflect on his future possible self by connecting his future goal (being an entrepreneur) to his present. This was not easy. It took months of dialogue: gentle at first, with Chris getting in the trenches with him, restraining his parental advice monster, slowly drawing Eddie out, and then giving judicious guidance and helping him see a path forward. The exams he had to take were not going to be fun, but he was perfectly capable of getting through them; on the other side was possibility, being an entrepreneur, having a car. Oyserman's road map is very useful here. We liked these four steps to help your children see and plan for some pathways to a future self. Oyserman is quick to point out that this takes time.* It is not a checklist you review with your child over dinner one night; rather, it's a process you work through over months like Chris did with Eddie:

- **Imagine.** Imagine yourself in one, two, five years. What would you like to be doing? Eddie imagined himself as an entrepreneur.
- **Identify steps.** Identify the steps to get there, including actions today. Eddie realized he needed to do well in his exams, and to do that, he needed to go to school and to study. He also needed experience, so he pursued an internship.
- **Reflect.** Reflect on the obstacles that might get in your way. Consider ways to deal with those. Chris helped Eddie see that his exams would be hard and Eddie might not want to study. What would he do then? Chris helped Eddie normalize that it's okay to feel discouragement but also useful to decide what skills help to persevere.
- **Interpret difficulty as importance.** Learn to understand difficulty as a sign of importance and meaning and not a signal to quit. Chris told Eddie that when he was discouraged it was not a signal to give up but evidence that he was making progress. Learning is hard. So is starting a business.

* For many more tips from Oyserman, see: *Pathways to Success Through Identity-Based Motivation* (New York: Oxford University Press, 2015).

Two years later, Eddie passed his exams. He enrolled in a local college in an entrepreneurship program. He started two businesses and finally, finally bought his own car. He went from refusing school to charting his own path, all with the help of a loving dad and some tips for imagining and planning for a possible future self.

Spot Their Strengths

One way to start thinking about future possible selves is to help your teens think about what place they might occupy in the world: not what job, but what set of skills. (We don't love the advice "Find your passion"—we prefer "Find your strengths and lean into your interests," which is clearly not as catchy.) Everyone has strengths and everyone has interests. These can change as kids grow. Telling a young person to find their passion feels a little like telling them to wait for the one true love that is out there for them.

For some kids, like Eddie, that path was clear. He wanted to be an entrepreneur. Samir found his passion in politics. But most kids don't yet know what they want to do. They have strengths and interests but can't see potential or possibility. They don't even know what's out there. For those kids, we turn to John Holland.

Holland struggled to find his way professionally, which will be ironic when you see what he became famous for. As he rooted around trying to find a career path, one question fascinated him: How did one's personality influence their career choice? His answer, published in a 1959 academic journal, would change the face of education and career placement. Holland believed that people fell into one of six personality types and that those personality types could be connected to different jobs or vocations.[18] He labeled them Realistic, Investigative, Artistic, Social, Enterprising, and Conventional but someone (thank you!) translated that into Doers, Thinkers, Creators, Helpers, Persuaders, and Organizers.[19] His theory was that by understanding themselves, and knowing more about the skills underpinning certain jobs, people could be better matched to work they loved. The "Holland Codes," as they came to be

THE HOLLAND CODES

DOERS

You like to work with things you can see and touch: the real and tangible vs ideas or concepts. You enjoy mechanical and/or physical tasks.

THINKERS

You enjoy logical thinking and like to learn how things work. You might be good at science, math, solving problems, doing research, and/or understanding data.

CREATORS

You enjoy expressing yourself creatively, possibly through dancing, acting, music, or writing. You like freedom, variety, and working creatively.

HELPERS

You like to work with people. You solve problems by talking about them. You like helping, understanding, and teaching others. You care about others' feelings.

PERSUADERS

You like to be in charge of your own work and take control. Competition doesn't scare you. You are willing to lead, supervise, and ensure the work gets done.

ORGANIZERS

You want to keep things in order. You like clear rules and instructions, and produce detailed, precise work. You are good with data and care about accuracy.

Source: John L. Holland, *Making Vocational Choices: A Theory of Vocational Personalities and Work Environments*, 3rd ed. (Odessa, FL: Psychological Assessment Resources, 1997).

known, are the foundation for today's field of career counseling and are used by everyone from the U.S. Labor Department to schools and colleges across the country.[20]

Over time, Holland and others made clear that people can have a mix of strengths and interests. He also recognized that there certainly were more than just these six. But it was a useful starting point to get people thinking about who they were and what they liked to do.

We like the Holland Codes for two reasons: They encourage us all to see and call out our kids' strengths, not just their annoying habits. They also help teens to see themselves in a broader way. We have seen the codes expand students' vision of the world along with their understanding of themselves in creative classrooms in Cajon Valley Unified School District in Southern California. But we all can use them.

In our interviews, young people consistently highlighted pivotal people in their lives who helped them see their strengths. The offhand supportive comment from a family member, teacher, coach, peer, or caring adult in the community can be the spark that moves an idea to an interest. And that interest may be what helps your child in Resister mode to get unstuck and jump into Explorer mode. This is what happened to Samir when his classmate noticed his love of local politics and invited him to his first political event.

If you are thinking, *My kid's only strength is gaming or social media, or emptying my fridge,* you are not alone. But the things that drive you bananas about your resisting kid might just be the spark that will lead them to change the world.

It's not enough to just help your kid identify what code or codes resonate with their strengths and interests. They need ways to test their ideas. Remember Tevin, the Cedar Rapids student who almost got kicked out of school for his resisting? His parents didn't have the Holland Codes in hand, but his doer and thinker strengths were obvious to them. They didn't just lean into his interests by helping him install CAD and asking about his drafts; they also took him to construction sites and suggested he get an internship. They planted seeds and

DECODING TEEN BEHAVIOR INTO HOLLAND CODES

HOLLAND CODE	THE TEEN VERSION
DOERS	Builds something, fixes something, jerry-rigs a marshmallow shooter out of a bicycle pump, hose, and old water gun (instead of doing homework).
THINKERS	Solves riddles and puzzles, points out every single inconsistency and discrepancy in your statements, tinkers with a slime recipe to figure out how to get the exact will-never-come-off-the-carpet consistency (instead of doing homework).
CREATORS	Decorates room to the nines, plays music, spends hours creating the perfect Minecraft world (instead of doing homework).
HELPERS	Spends hours on FaceTime supporting friends (instead of doing homework).
PERSUADERS	Throws a party, convinces older sister to buy the booze, ropes friends in to bring the food (instead of doing homework).
ORGANIZERS	Color-codes their closet, folding each item perfectly; fixates on the Colosseum LEGO set with two million tiny, annoying pieces that must be perfectly assembled (instead of doing homework).

connected dots for him. They didn't *tell him* to figure it out. They *helped him* to figure it out.

It is scary for young people to feel that they are stuck, or going in reverse, and it is terrifying as parents to feel helpless. But adults—parents, but also educators and coaches and pastors, rabbis, and imams—can clearly help turn things around. We can take Resisters' emotions seriously, investigate and get to the bottom of why they are resisting, and solve immediate problems that need solving (Serene's bullying, Annie's depression, Eddie's anxiety and school refusal, Antonio's overwhelm). These steps are crucial in getting kids in Resister mode to stop moving in reverse. But to get them to actually start moving forward, it's crucial to help them imagine and plan for their potential future selves—and eventually start testing those out. With a future possible self, they have somewhere to go.

With the right support, many kids in Resister mode move straight into Exploring mode. Remember, they have agency, just pointed away from their learning rather than toward it. Once they are redirected, with support and a vision for a better future, they can take off. Parents might have a few more gray hairs, and possibly a few good stories for later, but kids end up with the knowledge that they are integral to solving their own problems. They are reengaging in their learning and building Explorer muscles.

Takeaways

1. Kids in Resister mode have agency, but it's pointed away from their learning in school. They often need more serious interventions to overcome very real barriers to engagement.

2. The key to helping kids in Resister mode is establishing trust and building connections. They won't take advice from you without that foundation.

3. A key approach is taking resisting kids' emotions seriously, choosing an emotion-coaching approach.

4. Kids in Resister mode need us to help them get to the *why* of their resistance. Bullying, mental health struggles, and overwhelm are three common ones.

5. Once you have established trust and connection, and have gotten to the bottom of what's going on, you can help kids identify their strengths, interests, and values and imagine a future possible self they are excited about.

10

Exploring

Successfully Navigating a Lifetime of Learning

It's Friday morning in Carmen Arellano's fifth-grade classroom in Kramer Elementary School, a local public school nestled in a quiet suburb of Dallas, Texas. On a blustery January day, as the big oak trees bend in the wind outside the window, the students are sitting at tables in groups of three or four, writing down their reflections for the week.

There are big, multicolored posters around the room that read, "What's My Level of Engagement?"

Ms. Arellano teaches English, but alongside her poetry lessons, she also teaches her students about engagement. When were they most engaged? When were they least engaged? What is their goal for next week? What do they need to do differently to reach their goal, and is there any help they need to get there? They consult the posters with Amy Berry's Continuum of Engagement, illustrated by a rainbow of colors: purple for disrupting, blue for avoiding, dark green for withdrawing, light green for participating, yellow for investing, red for driving.[1]

Berry's continuum is a teachers' guide for making student engagement visible in their classrooms, and we drew on it as we developed the four modes of engagement. Kids in Resister mode are disrupting and avoiding in the purple and blue zones. Kids in Passenger mode are passively participating in the green zone. Kids in Achiever mode are investing in the yellow zone. And kids in Explorer mode are driving in the red.

Ms. Arellano's students pore over a printout of the continuum as they reflect on how engaged they were that week. Were there times they were in the blue zone, looking to leave the classroom for an extended bathroom break to avoid doing work? What was it that made them want to do that? Were there other times when they were just responding to questions the teacher asked, participating in the green zone? Perhaps in other activities they were in the red, setting a goal for themselves and seeking out more challenging activities? Do they remember what helped them get into the red zone?

Ms. Arellano walks between the tables, her petite frame and tight brown curls disappearing as she bends down to talk to her students and prompt them to think about their goals. One girl wants to do better on her next English test. How much better? She thinks about her last test. She didn't do that well; she's always struggled a lot in school. She is not the only one. A number of Ms. Arellano's students have Individualized Education Plans (IEPs) and have to work extra hard to keep up. Could she do better? She writes a number down she thinks is doable. It's a brave and hopeful act, committing publicly to a higher grade. What would she do to get that score? She decides that getting more feedback during the week would help. The students are building their Explorer muscles, figuring out where they want to go, assessing their progress, and learning how to ask for help to get there.

The kids in Ms. Arellano's class are learning how to recognize their modes of engagement and, importantly, how to move between them. They are learning that there are days when all they can muster is Passenger mode. They tell us this happens when they are tired, feel sick, or are really excited about something that is happening that day. The day we visit, the school awards ceremony is happening right after class, and one boy says that the anticipation is distracting him, so today he will just be participating (that is, in Passenger mode).

It's an exercise in self-awareness that Ms. Arellano swears by. She knows that students move all the time between different levels of engagement. Kids often react to their environment and subconsciously make split-second, gut-level decisions about which mode to use. Maybe the teacher is reviewing material they know and they are bored, so they decide to bug their peers to entertain themselves.

It's rare that students are given language to describe their level of engagement. Nor are they often taught that choosing to switch modes is an ability they can develop.

It's a skill all kids need and can nurture, including kids with learning differences and neurodivergent kids. Older kids find it useful too; we spoke to students in high school and college whose teachers had taught them about Berry's continuum, which helped to improve their learning.

There is a big difference between intentionally picking the slow lane and just ending up there. To change lanes purposefully, kids need the ability to look inward, self-assess, and have a toolkit of strategies to draw from. Ms. Arellano is clear that there are no rewards or punishments linked with their levels of engagement. "It is really important that it isn't used as a behavioral management tool," she says.[2]

Instead, Ms. Arellano wants her students to be able to notice when they switch modes and to use that observation to figure out how to make the lesson feel more rewarding. Should they skip ahead in the material? Ask a question that connects the material to something else they are learning? Help a friend who doesn't get it yet? Ask the teacher for suggestions of what else they could do? She is having them develop agency over their learning at a new level: nurturing the self-awareness to understand what mode they are in and strategically move between modes to maximize their learning.

Her work is paying off. She's seen a fifteen-point jump in their achievement levels over the first semester—from the class scoring an average of 70 to an average of 85. (This is a massive leap in education.) More importantly, as her students have learned to monitor their own engagement and dial it up or down, they have developed deeper reserves of motivation and agency. She's seen a profound shift, from students thinking, "I am going to be rewarded for getting a good score on my test," to "I've met that goal I set for myself and I feel good." These skills are essential in preparing them for navigating the rocky terrain of middle school. These are Explorer skills.

When kids are in Explorer mode, they're driving their own learning to productive and happy places. Unlike students in Resister mode, their agency is pointed *toward* their learning and engagement. They are getting help with things that commonly hold back teens in Passenger mode: more autonomy, more opportunities to investigate their interests, and support to manage their own learning-to-learn cycle. Likewise, they are getting help with the barriers commonly facing kids in Achiever mode: time to reflect on what they care about and want and encouragement to take risks and struggle productively.

This creates more Explorer moments. But they won't, and can't, be in Explorer mode all the time. To help them as they shift between the other modes, we, like Ms. Arellano, can coach our kids to be aware of their own engagement. Learning to recognize when they're in the four modes and developing the skills to switch between them intentionally are powerful tools for developing engagement and supercharging agency. Using the language of engagement isn't just helpful in school; it sets young people up for college and work. It gives them invaluable tools for building a meaningful life.

The Language of Engagement

For Ms. Arellano and other teachers we spoke to who use Amy Berry's Continuum of Engagement, the "lightbulb moment" is usually when students realize that there is a lot more to being a good student than just participating and coasting along in Passenger mode. When Emily Brokaw, a Dallas high school teacher, started using the continuum, her students were surprised. "A lot of what they thought it meant to be a good learner was in the participating part of the continuum," she says. "You show up to class, you do your work, you don't try to speak too much, you get through."

Brokaw is quick to note that teachers, including herself, are also surprised. When she started teaching, she thought that "if the students are doing the work, if the students aren't causing any trouble, if the students are answering my questions, that means they're engaged." It was a shock to learn that what she had thought was engagement "didn't really mean the kids were learning anything, or that their learning was going to have a deep, lasting impact."[3]

Learning well is an active, not a passive, undertaking. Full engagement requires digging in—to yourself and to the material. It requires the agency to drive one's own learning. Developing that agency is accelerated by having the language to understand what engagement looks like and how it can be managed.

Parents and teachers play a powerful role coaching kids to be aware of their own engagement. Without it, kids are on a learning journey without a useful map. For example:

- Stella didn't know the language of engagement: She stumbled into the realization that she needed to engage differently in chemistry. She protected herself by adopting Resister mode.
- For Amina, it took flaming out sophomore year at Yale to learn how to shift out of an Achiever identity to preserve her own well-being and actually enjoy learning.
- Samir is learning how to move more fluidly between gears after many years of operating in either overdrive or reverse.
- Mateo spends most of his time in Explorer mode but also marshals some Achiever mode for the classes he doesn't love.
- Isabel still spends a lot of time in Achiever mode but is learning to have a few Passenger and Explorer moments, too.

Engagement is a process, like development.

All the adults around kids—teachers, mentors, and, of course, parents—can coach teens to better understand what drives their learning, helping them to pick the mode that best fits the moment. "I don't just get in the fast lane and then live there the rest of my life," says Berry.[4] Being a good driver means knowing when you need to get into the slow lane and when you need to accelerate to avoid an obstacle on the side of the road. Any parent who has urged their perfectionist child to just turn in their essay—even if it isn't a masterpiece—is encouraging them to change lanes: Be a Passenger for this assignment in order to go to bed and get some sleep, take care of your health, and make it to the end of term without getting sick.

Less ambitious? Maybe. But more effective, definitely.

THE LANGUAGE OF ENGAGEMENT CHEAT SHEET

Are they doing the bare minimum to get by in school or in an out-of-school activity? → When? → PASSENGER MODE

Are they trying really hard to do well on an assigned task, in or out of school, to make sure they get a good grade or are assessed as performing well? → When? → ACHIEVER MODE

Are they disrupting their learning, in or out of school, by not doing work, refusing to participate, or making it hard for others to pay attention? → When? → RESISTER MODE

Are they taking actions to learn more about things they care about or tie what they are learning to things that matter to them? → When? → EXPLORER MODE

Believing in the Power of Learning Well

Adolescence is a tall task, figuring out how to stand out and fit in. To be a friend, to fall in love, to learn a lot of stuff and somehow from all of that, figure out who you want to be. It's a rough first draft with amazing possibilities for rewrites—as long as kids believe their story is always unfolding, that they are always capable of learning and growing, that there are many wonderful directions to travel. While your time by their side is fleeting, you are the one coach who stays with them forever. You are the most powerful force shaping their belief in the power of learning.

As in most things with parenting older kids, we're less directors and more advisers. We cannot bestow agency any more than we can pick our kids' interests or mold their personalities. As Alison Gopnik beautifully writes, we are gardeners, not carpenters, tending to the soil they grow in, not hammering away at the people they will become.[5] They have to discover their agency and feel it for themselves. We scaffold the journey, offering ideas and discussions that stretch and inspire. We use autonomy-supportive language, help them find time to reflect, and take their emotions seriously. We encourage them to struggle because that is the nexus of all rewarding things in life and the basis of resilience (we can do hard things because we have done hard things). We show them in a million ways how they matter beyond their achievements and help them find ways to belong: through new interests and passing passions. We afford them the respect they so desperately crave, modeling through words and actions what it is to be a respectful and caring adult.

Becoming better learners will help them throughout their long and rich lives. It will empower them as they pick college classes, manage their own time, and confront setbacks that you are not there to see. It will allow them to pursue a career they care about. It will help them to understand their own relationships, identify what supports they need, and ask for help. They will have language and strategies to know themselves in a way that is not narcissistic but rather deep and informative.

The shift toward engagement can be powerful for you too, and not just as a parent or teacher or coach. How we learn is foundational to who we are as humans, and understanding it is empowering. It can be painful and exhilarating (sometimes at the same time).

For Jenny, it took a lot of hair-raising, around-the-clock work covering high finance to realize how corrosive her Achiever tendencies could be. For a while, she thrived while powering through a full-time job at *The New York Times*, writing a book on behavioral economics, and managing two small kids. But her brother's cancer diagnosis put that to the test. Ultimately, losing her brother and wanting more time with her extended family—as an aunt and sister, daughter and wife as well as mother—made her realize the importance of all the modes, and not just the one driving at a hundred miles an hour.

This understanding set her free to have more Explorer moments, including venturing out of financial reporting and into education, a topic she had loved since she read Jonathan Kozol's *Savage Inequalities* at age sixteen. Now she enjoys the variety of modes: Passenger mode when it comes to sorting through complex academic source citations, Explorer moments working with start-ups rather than major media outlets, Achiever moments polishing a twentieth draft.

Rebecca, meanwhile, has learned that switching modes is essential to being able to juggle the many responsibilities she carries without burning out: leading a team at Brookings, conducting research, teaching, being a good (enough) parent, wife, sister, daughter.

It has taken her much trial and error, and support from an executive coach, to help her realize what parts of her day energize her and what parts sap her creative energy. She now coasts through budget meetings, keeping an eagle eye on two questions: How much money do we currently have? How much money do we need to accomplish our goals? After that, she lets others take the reins, paying attention only to the high-level numbers.

She now often counsels her younger team members to switch modes intentionally. She uses the language of grades because they do not have the language of engagement: You can't do A+ work on every task I give you, so learn to identify the ones where a C+ gets the job done just fine. Save the A+ effort for the really important tasks. If you don't know which tasks are which, ask.

This logic still feels counterintuitive to many. We've been heavily conditioned by the Age of Achievement and its benchmarks: giving 100 percent to everything at all times. No pain, no gain. And who doesn't love good results? The Age of Achievement endured because achievement feels good, and it pays. But the Age of Agency is here, and it requires different skills: less jockeying to win on the same narrow course, and more understanding how we learn so we can choose our own course and harness the energy to navigate it.

The Age of Agency

As we saw in chapter 1, assessment in the United States is beginning a tectonic shift away from measuring only academic achievement to also recognizing the value of skills like communication, collaboration, and creativity.

The rapid advance of technology, especially generative AI, is only accelerating these changes. AI can analyze data, recognize patterns, and synthesize information better than any human ever could. It shops for us, manages our travel, and tells us what to watch, whom to talk to, whom to fall in love with, and what's important in the world. It doesn't just retrieve information in certain expert domains; it can make sense of different kinds of information and communicate that in very human-like ways. The pace of progress is staggering. "There is no homework assignment the AI can't do," Ethan Mollick, a professor at Wharton and author of *Co-Intelligence,* told an audience at the ASU+GSV Summit in April 2024. "If you think it can't, you haven't used the paid version or used it enough."

AI is quickly making the skills prized by the Age of Achievement—processing and transmitting information quickly, synthesizing knowledge, and communicating it in a certain way—less unique to humans. To be prepared not only to navigate but also to thrive in this new landscape, we'll need to shift our priorities. AI *can't* replicate the depth of human creativity, empathy, ethical reasoning, and the ability to understand and navigate complex social and cultural contexts. It also cannot decide what goals are worth pursuing in the first place.

This is the hallmark of human agency. What type of person do you want to be? What type of life do you want to live? What type of society do you want to live in? As AI becomes more widespread, humans will need to get better at picking goals they care about and harnessing the motivation to meet them. For example, AI has revolutionized the process of mapping the structures of proteins. What once took scientists months and years now takes a matter of days.[6] This knowledge is essential to designing new drugs and curing diseases. But AI alone cannot transform this new insight into better medicine and healthcare that helps save lives. That requires deciding to invest in the research and development to develop the drugs and get them to market to save lives. The mapping is a critical tool. But it will help solve important problems in the world only if we choose to use it for that purpose.

We all need to work with AI but keep a firm grip on the steering wheel. This is especially true for our kids, who will increasingly need to collaborate with AI so they can map the journeys they want to take, rather than have AI map it for them.

Most important, to thrive in the Age of Agency, our kids will need to not only identify where they want to go but also be able to drive their own learning to get there. The AI-dominated future will favor not apathy and compliance, but the agency that comes from self-knowledge and the motivation to act. The language of engagement gives us a powerful tool for this, allowing our kids (and us) to understand ourselves as learners and direct our energies accordingly. It is an essential skill for adaptability. Helping kids stuck in Resister mode get out of reverse, students in Passenger mode shift out of neutral, and teens in Achiever mode not burn out in overdrive is the first step in a lifetime of up- and downshifting in response to the conditions around us.

Knowing you can pivot, change, adapt, and grow is an insurance policy against whatever the next wave of tech or automation or disruption will be. As author Todd Rose told us, "If you don't understand your own motivation and turn that into something productive, you are at an unbelievable disadvantage."[7] Explorers will meet the moment confidently, but not because we praised them or coddled them or forced them—consciously or not—to meet unreasonable demands. Their confidence will come from knowing themselves as learners and knowing how to learn better. With goals they care about, and motivation they have unlocked, they choose where to drive and can navigate various paths to get there.

In the Age of Agency, schools can help kids get better at understanding their own learning and to become more brave and resilient. They can be rigorous *and* engaging. They can be designed for individual human development *and* the collective work of making society function. They can help children acquire knowledge *and* develop the skills needed to apply what they know to drive action in the world. They can help build Explorers.

We know this because we have seen it. Pockets of brilliant innovation in education exist all over the globe, and especially in the United States. In a study Rebecca led across 160 countries, the United States was home to the largest number of education innovations.[8] These appear in schools that are new, old, charter, public, and private, and in and out of school programs. The common themes are more doing and less sitting, more connection to the real world and local communities and less time in classrooms with one teacher. Your kids have maybe experienced them, coming home fired up by an inspiring teacher, a challenging class, or a community project that had deep meaning attached to it.

We know the winds of change are blowing, from the architecture of assessment to the broader pathways many schools are offering to help kids identify, including learning and earning, dual credits, and apprenticeships. But we do not think this should be left to chance. You play a vital role. You've learned a lot in this book (we hope). You can also ask your kids' schools what they are doing to boost engagement and agency. Talk to your school board members. If they need inspiration, see the list we have provided in Advancing the Age of Agency: Organizations Leading the Way at the end of the book. It highlights organizations that can provide inspiration and work with schools in your community to give kids more Explorer opportunities.

A Lifetime of Learning

During our research, we visited Valor Collegiate Academies in Nashville, Tennessee. When we arrived, we noticed a sign on the wall that read: *Be the grown-up you needed.* Clearly, it is meant as an aspirational slogan for teachers. But when we saw it, we read it as parents, and it stopped us in our tracks.

So many kids need something from the adults in their lives that they fail to get. Support at the right moment. Stronger guidance in bumpy times. Unconditional love no matter how they show up. As parents and teachers, we want to be powerful, present forces for our children. But we often second-guess ourselves. What do our kids need? Can we provide it? How can we help them become resilient learners and humans? And how can we do it graciously, generously, and with as few slammed doors as possible?

It can be overwhelming to think about meeting your child's abundant and ever-changing needs, especially when you are just trying to get through the day: do laundry, put food on the table, make sure they do their homework and don't kill their sister. But at root, young people want two things from you: to feel loved for who they are, in all their brilliant, jagged individuality, and to feel they are being prepared for an uncertain and fast-changing world—to be challenged and to be supported. The more you can help them to have power over their learning, the more confident they will be in their ability to chart their own course, come what may.

Most kids can sit through thirteen or seventeen years of school and absorb enough to get by. But good learners will figure out how to take what they need from their learning, maneuver around barriers, ask for help, and dig in. This agency is central to living a good life. It's a skill that's available to anyone, from the kids of tech titans in Silicon Valley to kids of farmers in rural Brazil.

In the 1940s, a young, disaffected Brazilian lawyer named Paulo Freire was appointed to lead an education program for workers, many of whom lived in rural areas and could not read.[9] He was excited. Literacy was a precondition for voting in Brazil, and he knew the program had the potential to give the workers a voice.

He threw his heart and soul into his teaching but quickly figured out it wasn't working. Progress was slow even though interest was high. We imagine him holding forth with a textbook in hand, sweltering amid the humidity in a dusty building in one of the evening sessions he held for adults in the community, participants' motivation slowly diminishing as he droned on. After one of these evening sessions, his wife, Elza, turned to him on the way home and offered him some pointed feedback. She said, "You give the answers and the questions."[10] Paulo was crestfallen. He approached his work with dedication and told her he addressed the room with seriousness and respect.

Yes, Elza gently responded, but had he asked his students what they were interested in learning about?

It was a turning point for Freire. He began to shift his approach. Soon he was no longer standing at the front of the room posing the questions and the answers but holding learning circles where workers talked about their lives. Instead of him addressing passive listeners, the sessions became active and lively. Workers maybe discussed their problems trying to make ends meet with limited pay, issues with their bosses, and poor housing conditions.

He continued these conversations over several class sessions before prompting them to select one problem to focus on. They settled on housing. Freire instructed them to come to the next session with a picture they had drawn about their housing situation. As the workers discussed their pictures, we imagine them sharing the difficulties of poor sanitation, unforgiving landlords, and cramped quarters, and Freire writing down a list of their words. Then he picked one, like the word *favela,* meaning slum, and broke it down. *Favela* has three syllables.

Workers sounded out the word and soon were recombining the syllables to make new words. In one lesson, Freire had the workers making "twenty or thirty new words" from just learning *favela*.[11]

Freire had just discovered an essential truth about igniting learning. The key, he said, was not to think of someone learning a new skill as an empty vessel that needed to be filled with requisite knowledge and know-how. That "banking model" of education—depositing information in a student to be retrieved later—was devoid of human understanding. His students did not learn well by diagraming sentences that held no meaning for them. Instead, they needed to connect what they learned in class to relevant issues from their daily lives.

Over time, he refined his method and was able to teach adults to read in forty hours.

He wasn't just giving the workers the gift of literacy. Freire was giving them the power to talk about their world. He showed them that naming the world in their own words gave them a voice. With it, they could chart a meaningful path.

They started describing not only their problems but also how they wanted to change them. Mastering literacy gave them power to address problems in their lives. They were shifting into Explorer mode—setting their own goals, and developing the skills to pursue them.

Their education could be their liberation, a fact everyone who has had to fight for the right to go to school knows intimately. A government can take your home or land, or you can flee it; they can take your right to work or vote, but they cannot take what you know. Nor can they rob you of your power to learn. It's something that every dictator fears. When an authoritarian regime came into power in Brazil, they swiftly arrested Freire for instructing people and unleashing their agency through learning. He never returned to teaching in his home country, but he eventually escaped from Brazil. His ideas spread across the world.

Freire helped his Brazilian students to become better learners as well as to reflect on who they were and where they wanted to go. By helping our kids name their world, we, too, can help them name the world they want to see. It will be a gift they can carry through life to fuel them toward the things they love and buffer them against the storms that come.

Hope can feel in short supply these days. The drumbeat of wars, rising authoritarianism, polarization, and anger feels steady and at times deafening. Amid this, our teens are in formation, trying hard to figure out who they want to be. As parents, we cannot control the world around them, but we are uniquely placed to help them unleash their agency to control what they can and go after what they want. To be brave in a messy world.

Agency, rooted in being an Explorer, is key to building this hope. Things can be changed because we are adaptable. We can do hard things because we have tried hard things and made it through. Struggle in learning is not a sign of weakness, but a sign that growth is happening. Working hard is not just a means to getting a meaningful job but also part of a thrilling life.

To learn well is an essential ingredient to what it means to live well.

Being an Explorer requires bravery to write down the grade you want to get and vulnerability to ask for the help you need to get there. It is a powerful alternative to the vortex of isolation and overstimulation sometimes permeating young people's lives. Our collective way back to civility and an enduring democracy will require much more than just unlocking engagement and building better learners. But it will be next to impossible without it.

RESOURCES

Ending the Tech Wars

Boosting Real Engagement

Parents frequently ask us about how to help their stressed-out or struggling kids engage with learning in a world awash with technology.

If you are like us, you have probably explained to your kids that tech is ruining their brains/lives/study habits/friendships. No, the brain can't multitask that much; no, you can't listen to and sing along with Drake and actually learn what a system of checks and balances was meant to protect against; yes, watching celebrities apply eye masks is a mug's game; and no, more time on the console is not going to make you an influencer or get you into college.

Are we old and clueless? Probably. Socrates warned that the written word could have dire consequences for our memory and face-to-face conversation.[1] Every generation panics about new technology. Dime novels, radio dramas, comic books, and cable TV have also been the focus of society's concerns: They too were thought to increase anxiety, decrease sleep, and foster antisocial behavior.[2] We are just the latest generation to freak out.

And yet there are important reasons to worry about today's tech. It's fundamentally changed how we live, causing us to spend less time sleeping and more time alone in front of screens.[3] When things go wrong for kids, especially with cyberbullying, there is nowhere to hide. An iPhone loaded with TikTok, Snapchat, Instagram, Discord, Netflix, Hulu, and WhatsApp is not the same as the family TV: Kids carry it with them to class, to parties, and on dates. Trillion-dollar tech companies spend staggering amounts of money to hijack and monopolize everyone's attention—a pursuit they ironically call "engagement." According to a 2023 report from Common Sense Media, on a typical day, survey respondents—a diverse sample of about two hundred eleven- to seventeen-year-olds—received a median of 237 notifications. Of those, about a quarter arrived during the school day, and 5 percent at night.[4]

Schools are catching on and starting to ban phones. In 2023, England followed the lead of about fifty other countries and said no more.[5] Research shows that students regularly get distracted in class by cell phones and that such bans lead to improvements in high-stakes testing as well as more time spent playing and exercising at school.[6] We spoke to one middle school principal in Washington, D.C., who banned phones because 80 percent of the behavior incidents during school hours had started on social media. Her school is much safer now.

But smartphones aren't going away any more than TVs did. And us lecturing teens about the idiocy of it all (often while texting a work colleague and liking a friend's Instagram post) is not just hypocritical, it's ineffective.

It also overlooks the many ways that technology plays an important and constructive role in kids' lives. The young people we spoke to all saw the downsides of tech. They didn't love feeling addicted, but they also talked about the myriad ways they used tech to help them learn, connect, reach out for help, and find communities that shared their interests. For some kids struggling deeply with peers in school, their connection to caring friends online was literally lifesaving. Plus, plenty of schools use tech in the classroom—apps that help dyslexic kids read, generative AI that lets teachers devise lesson plans, TED-Ed videos that help with research, and so on. When your kids say they need to be on screens at night to do their homework, it's often true.

So what's a desperate parent to do? How do you harness the good and manage the bad of tech? The truth is that technology is not *inherently* a problem. When studies look broadly at adolescents who use technology, including those who are not using it excessively, they find that tech has only a limited effect on kids' well-being.[7] Tech becomes a problem when it stops fueling learning, belonging, and exploration, and instead fuels disengagement, apathy, and isolation. The good news is that parents can influence whether tech shows up in our kids' lives as Dr. Jekyll or Mr. Hyde. We can limit the ways technology fuels disengagement and support the ways it fosters exploration.

How Tech Intensifies Disengagement

When Kia was obsessively scrolling on her phone instead of doing homework, then feeling bad about it, then scrolling some more to escape her guilt, she was caught in the procrastination cycle. Technology wasn't the reason Kia started to check out at school. The reason was that the work started getting hard and uninteresting. Tech certainly was a major *disengagement enabler.* It was there for her when she was bored, when she was frustrated, when she felt guilty, when she felt stressed. It helped her numb her feelings rather than face them. There are plenty of other ways people do this, but we have made most of them, like alcohol, illegal for children.

For plenty of kids, tech enables disengagement because it intensifies the feeling that they do not belong. One high school student we spoke to struggled with social media. She felt she needed to be on it but often didn't enjoy it: "It's not a good feeling to be scared to check your notifications." As we've mentioned, during the teen years, neurobiological and hormonal changes elevate teens' desire to feel a sense of belonging, to be respected and admired, and to find meaning. At that moment of peak vulnerability, technology enters with Snap Maps showing where everyone is gathering (and your kid is not) and "like" buttons creating a "tyranny of metrics" ("How many likes did I get?").[8] Endless scrolling, which teens don't even know is a thing because it's all they've ever known, is the equivalent of junk food: empty calories that never sate but rather create more hunger. It's not just that tech is designed to be addictive. It's that our kids' place in the virtual world becomes yet another forum, in addition to the middle school cafeteria and prom, for the all-important work of crafting their identity and finding their place in the world. Looking perfect and winning the next game is urgent; geometry and diagramming a sentence, less so.

Another way to see how tech exacerbates underlying problems with engagement is to monitor its opportunity costs. Some of the most compelling evidence shows that when tech does have a negative effect it is often because of what it displaces. According to Gallup data, American teens spend about five hours a day just on social media platforms.[9] These figures don't include time spent on screens for homework.

This is a lot of time that they don't get to spend being with friends in person, doing activities, playing sports, working, and studying, not to mention the downtime that is so needed for the type of reflection and daydreaming that boosts creativity and makes room for meaning making and identity development. We described in chapter 8 why this type of powerful reflection requires kids to have time and space when they are not responding to external inputs and stimuli. External inputs includes hours of gaming, getting lost in TikTok and Snapstreaks (exchanges of photos between two people every day on Snapchat for at least three consecutive days).

But the biggest opportunity cost of the mind-bending amount of time spent on tech is that teens do not get nearly enough sleep. Over half of middle school students and over 70 percent of high school students do not get the eight to twelve hours of sleep they need.[10] This is a full five-alarm fire for education experts.* Without enough rest, kids cannot engage well in learning. Lack of sleep seriously messes with brain function, including essential building blocks of learning: mem-

* The American Academy of Sleep Medicine recommends that children six to twelve years of age should sleep nine to twelve hours per night and teenagers thirteen to eighteen years of age should sleep eight to ten hours per night for optimal health. See their Sleep Education website at https://sleepeducation.org.

ory, processing information, attention, and problem-solving.[11] Learning while you're tired is like playing basketball with one hand or trying to paint with your eyes closed. Perhaps one of the best ways we can boost teens' engagement—and ultimately their grades, test scores, and enjoyment of learning—is to take away their tech at night. A meta-analysis of twenty cross-sectional studies of children ages six to nineteen years old revealed a strong association between bedtime access to and use of media devices and inadequate sleep quantity and quality.[12] Common Sense Media asked a panel of teens and tweens about school-night usage of tech—defined as any use Monday through Friday during the hours of midnight to 5 A.M. (not including holidays). More than half of participants—59 percent—used their phones on school nights.[13]

Lack of sleep also messes with friendships and can hamper social interactions.[14] Studies show that teens who struggle with sleep have fewer social connections than students who sleep well.[15] Being over-tired hurts their learning, impedes their ability to make friends, and makes them a whole lot more difficult to be around (apparently, we're not the only ones to notice it). Research shows what common sense dictates: that kids who are sleep-deprived are more cranky and irritable.[16] Staying up late glued to a phone is harming kids' health. Serious lack of sleep or sleep disturbance is one of the most common symptoms of depression among adolescents.[17]

Many young people we spoke to had a love-hate relationship with their phones. They struggled to maximize the upside and limit the downside. We want to be very clear here: It is an absolutely absurd premise to think that kids should simply "control themselves" in the face of trillion-dollar companies weaponizing technology to attract and hold our attention. Big Tech and social media companies need to be regulated. We've regulated tobacco and drugs and food. When it comes to tech, we are the product. But since Big Tech also has very big lobbying budgets and the United States has a deeply libertarian streak, and we parents are on the front lines now, it's on us to put some limits on tech. Whether we like it or not, we're the best option to help kids regain some agency over their time, learning, and lives.

Give Kids the Power to Stop

Here's what parents can do.

SET LIMITS

Don't be afraid to set limits on screentime. First and foremost: no screens in the bedroom after 9 P.M. Other options include screen-free meals, turning off notifications, and turning on grayscale to make kids' phones less enticing. Rather than coming up with these limits on your own and passing them down as edicts, talk with your kid about why this is important for them. Bringing them into the process will help them develop some ownership over it. You may be surprised at the ideas they come up with and their receptivity to gaining some control over their tech use, and feeling supported, not judged, in doing so.

DON'T MAKE EXCEPTIONS FOR HOMEWORK

Parents we spoke to were frequently frustrated that they try to set limits but their kids insist they need their devices to do their homework. Maybe they need to access a Quizlet, or all their study guides are loaded on Google Classroom, or they have online problem sets, or they need to FaceTime a friend to get some help. These are all legitimate reasons to need screens. Parents can work with kids to set time limits on their apps (although many kids we spoke to have creative ways to get around controls parents and teachers put on school technology). But until schools go back to using just books and paper, which is likely to be never, parents need to set screentime limits and stick to them—even if this means they don't always get their homework done. That's a lesson too: Knowing they have to go off screens every evening at a certain time might inspire them to get started earlier. One veteran educator told us that bedtime in her house is 8:45 P.M. for her twelve-year-old son. "If he hasn't finished his homework, it's too bad. I'm a teacher, and I'm still like, 'Life is more important than homework.'" She knows sleep is one of the most important things she can give his developing body and brain, and one of the best ways to help him keep his GPA up even if he doesn't do all his homework occasionally. Parents with older children may find it harder to follow this rule. But it is still doable even when their bedtimes are later. Turn all tech off at 10:30 P.M. Period. You bought the phone, you pay for the internet; you can put limits on them.

MODEL HEALTHY TECH USE

If you, one of the main adults in their life, are scrolling through Instagram for hours on end, good luck telling your kids to put their phone away during homework time. We need to model some self-control. Try to avoid interrupting conversations, especially with them, to check our texts or emails or to take a call. We know work beckons (or the news, or an update from your best friend, or a sale). If you need to do something, articulate that it's time sensitive and urgent. Don't lie about it; they will know (they are the masters of making it seem as if they are paying attention when they are really down an Instagram rabbit hole). If they see you controlled by your phone, not only will they discount your "advice" as being hypocritical, but they will also be able to justify that successful and happy parents like you can use social media all the time and be *just fine.*

ARTICULATE HOW BIG TECH IS MONETIZING THEM

One of the best ways to help teens increase their power over tech is to help them understand the starring role they play in Big Tech's bottom line. Helping them understand why they should want to exert some control over how they use tech can often be a better use of your time, and theirs.

"Are you using tech or is tech using you?" This is a line that award-winning poet and storyteller Max Stossel asks teens when he talks to them, which is a lot.[18] He asks how many of them have Snapstreaks. Hundreds of hands shoot up. "How many of you have taken pictures of your ceiling to keep up a streak?" Almost all the hands stay up. "How many of you want to stop?" The hands *stay up.*

"Isn't that amazing?" he says. We spend our time doing something we don't have to do, don't want to do, but feel compelled to do. Stossel is empathetic, not judgmental. He knows that having a streak with a friend feels important, a way of feeling popular and that you matter. "It feels real," he says.[19]

The problem is, it's no accident that kids are doing something they don't really want to do. Silicon Valley designs its products to maximize our insecurities, including our desperate fear of missing out—and our drive to seek affirmation through generating as many "likes" as possible. It pours billions of dollars into creating tools to get us hooked (the "like" button), keep you (endless scroll), and make you feel bad (Snap Maps). The negative feelings are not an unintended consequence. They are not a bug of the system, but a central feature.

Stossel is not alone in explaining clearly how much Silicon Valley executives are using our attention—our most precious resource—to line their pockets. As an employee at one of the top tech firms in Silicon Valley, Tristan Harris loved tech until he didn't. He went to Stanford, studied "persuasive technology" with the famous B. J. Fogg, and worked at Google. But he started to notice that no human brain could withstand the sophisticated tools Big Tech was deploying to capture people and keep them online as long as possible. In 2013, he created a presentation inside Google, "A Call to Minimize Distraction and Respect Users' Attention," that quickly went viral.[20] But not much changed inside the tech giant. He quit in 2015 and started a campaign called Time Well Spent. In 2018, he founded the Center for Humane Technology to educate, raise alarm bells, and lobby for better protections.* Since then, Harris has been on a mission to try to get people to see that

---

* Some of the people who invented the tools he talks about (the "like" button, endless scroll) are advisers.

Google, Facebook (which owns Instagram and WhatsApp), and TikTok have one goal: to make money. And they use all of us to do that.

The way to appeal to teens about their tech use is to harness their incredible desire for fairness and justice and their proclivity for outrage and to point it at Big Tech. Daren Dickson, the chief culture officer of Valor Collegiate Academies, says that this is the best way he has found to help high school students, especially eleventh and twelfth graders, have a healthy relationship with tech. "I teach them about the attention economy, that there are these multinational billion-dollar corporations that sit in tiny little rooms, and they talk about your attention and how they want to monetize it. They're making money off your attention and you're basically letting them do it. So the most rebellious thing you could do is to get control of your own attention and put it where you want to put your attention," he tells us.[21]

The "you're being manipulated by the man" approach has been very effective in shifting teen behavior in other areas too, like healthy eating. In an experiment with more than 350 eighth graders at a Texas school, half of the kids were offered an exposé-style article highlighting how the food industry methodically engineers foods that are both bad for us and incredibly addictive, targeting poor people and children, who are more vulnerable. The other half of the class was offered lessons about nutritional choices and factual information about calories and what kind of food is good for us. The kids who learned that Big Food was manipulating and trying to monetize them made healthier eating choices for the last three months of the school year. The effects were particularly striking for boys, who reduced their daily purchases of unhealthy drinks and snacks in the school cafeteria by 31 percent compared to the control group. "Adolescents have this craziness that we can criticize—or we can tap into," Ron Berger, chief academic officer at EL Education, a nonprofit supporting schools across thirty states, told *The New York Times*. "This is a time in their lives when justice matters, more than any other time."[22]

We need to recognize and harness those strengths. When parents work with their kids to not only set limits but understand the very significant forces at work, it can help them to manage their tech use now. It might also help them when they are older and there's no one there to put their phone in a lock box at 9 P.M.

TRY THE "CHOOSING TIME VERSUS KILLING TIME" ACTIVITY

One of the first steps toward gaining agency over tech is helping our kids become aware of how they are interacting with it in the first place. We really like an activity we call Choosing Time Versus Killing Time.[23] We were inspired by speaking with Alison Link, a practitioner in the academic field of leisure studies, which examines how kids and adults manage leisure time to promote meaningful engagement and positive experiences.[24] Link works at Lamoille Family Center in rural Vermont, where she collaborates with Linda Caldwell, a professor at Penn State, to support schools to use the TimeWise: Taking Charge of Leisure Time curriculum.* They share an example: A teacher asked his students to pull out their phones and look at their analytics from the weekend. He then asked the students to write down three things: how much time they spent in each app, what they did in that app, and what they got out of it.

The students could do the first, but not a single one could do the second two. No one. They had no idea what they had gotten out of it because they couldn't even remember what they had been doing when they were in each app. But according to their analytics, they spent hours and hours there. The activity illustrates the difference between "choosing time" and "killing time": a choice we all have but, without realizing it, decline to make.

Parents can easily try this. Once a week, over dinner (or whenever you gather as a family), ask everyone to bring out their phones and look at the analytics. You have to join too (you may well need some limits).

---

* The principles in the curriculum have been tested in a range of contexts including the United States, Malaysia, and South Africa and the goal is to help students develop self-awareness around how they use their time.

Write down how many hours you spent on each app in the past two days, what you did on it, and what you got out of it. If your teen writes down four hours of YouTube and says she mainly learned all about great skin care products and the latest and greatest happenings of SZA, then no problem. They are teens. They are expressing themselves, exploring things they are choosing to care about, staying in the know with their friends at school.

But if they (or you) can't remember what you did, that is a signal that you are killing time rather than choosing time. Half a day, handed to the billionaires masterminding our tech universe.

HELP THEM ASK: IS TECH BRINGING ME DOWN, OR BUILDING ME UP?

Everyone needs downtime. And most of us turn to the latest media to enjoy that downtime. Boomers delighted in TV. Gen X loved their MTV. Millennials populated Facebook. And Gen Z has, well, the entire social media universe.

Whatever the medium, some of it is fine. It's a way of staying current, of being entertained, of kicking back and hopefully restoring our energy. The challenge is figuring out when it restores us versus when it depletes us. Elizabeth Weybright is a professor at Washington State University who also studies leisure, including what she calls the tipping point. "The same activity can be good or bad depending on how much I am doing it or why I am doing it," she says.[25]

There's no magic number for when that tipping point occurs. Different people need different levels of downtime. A good day may not require downtime. A bad one might require lots. The issue is how in control our kids feel. Do they feel like they can stop and move on to something else? Or do they feel sucked into the Big Tech vortex, unable to stop whatever they are doing? When the feeling shifts from self-control to out-of-control, that's the tipping point between restorative and depleting.

Link, who works with young people in Vermont, not surprisingly, uses this when parenting her own adolescent kids. When they have been playing video games or watching TV for a while, she asks them to do a "check-in." How are they feeling? Are they still in control, or is it time to move on to something else? "It's a skill to be able to know when to stop and to choose something new," she says. Academics call this skill "restructuring," the practice of assessing your own tipping point and making a switch when necessary.[26] Ultimately, restructuring is about agency: building the self-reflection and self-regulation practices necessary to be in control of your time.

Building kids' awareness about their time takes time and will require repeated conversations. You will need Herculean levels of patience.

Acknowledge the Beauty of Tech

Helping our kids develop self-control over their use of tech serves a dual purpose: it helps them minimize the negative impacts of tech and maximize the beneficial ones. Numerous kids we spoke to used tech in all its different forms to boost their engagement. Francisco, who has dyslexia, loves books thanks to his audiobook app and has good grades thanks to his school's Read&Write app, which lets him show what he knows through speech-to-text conversion.[27] Serene shared her story about overcoming bullying and built her confidence thanks to being invited to film a TEDxKids YouTube video. Samir became an expert on school policies after plumbing the depths of his school district policies online. Tevin explored his love of architecture through practicing drafting at home on his computer. Kia reconnected with her love of learning by doing studios where she used tech, including making a podcast. According to Pew Research, about two-thirds of teens say phones make it easier for them to pursue interests and be creative.[28]

Multiple kids we spoke to found a place to belong online when their home and school life didn't offer that. Kids who were gay but feared coming out to their families found real connection and acceptance with peers online. Students who ate alone in their middle school cafeteria didn't always feel lonely; many had deep friendships with peers online, interacting and talking daily through shared video games. Some kids found just the support they needed to get through hard math sets every night: FaceTiming a friend and doing their homework together. The trick for parents is to foster your kid's use of tech when it is an *engagement enabler*—when it helps them have more Explorer moments. Following are some of the ways tech can do this.

PLAYING

Susan Rivers, the cofounder of the Yale Center for Emotional Intelligence who now runs the iThrive Games design studio and co-leads the History Co:Lab, uses games to advance young people's social and emotional learning. She's also a parent. When her son was young, around nine, he got his first computer in his bedroom. She and her husband were busy at work, and, like most parents in wealthy countries today, they worried he was spending too much time playing video games. She recalls going into his room, irritated, and asking him, *Why are you spending your time on this? You're wasting your time!*[29]

Almost instantly, she regretted the overture. Her son loved games deeply. By criticizing his interests, she realized, she was inadvertently shaming *him.* "When we say things that promote shame, it can be devastating," she said. Saying to a kid who loves video games that their games are dumb is saying, "Your identity is dumb."

She tried a different tack, one we can learn from. She got curious. "The way one gets curious about a kid is to be curious about the things he enjoys," she told us. Rivers asked her son what games he liked and why. She asked him to teach her to play. She wondered about the qualities of certain avatars and what made for a good teammate. She asked how he figured out the strategies to advance to the next level. In other words, she leaned into his interests and asked him to use his expertise to teach her something she did not know how to do.

She of course set limits. He was young and still needed to learn how to regulate his playtime. She collaborated with him to establish the times he could play and for how long. But the conversation was constructive, and the relationship shifted from antagonism to respect.

Getting interested in his games didn't just improve their interactions; it helped to launch the next phase of her career. Around 2015, Rivers noticed how little attention was spent helping teens build social and emotional skills in smart ways. She knew how much video games engaged kids. Could the two be combined? In 2016 she left Yale to become the executive director and chief scientist at iThrive Games, whose purpose was to intentionally build prosocial learning experiences into the fabric of game design. Face a challenge in the game? *How will you prepare?* About to die? *Who can you call for help?* Died? *What will you do differently in your next life?* (Skill development in order: developing executive function skills, self-advocacy and teamwork skills, and problem-solving.)

We spoke to many parents who were worried that games were rotting their kids' brains. But the truth is that many games are excellent spaces for exactly the kind of engagement and exploring kids need. *Minecraft* lets young people construct their entire world—it's a prime playground for practicing Explorer skills. (This is just what Samir did with his two best friends in elementary school.)

Worried parents can take advice from Rivers. Limit the activity, but don't shame the user (i.e., your kid). Don't get caught in the negative spiral: *You're not spending your time on great things; you're not going to have the right opportunities; you're going to fail in life.* Instead: Get curious. Learn about the worlds they create or conquer. It's a way to connect, to be curious about their interests, and for them to teach us something.*

* Jordan Shapiro, author of *The New Childhood,* agrees. Fighting with the future will not bring back the past, he said. We fight because we don't understand—the technology or the future. But we can't stop the future (the only constant in life is change, said Jenny's dad and Heraclitus, apparently). Help them to courageously walk into the future by getting involved in the tech they love.

LEARNING

Tech can not only complement but accelerate learning at school. From YouTube videos on the Civil War to reading kid-friendly news on Newsela to learning about how the U.S. democratic system works by playing the iCivics video game, we have a million new ways to consume content, many of which are way more accessible than a teacher directing a class.

Testing apps are powerful tools for recall and consolidation—one of the most effective ways to learn. Didn't pay attention in math? Catch up on Khan Academy. Didn't understand a word of Shakespeare? Plenty of tools to help with that.

Tech can also help kids explore their interests outside of school. From Diego's obsession with weather to Brianna's passion for social justice to Mateo's coding, teens pursue their interests via all sorts of tech platforms. There is literally nothing you can't learn on YouTube, BrainPOP, and Outschool to name a few.

At the time of writing this book, generative AI is only just beginning to be harnessed for learning in school. Initially, after ChatGPT was released in November 2022, discussion was dominated by issues of cheating, plagiarism, and generative AI bans. How students will collaborate with AI to grow their skills, advance their learning, and spend more time in Explorer mode is still an open question. We do know that its existence challenges Age of Achievement teaching and learning practices and provides further fuel to the Age of Agency. If AI can respond to essay questions and solve math problems, young people will need to become good at asking questions, not just finding answers. They will need to think critically, to seek out meaning, and to tap into their creativity. This will benefit those with agency—the ones who know their goals and have the motivation to pursue them.

RECHARGING

Teens' lives are stressful, and tech can replenish kids. We know there is a tipping point when replenishment turns into depletion, and we can help them identify that point *for themselves.* But tech as a way to escape, laugh, and enjoy life is good. Kids are not meant to be productive all the time, or even reflective all the time. A little bit of mindless scrolling is today's equivalent of bad TV. We don't know about you, but Jenny watched plenty of it in the 1980s and 1990s (and Rebecca wished she did, but her parents did not own a TV because it "rots the mind").

CONNECTING

Being connected matters, and tech can help kids connect with friends. A lot. As author danah boyd argues, teens aren't in love with tech; they are in love with each other.[30] Tech is just the medium. This was the number one thing teens told us they most valued about tech.

Every teen we spoke with loved finding funny videos, sharing them, and laughing with friends. They also regularly consulted their friends—over FaceTime or through texting or even occasionally by a good old-fashioned phone call—with questions about homework assignments. Plenty of evidence shows that peer-to-peer learning is a powerful way to learn and that teaching a friend a concept is an effective way to deepen one's understanding of it.[31]

We also spoke to kids whose lives were changed through the connection they found online. When Calista, an eighteen-year-old living in Oklahoma City, graduated from high school, it was a profound accomplishment. School was brutally hard for her, mostly because of a friendship at school that turned toxic and abusive, initiating a vicious downward cycle of anxiety, depression, self-harm, and multiple suicide attempts.

Calista found her way out with help from three separate psychiatric facilities, her mother, and two incredible teachers. But she also credits finding a sense of belonging and catharsis by connecting to peers through an online gaming platform. Calista is an artist—she loves to draw, and she loves making games. It isn't something she shares with people at school much. During COVID, she made her art at home in her room. One day when she was scrolling on Instagram, she found a girl with an account she loved. She messaged her immediately. "I told her [that] her art was super good. And then we kind of got together to make a Discord server [meeting point for like-minded people] for fan games [games created by fans]," Calista told us. The girl whose art she admired joined as a cocreator. Two others came in quickly. "And we've kind of all clicked really easily. And we're still friends to this day." She built a community, she was creating games, she was getting positive feedback, and she was able to invest energy because she was interested. It didn't matter that she wasn't getting school credit for it. She had all the conditions to fuel her engagement in learning. It was feeding her soul. It was her place to explore.

During her senior year, Calista's life was clearly on the upswing. She had a boyfriend she loved who buffered some of the social challenges at school. She applied to college and was planning to go in the fall. But the thing she was most excited about was the new game she was making: a role-playing game where people get lost in their fears of missing each other even when they want to stay close. It was her way of processing, in a healthy way, the impending separation from her boyfriend. Her peers in the online gaming community, she said, had given her the courage to make it.

We can help kids engage in their learning online as well as IRL (in real life). Tech is and will continue to be everywhere, a tool our kids will have to understand, manage, and maybe one day improve. That requires some trial and error around use and reflection on how it messes with good things in life but also makes things better.

The more we can support our kids to develop agency over their tech use, the more they can use tech to pursue goals that are meaningful to them. Algorithms, even the most powerful ones, cannot decide what those goals are. Humans can.

Advancing the Age of Agency

Organizations Leading the Way

There are many approaches to supporting student engagement in school. If you want to move beyond supporting your own child and be part of advancing the Age of Agency for all kids in your community, we have some suggestions to get you started.

The first step is to ask your child's school, district, or community leaders what they are currently doing to support engagement. Often educators are using a wide range of things behind the scenes to help support creative teaching and learning approaches.

If you want more inspiration, you can investigate and share some of the organizations listed in this section. They are all nonprofits with proven track records, most of them working with a wide range of schools from public to charter to private. Some also work in communities to spread awareness about the importance of active and engaging learning environments for children. We picked fourteen organizations, and provided a description at the time of writing, but this is by no means an exhaustive list.

Some of these groups offer radical new school design models while others have programs that can be incorporated into any school setting to boost students' engagement and agency. While some work nationally, others focus their attention in a particular city or state. We've included them because they offer interesting approaches.

Change is always challenging, and the Age of Agency needs advocates everywhere. Alongside teachers and education leaders, parents and families, community, business, and philanthropic leaders can play a major role in making sure more kids have better opportunities to explore. And congrats if you choose this route: You are being Explorers in digging into how to make learning better.

Big Picture Learning

HTTPS://WWW.BIGPICTURE.ORG

Founded in 1985, Big Picture Learning (BPL) supports a network of more than one hundred schools in twenty-seven U.S. states as well as one hundred other schools across twelve countries. The BPL approach prioritizes interests, hands-on practice, and relationships. Each week students split their time between classes in school and working closely with adult mentors, often through internships in organizations and businesses in the community. Students choose the places they work based on topics they are curious to explore. They are evaluated on the skills they develop in and out of school, with opportunities to demonstrate how they use their knowledge to solve problems in real-world settings. Students are supported across all their high school years not only by teachers and workplace mentors but also by advisers (usually an educator in the school), whom they meet with weekly to troubleshoot problems and check in emotionally. The BPL model can be adopted by public, private, and charter schools.

Big Thought

HTTPS://WWW.BIGTHOUGHT.ORG

Based in Dallas, Big Thought offers a wide variety of education programs during school, after school, and in summer. Founded in 1987, the organization works to provide young people multiple opportunities to develop skills to understand themselves and others, to learn to use their voice, and to exercise their agency. They do this through using hands-on learning and trauma-informed practices. Examples of their after-school programs include Artivism, a program that lets youth explore social justice issues through art; Thriving Minds, a program for elementary and middle school students to build problem-solving and critical thinking skills (while strengthening academic abilities); and Creative Solutions, a program that uses the performing and digital arts to help youth who have encountered the justice system to build their skills, envision a positive path forward, and be ready for employment.

Challenge Success

HTTPS://CHALLENGESUCCESS.ORG

Challenge Success is a nonprofit affiliated with Stanford University. Founded in 2011, the organization conducts research on student engagement and well-being, and translates that research into strategies to support schools, students, and parents to shift practices. It works with a variety of K–12 schools from private schools to public schools and charter schools in California and across other states. Through consultations and workshops, it aims to help schools, parents, and students develop ways to maximize student well-being, belonging, engagement, and sleep while decreasing stress and anxiety, depression, and overload.

Education Reimagined

HTTPS://EDUCATION-REIMAGINED.ORG

Education Reimagined is a national group founded in 2015 and dedicated to spreading awareness and information about putting learner agency at the center of public education experiences. It connects leaders working on learner-centered approaches; shares ideas across K–12 public education, homeschooling, and youth development programs; and publishes a magazine highlighting stories about learner-centered education experiences.

EL Education

HTTPS://ELEDUCATION.ORG

EL Education is a national group that supports teachers, schools, and districts in using expeditionary learning approaches. In EL schools, students take part in class instruction inside school and fieldwork outside the classroom. They conduct research and do projects in their communities and present their findings to an audience of educators, peers, and family members. Young people also take part in what the organization calls crew, where each year students have a core teacher and a group of peers to support them as they navigate their education journey. The approach focuses on an expanded definition of student success, including mastery of knowledge and skills, building character, and demonstrating high-quality work. The organization supports hundreds of schools and districts in more than twenty states through its curriculum, instructional practices, and professional development for teachers and other education personnel.

High Tech High

HTTPS://WWW.HIGHTECHHIGH.ORG

High Tech High (HTH) was founded in 2000 as a public charter school in San Diego, California. It has since grown into a network of sixteen charter schools in the state, a teacher credentialing program, and a graduate school of education. A hallmark of the HTH approach is allowing students to develop their skills based on their interests through classwork, four-week offsite internships, and presentations to their peers. Principles of equity, personalization, authentic work, and collaborative design drive their approach, showing up in the school's small class size, home visits, advisories, and team approach to projects.

Iowa Big

HTTPS://IOWABIG.ORG

Iowa Big is a collaborative high school program located in Cedar Rapids serving high school juniors and seniors across several school districts. Students typically spend half their time at their traditional high school taking academic classes, playing on the sports teams, and participating in school social events. The other half of their time they practice applying their academic learning to real-world problems in their community. These are either requested by community leaders, such as city government or local businesses or nonprofits, or developed by the students themselves. The approach focuses on helping students develop agency, efficacy (the ability to get things done), and passions.

JA (Junior Achievement) Worldwide

HTTPS://WWW.JAWORLDWIDE.ORG
HTTPS://WWW.3DESCHOOLS.ORG
HTTPS://JAUSA.JA.ORG

JA Worldwide is a global organization that delivers hands-on learning to students across more than one hundred countries.* Their programs are delivered in and out of school and focus on entrepreneurship, work readiness, and financial health. Students work in teams to develop an idea, fundraise for it, and launch new businesses, with support from business volunteers in their communities. Young people get exposed to a wide range of careers and develop key skills, including creative and entrepreneurial thinking, to help them succeed in the workplace. In the United States, two organizations help bring this approach to schools. JA USA has partnered with 3DE Schools, a nonprofit working with high schools across the country, to integrate instructional models from JA with the aim of delivering engaging, relevant, project-based learning that is connected to the real world.

* At the time of writing, Rebecca was a member of JA Worldwide's Board of Governors.

Montessori Schools

HTTPS://MONTESSORI-AMI.ORG
HTTPS://AMSHQ.ORG
HTTPS://WWW.PUBLIC-MONTESSORI.ORG

Maria Montessori, the first female medical doctor in Italy, developed the Montessori approach in the early 1900s. It has evolved over the last century and is implemented differently around the world, but it retains several core principles. Students learn in mixed-age classrooms, instruction is minimalist, and students choose how to move through various hands-on activities, where they can spend as much or as little time as they like exploring in indoor and outdoor settings. The Montessori name is not trademarked or copyrighted, but there are a variety of organizations committed to advancing the approach around the globe. The Association Montessori Internationale (montessori-ami.org) was founded by Maria Montessori and has branches around the world, including in the United States. The American Montessori Society (Amshq.org) is the U.S. advocacy organization to support the use of Montessori approaches in education, and the National Center for Montessori in the Public Sector focuses on helping U.S. public schools take up Montessori methods (public-montessori.org).

Next Education Workforce Initiative

HTTPS://WORKFORCE.EDUCATION.ASU.EDU

Next Education Workforce Initiative, started in 2020, works with dozens of schools and districts in Arizona and beyond to reimagine the one-teacher, one-classroom model. The goal is to give students deeper and more personalized learning experiences while also providing educators more rewarding professional lives. The initiative uses teams of teachers, school leaders, community educators, and paraprofessionals working together. Drawing on the strengths of diverse community members and new staffing structures, the model aims to provide more dynamic learning environments, more flexible schedules, and improvements in the working lives of teachers. The initiative is part of Arizona State University's Mary Lou Fulton Teachers College.

NYC Outward Bound

HTTPS://NYCOUTWARDBOUND.ORG

NYC Outward Bound was founded in 1987 and works with over seventy New York City public schools. It draws on expeditionary learning approaches, including a focus on incorporating outdoor adventure as part of the learning experience. Students are part of a crew, with an adviser and a small group of peers accompanying them throughout their high school journey, seeking to help build belonging. They also use project-based learning and diverse assessment approaches to enable students to demonstrate what they can do with their knowledge in various ways. They help schools support rigorous learning by creating environments that support student belonging and give young people opportunities to exercise their voice and agency.

Remake Learning

HTTPS://REMAKELEARNING.ORG

Remake Learning is a network of educators and innovators in the Pittsburgh region that shares ideas and strategies for making learning more engaging and relevant. Their network draws a wide variety of people from teachers, artists, employers, academics, childcare professionals, and school leaders to museum program heads to showcase new and engaging ways to learn. The network raises awareness about the need for new approaches to education that are more engaging and active and shares specific ideas about how to do that in and out of school. One of their signature ways to do this is through Remake Learning Days, community-wide events focused on hands-on learning held in hundreds of communities across the country.

Summit Public Schools

HTTPS://SUMMITPS.ORG

HTTPS://WWW.SUMMITLEARNING.ORG

Summit Public Schools is a network of nine tuition-free and open-enrollment public charter schools in California and Washington State. At the center of the model is a personalized learning plan that each student develops for themselves with support from their teachers and families. Every student has a laptop and uses it to set goals for themselves and make plans to achieve those goals for the day, week, and year. Each day, there is dedicated planning time where kids are taught the skills they need to independently develop and manage their learning plans. Students follow these plans at their own pace. They receive support from teachers and mentors through class instruction, online learning, and annual projects that they do in their communities. Summit Learning (summitlearning.org), a separate nonprofit, was developed to share the model with others outside of the nine Summit schools. Any school interested in using the Summit approaches can do so through coaching, training, and materials provided by Summit Learning.

Transcend Education

HTTPS://TRANSCENDEDUCATION.ORG

Transcend has worked directly with hundreds of schools and leaders in over thirty states. It uses a community-driven approach, partnering with schools or districts to reimagine and redesign students' learning experiences to be more engaging and equitable. They work directly with schools on "design journeys" while also sharing powerful models, tools, and insights from across the sector. The organization's focus is collaborating with public and charter schools to help each find their own tailored approach to education redesign.

Acknowledgments

If it takes a village to raise a kid, it takes a sprawling metropolis to write a book. Thank you to the many young people who patiently answered endless questions about what it is like to be in school today. Your honesty and insights impressed us and profoundly shaped our thinking. You give us tremendous hope about the future of learning, as well as the future in general.

Thank you also to the parents who shared their kids with us, and shared themselves, digging into their own struggles and triumphs with this very tricky human endeavor called parenting. There were many characters who did not make it into the final draft but whose stories we learned so much from.

We are grateful to the many teachers, educators, school counselors, administrators, school heads, and district leaders who opened their classrooms, shared their insights, and so generously carved out time for us amid the one million things you do every day. Your creativity and your dedication to fostering a love of learning inspired us while writing this book.

To educators everywhere: We see you changing lives. Thank you.

Huge thanks also to the hundreds of brilliant academics, researchers, innovators, and leaders of education organizations who helped us understand the scope of the disengagement crisis and the complex factors underpinning it. Your work elevating student engagement and advancing student well-being is powerful. We hope we have helped to spread the message far and wide that unlocking more agency will not compromise kids' learning, but empower it.

We are grateful to our agent, Todd Shuster and our editor, Leah Trouwborst. Without you, this book would not exist. Thank you for believing in us, for taking a chance on us, and for guiding us along the way. We are deeply indebted to Gareth Cook and the team at Verto for getting us over the finish line; what a memorable three weeks. Thank you to Gillian Blake for your keen eye and your support on this project, and Libby Burton for stepping in to help so adeptly. To Ashley Pierce, Dustin Amick, Elisabeth Magnus, Aubrey Khan, Yang Kim, Tammy Blake, Kimberly Lew, Rachel Rodriguez, and the entire Crown team: we are so grateful for your attention and expertise. Cierra Hinckson: you are a star. Will you miss all our emails?

We do not have the space to name all the people who meaningfully informed this book, but there are a few who deserve our deepest thanks. First and foremost, to Erik Jahner, who provided invaluable research assistance, thought partnership, editorial advice, and an endless supply of good humor and moral support. This book is better because of your input, your patience, your stamina, and your keen insights into young people and the brain.

To Claudia Barwell, for your powers of community building: This book is etched with Oppi love and expertise. To McKenzie Cerri, Vicki Phillips, and Kelly Young, for your pivotal role in helping us find language for the modes. To Amy Berry, Anindya Kundu, Jennifer Fredricks, Johnmarshall Reeve, and Sandra Christenson, for your incredible work on student engagement and agency that was so helpful in guiding our path. To the experts who went above and beyond, including Pam Cantor, Ron Dahl, Andrew Frishman, Daren Dickson, Sarah Peterson, Denise Pope, and Mary Helen Immordino-Yang.

We are so thankful to the many colleagues and friends who spent an inordinate amount of time reading drafts, giving us feedback, and helping us improve our thinking and writing: Ronald Dahl, Brad Olsen, Sandra Christenson, Vicki Foley, Patrice Keet, Jennifer Fredricks, Vicki Phillips, Sarah Peterson, Jeff Wetzler, Pilar Guzmán, Jason Karaian, Krista Haregrave, Brooke Singer, Annaliese Griffin, Kim Newell Green, Tom Ralston, Jordan Shapiro, Fernande Raine, and Imogen Barker.

A warm thank-you to Mike Bond and the entire team of Bond and Coyne for the incredible illustrations. Your creative eye has helped bring the heady concepts of student engagement and agency to life and added an important dimension to this book.

Lastly, we are deeply grateful for the Brookings team and all their partners. We chose to list authorship alphabetically and this book drew heavily on a wide range of research conducted by Rebecca and her colleagues at the Center for Universal Education at Brookings. Thank you to Youssef Shoukry, David Nitkin, Juetzinia Kazmer-Murillo, and Jeff Wetzler at Transcend for your warm spirit and passion in partnering with us, surveying parents, and conducting novel analysis of student survey data. This joint Brookings-Transcend research has helped shape how we see the problems of engagement in our country.

Thank you to the many partners in the Brookings Family Engagement in Education Network who helped us gain deep insights into what families need from schools through surveys and focus groups with parents and caregivers, teachers, educators, and students. Thank you to all the Brookings colleagues who have advanced this work over the years with such dedication and passion: Natasha Luther, Andrés Villalba, Chloe Baldauf, Max Lieblich, Dakshesh Thacker, Omaer Nasem, Laura Nora, Erin Thomas, Esther Lee Rosen, Richaa Hoysala, Francesca Braun, Akilah Allen, Lauren Zeigler, Claire Sukumar, Ashleigh Ekwenugo, Richaa Hoysala, Nina Fairchild, and Ariana Sharghi. A special thanks to Emily Morris and Jennifer O'Donoghue, for your thought partnership and leadership on better understanding young people through investigating their perspectives and the perspectives of the adults in their lives, including caregivers, teachers, and mentors. Thank you to Joanne McPike, for all the many ways you have supported the development of this work. A final note of thanks goes to

Sophie Partington, whose grace, strategic guidance, and efficiency played a major role in ensuring the high quality of our work, which helps advance the understanding of the relationships between families, student engagement, and school.

• • •

We are also deeply grateful to our families and loved ones. Not only for their patience, but for all they have taught us about helping kids learn.

From Jenny: Thank you to the family, friends, and neighbors who stepped up with driving and general caregiving over the long "final" sprint. To Dayle and Ash for keeping me strong, to Scott for your love and care of Tiggy, to Sanam Vakil for the runs, to my POW peeps, and to the Ladies for the bottomless support. Thanks to Charlie Duhigg and Sue Dominus for answering my many panicked emails; Pilar Guzmán for your editorial insights and sage life advice; and Larry Ingrassia for taking a chance on me way back when. To my mom, whose love is boundless and whose wisdom about relationships is golden; and my (late) dad, who embodied Explorer mode more than anyone I know. To Robbie: You would have teased me mercilessly for writing this book, but I know you would have been proud. To Thorold: You are my everything (including excellent editor). Thank you. To Ella and Tess: Thank you for your very direct insights, your patience at never getting fed on time, and your general awesomeness. You blow me away every day with your brilliant questions, kindness, and keen observations. Every hug helped. I cannot wait to see what you choose to explore in life.

From Rebecca: First and foremost, thank you to Santi and Nico for being the lights of my life, for sharing your learning journey with me, and for expressing your thoughts and (strong) opinions about ideas in the book. Your enthusiastic encouragement during the final stages of writing kept me going. Every "You got this, Mom!" gave me renewed energy. Your boundless curiosity brings me joy and helped me see all the ways young people can get into Explorer mode. Jean-Marc, thank you for being an incredible partner, holding things all together when I am stretched across the globe, and for your ideas and thoughtful critique. You show us all what Explorer mode looks like every day. Thank you, Mom and Dad, for your love and guidance throughout my life and your unflagging moral support in the long process of writing this book. Thank you for all the many ways you keep our family running. Mom, thank you for reading the book in one sitting and for the wise counsel and feedback on how to improve it. Thank you, Anna and Eleni, for your love and support and for the many discussions about parenting our own children—helping me be a better mom and also a better author.

Notes

Introduction

THE DISENGAGEMENT CRISIS

1. Organization for Economic Cooperation and Development, *PISA 2022 Results,* vol. 1: *The State of Learning and Equity in Education* (Paris: OECD Publishing, 2023), https://www.oecd.org/publication/pisa-2022-results.
2. OECD, *PISA 2022 Results* (vol 1): 2023.
3. In the history of the PISA test, scores have only ever varied by 4 percentage points. This recent decline is a decline of approximately 15 percentage points, which greatly worries educationalists.
4. Multiple sources show low levels of student engagement in the United States. The U.S. Census provides a nationally representative snapshot of student engagement in 2014 and 2020 through its Survey of Income and Program Participation (SIPP). In 2014, the SIPP showed that only 35 percent of students were highly engaged in school. Based on authors' calculations of the 2020 SIPP results, that number dropped to approximately 27 percent during the height of the COVID-19 pandemic. There is not one way to measure student engagement, making it difficult to precisely compare findings. But all the surveys of student engagement we examined show low engagement levels, including: state-level surveys, Gallup's Student Poll, and the Challenge Success-Stanford Survey of Student Experiences, among many others. The trend is quite clear: Engagement is low, has been for some time, and got worse in the pandemic.
5. Disengagement in school has been low since 2010 and remained fairly stable even though the presence of technology in children's lives has changed dramatically. For example see: Challenge Success, *Student Voice Report: A Review of Quantitative and Qualitative Data from 2010–2023 Examining High*

School Students' Emotional and Physical Health, Sense of Connection and Belonging in School, and Engagement With Learning, (June 2024), https://challengesuccess.org/wp-content/uploads/2024/06/Challenge-Success-2024-Student-Voice-Report.pdf.

6. For the United States: Rebecca Winthrop, Youssef Shoukry, and David Nitkin *The Disengagement Gap: Why Student Engagement Isn't What Parents Expect* (Washington, DC: Brookings Institution, 2025); For Chile: In Chile, many schools take the Diagnóstico Integral de Aprendizajes, which is administered by La Agencia de Calidad de la Educacion. Recent results showed low levels of student satisfaction with the quality of education they receive. "Diagnóstico Integral de Aprendizajes," accessed June 28, 2024, https://diagnosticointegral.agenciaeducacion.cl.
7. Jennifer A. Fredricks, Amy L. Reschly, and Sandra L. Christenson, eds., *Handbook of Student Engagement Interventions: Working with Disengaged Students* (London: Academic Press, 2019).
8. Winthrop, Shoukry, and Nitkin, *The Disengagement Gap.*
9. Johnmarshall Reeve et al., *Supporting Students' Motivation: Strategies for Success* (Abingdon, Oxon: Routledge, 2022).
10. Anindya Kundu, *The Power of Student Agency: Looking beyond Grit to Close the Opportunity Gap* (New York: Teachers College Press, 2020). See also multiple scholars who have demonstrated the importance of student engagement and student agency for the most marginalized students. For example, the work of Pedro Noguera. For rigorous empirical research demonstrating the importance of student engagement for the most marginalized, see the numerous studies coming out of the Check and Connect program spearheaded by Sandra Christenson and colleagues: Sandra L. Christenson et al., "Check and Connect: The Role of Monitors in Supporting High-Risk Youth," *Reaching Today's Youth: The Community Circle of Caring Journal* 2 no. 1 (Fall 1997): 18–21; Mary F. Sinclair et al., "Facilitating Student Engagement: Lessons Learned from Check & Connect Longitudinal Studies," *The California School Psychologist* 8, no. 1 (January 2003): 29–41, doi.org/10.1007/bf03340894; and Amy R. Anderson et al., "Check & Connect: The Importance of Relationships for Promoting Engagement with School," *Journal of School Psychology* 42, no. 2 (March 2004): 95–113, doi.org/10.1016/j.jsp.2004.01.002.
11. Winthrop, Shoukry, and Nitkin, *The Disengagement Gap.*
12. Dana Goldstein and Audra Melton, "A School with 7 Students: Inside the 'Microschools' Movement," *New York Times,* June 17, 2024, https://www.nytimes.com/2024/06/17/us/public-schools-education-voucher-microschools.html.
13. One of the leading academics on the role of parents in shaping children's motivation, including in relation to school, is Wendy S. Grolnick, professor of psychology at Clark University. See her body of work for two decades of research uncovering how and when parents and caregivers shape children's motivation. See also chapter 6 for a more detailed review of the evidence on parental influence on student engagement. Teachers clearly have an important influence on student engagement inside the classroom, and peers particularly

influence behavioral engagement. In the following study, parents were found to shape student engagement across multiple domains: Ming-Te Wang and Jacquelynne S. Eccles, "Social Support Matters: Longitudinal Effects of Social Support on Three Dimensions of School Engagement from Middle to High School," Society for Research in Child Development, April 2012. See also, Ming-Te Wang and Salam Sheikh-Khalil, "Does Parental Involvement Matter for Student Achievement and Mental Health in High School?" *Child Development,* vol. 85, no. 2 (April 2014): 610–625.

14. See chapter 3 in "PISA 2022 Results (Volume II): Learning During—and From—Disruption," *OECD,* December 5, 2023, doi.org/10.1787/a97db61c-en.
15. This research was done jointly by the team at the Center for Universal Education at Brookings and Transcend. Together, we developed a novel analysis of Transcend's existing survey data of students, and we jointly surveyed parents to better understand their perspectives of student engagement. The full methods are described in Winthrop, Shoukry, and Nitkin, *The Disengagement Gap.*
16. Anthony S. Bryk, "Organizing Schools for Improvement," *Phi Delta Kappan 91,* no. 7 (April 2010): 23–30, doi.org/10.1177/003172171009100705.
17. See Robert Crosnoe, *Fitting In, Standing Out: Navigating the Social Challenges of High School to Get an Education* (Cambridge: Cambridge University Press, 2011); a distinguished professor in the School of Public Health, Dahl first heard this from Wouter van den Bos from the University of Amsterdam: Ronald Dahl, University of California, Berkeley, interview with the authors, June 2024.

Chapter 1

THE POWER OF ENGAGEMENT: UNLOCKING EVERY KID'S POTENTIAL

1. CDC, Adolescent and School Health, *Youth Risk Behavior Survey: Data Summary and Trends Report, 2011–2021,* February 2023, https://www.cdc.gov/healthyyouth/data/yrbs/pdf/YRBS_Data-Summary-Trends_Report2023_508.pdf.
2. "YRBSS Data Summary & Trends," *Centers for Disease Control and Prevention,* April 27, 2023, https://www.cdc.gov/healthyyouth/data/yrbs/yrbs_data_summary_and_trends.htm.
3. Sally C. Curtin et al., "Death Rates Due to Suicide and Homicide Among Persons Aged 10–24: United States, 2000–2017," *NCHS Data Brief* no. 352, October 2019, https://www.cdc.gov/nchs/products/databriefs/db352.htm.
4. U.S. Surgeon General, *Protecting Youth Mental Health,* 2021, https://www.hhs.gov/sites/default/files/surgeon-general-youth-mental-health-advisory.pdf.
5. Jean M. Twenge, *Generations: The Real Differences Between Gen Z, Millennials, Gen X, Boomers, and Silents—and What They Mean for The Future* (New York: Atria Books, 2024), alcohol and sex, 272, 393; loneliness, 393.
6. Attendance Works, "Chronic Absence Remained a Significant Challenge in 2022–23," Attendance Works Blog, October 2023, https://www.attendanceworks.org/ chronic-absence-remained-a-significant-challenge-in-2022-23/.
7. Brandon Busteed, "The School Cliff: Student Engagement Drops with Each Year in School," Gallup, January 7, 2013.

8. Across all our research, we were especially inspired by two excellent books demystifying student engagement for teachers: Jennifer A. Fredricks, *Eight Myths of Student Disengagement: Creating Classrooms of Deep Learning* (Thousand Oaks, CA: Corwin, 2016) and Amy Berry, *Reimagining Student Engagement: From Disrupting to Driving* (Thousand Oaks, CA: Corwin, 2023).
9. Winthrop, Shoukry, and Nitkin, *The Disengagement Gap.*
10. We are sparing you a review of all the different engagement researchers, their theoretical underpinnings, and the differences in how they measure student engagement. Many scholars measure similar things but call them different things or put them in different categories. Still others are expanding the field by testing out different constructs and dimensions. We have chosen to focus on four dimensions of engagement (behavioral, emotional, cognitive, agentic) because they resonated with the student interviews we did and they are deeply evidenced in the academic literature. Academics have coalesced around the presence of at least three dimensions of engagement: behavioral, emotional, and cognitive; see Jennifer A. Fredricks, Amy L. Reschly, and Sandra L. Christenson, eds., *Handbook of Student Engagement Interventions: Working with Disengaged Students* (London: Academic Press, 2020). We use the articulation of these three dimensions found in Ming-Te Wang and Stephen C. Peck, "Adolescent Educational Success and Mental Health Vary Across School Engagement Profiles," *Developmental Psychology* 49, no. 7 (July 2013): 1266–76, doi.org/10.1037/a0030028. We have chosen to add the dimension of agentic engagement to these three, using Johnmarshall Reeve's conceptualization (see Johnmarshall Reeve and Hyungshim Jang, "Agentic Engagement," *Handbook of Research on Student Engagement,* 2020). This is both because his research is sound and convincing on the importance of examining student's proactive behaviors in their learning. It is also because we believe that to thrive in today's world, students need more agency, not less.
11. Plato, "Phaedrus," trans. Benjamin Jowett, Project Gutenberg ebook, last updated January 25, 2013, https://www.gutenberg.org/files/1636/1636-h/1636-h.htm.
12. Plato, *Plato's Meno,* trans. George Anastaplo and Laurence Berns (Newburyport, MA: Focus Publishing/R. Pullins, 2004); and Jordan Shapiro, personal communication, June 20.
13. Robert H. Winthrop, "Norm and Tradition in American Benedictine Monasticism" (PhD diss., University of Minnesota, 1981).
14. Jenny Anderson, "Google's Former Ethicist Says Better Design Is Key to Tackling Our Tech Addiction," *Quartz,* February 8, 2018, https://qz.com/1201583/how-tristan-harris-an-ex-google-ethicist-wants-to-design-tech-to-make-our-kids-less-addicted-to-it.
15. David Yeager, *10 to 25: The Science of Motivating Young People: A Groundbreaking Approach to Leading the Next Generation—and Making Your Life Easier* (London: Avid Reader Press, 2024).
16. David Yeager, professor, University of Texas at Austin, interview with the authors, May 2024.
17. "Former Google Ethicist on Tech's 'Race to the Bottom of the Brain Stem,'" YouTube, May 7, 2019, https://www.youtube.com/watch?v=l2tZLesCX4M.

18. John Hattie and Kyle Hattie, *10 Steps to Develop Great Learners: Visible Learning for Parents* (Abingdon, Oxon: Routledge, 2022), xiii.
19. Christina D. Bethell, Narangerel Gombojav, and Robert C. Whitaker, "Family Resilience and Connection Promote Flourishing Among US Children, Even amid Adversity," *Health Affairs* 38, no. 5 (May 2019): 729–37, doi.org/10.1377/hlthaff.2018.05425.
20. Bethell, Gombojav, and Whitaker, "Family Resilience and Connection Promote Flourishing Among US Children."
21. Ajmel Quereshi and Jason Okonofua, "Locked Out of the Classroom: How Implicit Bias Contributes to Disparities in School Discipline," *SSRN*, February 16, 2024, https://ssrn.com/abstract=4702736.
22. Verone Kennedy, executive director of knowledge management at New York City Department of Education, interview with the authors, December 2023.
23. Johnmarshall Reeve and Hyungshim Jang, "Agentic Engagement," in *Handbook of Research on Student Engagement*, ed. Amy L. Reschly and Sandra L. Christenson (Cham, Switzerland: Springer, 2022), 95–107, doi.org/10.1007/978-3-031-07853-8_5.
24. Winthrop, Shoukry, and Nitkin, *The Disengagement Gap.*
25. Ben Steverman, "Why Aren't American Teenagers Working Anymore?," Bloomberg.com, June 5, 2017, https://www.bloomberg.com/news/articles/2017-06-05/why-aren-t-american-teenagers-working-anymore.
26. Jennifer Breheny Wallace, *Never Enough: When Achievement Culture Becomes Toxic—and What We Can Do about It* (New York: Portfolio/Penguin, 2023), 41.
27. Ronald Dahl, distinguished professor in the School of Public Health, University of California, Berkeley, interview with the authors, June 2024.
28. Elizabeth H. Weybright, John Schulenberg, and Linda L. Caldwell. "Bored Today Than Yesterday? National Trends in Adolescent Boredom from 2008 to 2017," *Journal of Adolescent Health* 66, no. 3 (2020): 360–65.
29. Jenny Anderson, "The Unlikely Champion for Testing Kids Around the World on Empathy and Creativity," *Quartz*, February 22, 2019, https://qz.com/1540222/how-changing-the-pisa-test-could-change-how-kids-learn.
30. Andreas Schleicher, director for education and skills at OECD, personal communication, May 2023.
31. Linda Darling-Hammond et al., *Criteria for High-Quality Assessment* (Stanford, CA: Stanford Center for Opportunity Policy in Education; Los Angeles: Center for Research on Student Standards and Testing, University of California at Los Angeles; Chicago: Learning Sciences Research Institute, University of Illinois at Chicago, 2013), https://edpolicy.stanford.edu/sites/default/files/publications/criteria-higher-quality-assessment_2.pdf.
32. Victoria Masterson, "Future of Jobs 2023: These Are the Most In-Demand Skills Now—and Beyond," World Economic Forum, May 2023, https://www.weforum.org/agenda/2023/05/future-of-jobs-2023-skills/.
33. Jenny Anderson, "The Way We Assess What Kids Are Learning Is Changing," *Time*, January 18, 2024, https://time.com/6563787/american-students-skills-assessments-education/.
34. David Coleman, College Board CEO, presentation at SXSWEDU, March 2024.

35. Randi Weingarten, president of the American Federation of Teachers, interview with the authors, January 2024.

Chapter 2

PASSENGER MODE: QUIETLY QUITTING

1. Rebecca Winthrop, Youssef Shoukry, and David Nitkin, *The Disengagement Gap: Why Student Engagement Isn't What Parents Expect* (Washington, DC: Brookings Institution and Transcend, 2025).
2. Shannon M. Suldo and Janise Parker, "Relationships Between Student Engagement and Mental Health as Conceptualized from a Dual-Factor Model," in *Handbook of Research on Student Engagement,* 2nd ed., eds. Amy L. Reschly and Sandra L. Christenson (Cham, Switzerland: Springer, 2022), 217–38; and Ming-Te Wang and Stephen C. Peck, "Adolescent Educational Success and Mental Health Vary Across School Engagement Profiles," *Developmental Psychology* 49, no. 7 (July 2013): 1266, doi.org/10.1037/a0030028.
3. Johnmarshall Reeve, professor, Institute for Positive Psychology and Education, Australian Catholic University, interview with the authors, January 2024.
4. Daren Dickson, chief culture officer, Valor Collegiate Academies, interview with the authors, March 2023.
5. Lev S. Vygotsky, *Mind in Society: The Development of Higher Psychological Processes* (London: Harvard University Press, 1978).
6. Sonja Santelsises and Joan Dabrowski, *Checking In: Do Classroom Assignments Reflect Today's Higher Standards?* (Washington, DC: Education Trust, 2015), 4.
7. See the nonprofit Made by Dyslexia (https://www.madebydyslexia.org/), which has a repository of data on dyslexia, including the percentage of self-made millionaires who are dyslexic.
8. American Psychiatric Association, *Diagnostic and Statistical Manual of Mental Disorders,* 5th ed. (Washington, DC: American Psychiatric Association, 2013).
9. For the definition of *neurodiversity,* see Nick Chown, "Neurodiversity," in *Encyclopedia of Autism Spectrum Disorders,* 2nd ed., ed. Fred R. Volkmar (Cham, Switzerland: Springer, 2021): 3134–35, doi.org/10.1007/978-3-319-91280-6_102298. For the national statistics on neurodiversity see "Interactive Data Query: National Survey of Children's Health (2022–present)," Data Resource Center for Child and Adolescent Health, accessed March 24, 2024, https://www.childhealthdata.org/browse/survey.
10. Ashley Major, Rhonda Martinussen, and Judith Wiener, "*Self-Efficacy for Self-Regulated Learning in Adolescents with and without Attention Deficit Hyperactivity Disorder (ADHD)*," Learning and Individual Differences 27 (October 2013): 149–56, doi.org/10.1016/j.lindif.2013.06.009.
11. See the nonprofit Made by Dyslexia (https://www.madebydyslexia.org/) for data on employers who are looking for skills people with dyslexia usually are strong in.
12. The U.S. Census provides a nationally representative snapshot of student engagement in 2014 and 2020 through its Survey of Income and Program Participation (SIPP).

13. "Results from the 2019 NAEP High School Transcript Study," The Nation's Report Card, accessed June 6, 2024, https://www.nationsreportcard.gov/hstsreport/#coursetaking_1_0_el.
14. "Men Adrift," *The Economist,* May 30, 2015.
15. National Center for Education Statistics, "Degrees Conferred by Postsecondary Institutions, by Level of Degree and Sex of Student: Selected Years, 1869–70 through 2029–30" *Digest of Education Statistics,* Table 318.10, https://nces.ed.gov/programs/digest/d18/tables/dt18_318.10.asp.
16. Richard Reeves, *Of Boys and Men: Why the Modern Male Is Struggling, Why It Matters, and What to Do About It* (Washington, DC: Brookings Institution Press, 2022), 9.
17. Javier Valbuena et al., "Effects of Grade Retention Policies: A Literature Review of Empirical Studies Applying Causal Inference," *Journal of Economic Surveys* 35, no. 2 (December 15, 2020): 408–51, doi.org/10.1111/joes.12406.
18. Jordan Shapiro, associate professor at the College of Liberal Arts, Temple University, interview with the authors, January 2023.
19. Ronald Dahl, distinguished professor in the School of Public Health, University of California, Berkeley, interview with the authors, June 2024.
20. Big Picture Learning, home page, accessed April 30, 2024, https://www.bigpicture.org.
21. Jennifer A. Fredricks et al., "Spilling Over: How Participating in After-School Organized Activities Predicts Students' Engagement," in *Handbook of Student Engagement Interventions: Working with Disengaged Students* (San Diego, CA: Elsevier Academic Press, 2019), 231–43, doi.org/10.1016/B978-0-12-813413-9.00016-4.
22. Kaya Henderson, former chancellor of the Disrict of Columbia Public Schools, interview with the authors, October 2023.
23. Suzanne Hidi and K. Ann Renninger, "The Four-Phase Model of Interest Development," *Educational Psychologist* 41, no. 2 (June 2006): 111–27, doi.org/10.1207/s15326985ep4102_4.
24. Peter L. Benson, *Sparks: How Parents Can Ignite the Hidden Strengths of Teenagers* (New York: John Wiley, 2008), 23.
25. Richard M. Lerner, *The Good Teen: Rescuing Adolescence from the Myths of the Storm and Stress Years* (San Francisco: Jossey-Bass, 2009).
26. Ann K. Renninger and Suzanne E. Hidi, "To Level the Playing Field, Develop Interest," *Policy Insights from the Behavioral and Brain Sciences* 7, no. 1 (March 2020): 10–18, doi.org/10.1177/2372732219864705.
27. Dustin B. Thoman, Jessi L. Smith, and Paul J. Silvia, "The Resource Replenishment Function of Interest," *Social Psychological and Personality Science* 2, no. 6 (March 28, 2011): 592–99, doi.org/10.1177/1948550611402521.
28. Ulrich Trautwein et al., "Using Individual Interest and Conscientiousness to Predict Academic Effort: Additive, Synergistic, or Compensatory Effects?," *Journal of Personality and Social Psychology* 109, no. 1 (July 2015): 142–62, doi.org/10.1037/pspp0000034.
29. Catherine H. Crouch et al., "Life Science Students' Attitudes, Interest, and

Performance in Introductory Physics for Life Sciences: An Exploratory Study," *Physical Review Physics Education Research* 14, no. 1 (March 5, 2018): 010111, doi.org/10.1103/PhysRevPhysEducRes.14.010111; Galit Hagay and Ayelet Baram-Tsabari, "A Shadow Curriculum: Incorporating Students' Interests into the Formal Biology Curriculum," *Research in Science Education* 41, no. 5 (August 3, 2010): 611–34. doi.org/10.1007/s11165-010-9182-5.

Chapter 3

ACHIEVER MODE: THE PERILS OF PERFECTION

1. Jennifer A. Fredricks, Amy L. Reschly, and Sandra L. Christenson, "Interventions for Student Engagement: Overview and State of the Field," in *Handbook of Student Engagement Interventions: Working with Disengaged Students,* eds. Jennifer A. Fredricks, Amy L. Reschly, and Sandra L. Christenson (London: Academic Press, 2019), 1–11; and Amy L. Reschly and Sandra L. Christenson. "Jingle, Jangle, and Conceptual Haziness: Evolution and Future Directions of the Engagement Construct," in *Handbook of Research on Student Engagement, eds.* Sandra L. Christenson, Amy L. Reschly, and Cathy Wylie (Cham, Switzerland: Springer, 2012), 3–19.
2. Robert Rudolf and Dirk Bethmann, "The Paradox of Wealthy Nations' Low Adolescent Life Satisfaction," *Journal of Happiness Studies* 24, no. 1 (October 26, 2022): 79–105, doi.org/10.1007/s10902-022-00595-2.
3. Ming-Te Wang and Stephen C. Peck, "Adolescent Educational Success and Mental Health Vary Across School Engagement Profiles," *Developmental Psychology* 49, no. 7 (July 2013): 1266–76, doi.org/10.1037/a0030028.
4. Rudolf and Bethmann, "The Paradox of Wealthy Nations' Low Adolescent Life Satisfaction."
5. Claude M. Steele, "A Threat in the Air: How Stereotypes Shape Intellectual Identity and Performance," *American Psychologist* 52, no. 6 (June 1997): 613–29, doi.org/10.1037/0003-066x.52.6.613; Suniya S. Luthar, "Vulnerability and Resilience: A Study of High-Risk Adolescents," *Child Development* 62, no. 3 (June 1991): 600–616, doi.org/10.1111/j.1467-8624.1991.tb01555.x.
6. Jason W. Osborne and Christopher Walker, "Stereotype Threat, Identification with Academics, and Withdrawal from School: Why the Most Successful Students of Colour Might Be Most Likely to Withdraw," *Educational Psychology* 26, no. 4 (August 2006): 563–77, doi.org/10.1080/01443410500342518.
7. Luthar, "Vulnerability and Resilience."
8. Denise Pope, cofounder and strategic adviser of Challenge Schools, interview with the authors, July 2023.
9. Johnmarshall Reeve, professor at Australian Catholic University, interview with the authors, January 2024.
10. Dennis Shirly and Andy Hargreaves, *Five Paths of Student Engagement: Blazing the Trail to Learning and Success* (Bloomington, IN: Solution Tree Press, 2021).
11. Thomas Curran, assistant professor of psychological and behavioral sciences at the London School of Economics and Political Science, interview with the authors, July 2023.

12. Rudolf and Bethmann, "The Paradox of Wealthy Nations' Low Adolescent Life Satisfaction."
13. Denise Clark Pope, *"Doing School": How We Are Creating a Generation of Stressed Out, Materialistic, and Miseducated Students* (New Haven, CT: Yale University Press, 2003).
14. Thomas Curran and Andrew P. Hill, "Perfectionism Is Increasing over Time: A Meta-Analysis of Birth Cohort Differences from 1989 to 2016," *Psychological Bulletin* 145, no. 4 (April 2019): 410–29, doi.org/10.1037/bul0000138.
15. Thomas Curran, assistant professor of psychological and behavioral sciences at the London School of Economics and Political Science, interview with the authors, July 2023; Karina Limburg et al., "The Relationship Between Perfectionism and Psychopathology: A Meta-analysis," *Journal of Clinical Psychology* 73, no. 10 (2017): 1301–26, doi.org/10.1002/jclp.22435; Gail Cornwall, "The Psychological Toll of Wanting Your Kid to be 'Perfect,'" *Salon*, September 12, 2021.
16. Thomas Curran and Andrew P. Hill, "A Test of Perfectionistic Vulnerability Following Competitive Failure Among College Athletes," *Journal of Sport and Exercise Psychology*, preprint, September 18, 2018, doi.org/10.31234/osf.io/te2a3.
17. Andrew P. Hill et al., "The Cognitive, Affective and Behavioural Responses of Self-Oriented Perfectionists Following Successive Failure on a Muscular Endurance Task," *International Journal of Sport and Exercise Psychology* 9, no. 2 (June 2011): 189–207, doi.org/10.1080/1612197x.2011.567108.
18. Thomas Curran and Andrew P. Hill, "Young People's Perceptions of Their Parents' Expectations and Criticism Are Increasing over Time: Implications for Perfectionism," *Psychological Bulletin* 148, no. 1–2 (January 2022): 107–28, doi.org/10.1037/bul0000347.
19. Thomas Curran, assistant professor of psychological and behavioral sciences at the London School of Economics and Political Science, interview with the authors, July 2023.
20. Richard Weissbourd, senior lecturer at the Harvard Graduate School of Education, interview with the authors, July 2023.
21. Jennifer Breheny Wallace, "Students in High-Achieving Schools Are Now Named an 'At-Risk' Group, Study Says," *Washington Post,* October 24, 2019, https://www.washingtonpost.com/lifestyle/2019/09/26/students-high-achieving-schools-are-now-named-an-at-risk-group/.
22. C. Ryan Dunn et al., "The Impact of Family Financial Investment on Perceived Parent Pressure and Child Enjoyment and Commitment in Organized Youth Sport," *Family Relations* 65, no. 2 (April 2016): 287–99, doi.org/10.1111/fare.12193.
23. Lisa Damour, clinical psychologist and bestselling author, interview with the authors, February 2024.
24. Damour interview.
25. S. B. Dale and A. B. Krueger, "Estimating the Payoff to Attending a More Selective College: An Application of Selection on Observables and Unobservables," *Quarterly Journal of Economics* 117, no. 4 (November 1, 2002): 1491–1527, doi.org/10.1162/003355302320935089.

26. Raj Chetty et al., "Social Capital II: Determinants of Economic Connectedness," *Nature* 608, no. 7921 (August 1, 2022): 122–34, doi.org/10.1038/s41586-022-04997-3.
27. Challenge Success, "A 'Fit' over Rankings: Why College Engagement Matters More Than Selectivity," brief, October 2018, https://challengesuccess.org/wp-content/uploads/2023/03/College-Brief-Web.pdf.
28. Challenge Success, "A 'Fit' over Rankings."

Chapter 4

RESISTER MODE: DRIVING IN REVERSE

1. Karissa Leduc et al., "School Refusal in Youth: A Systematic Review of Ecological Factors," *Child Psychiatry and Human Development,* preprint, November 24, 2022, 1–19, https://www.ncbi.nlm.nih.gov/pmc/articles/PMC9686247.
2. Emma Dorn et al., "Covid-19 and Education: An Emerging K-Shaped Recovery," McKinsey, December 14, 2021, https://www.mckinsey.com/industries/education/our-insights/covid-19-and-education-an-emerging-k-shaped-recovery.
3. Attendance Works, "Rising Tide of Chronic Absence Challenges Schools," *Attendance Works Blog,* October 2023, https://www.attendanceworks.org/rising-tide-of-chronic-absence-challenges-schools.
4. Edward Fergus, Pedro Noguera, and Margary Martin, *Schooling for Resilience: Improving the Life Trajectory of Black and Latino Boys Boys* (Cambridge, MA: Harvard Education Press, 2014).
5. Pedro Noguera, "Grit, Overemphasized—Agency, Overlooked," *Motion Magazine,* March 3, 2015, https://www.inmotionmagazine.com/er15/pn_15_grit_and_agency.html.
6. Early studies of student engagement identified the importance of students feeling a sense of identification with school, including feeling like an important member of the school community, as one of the essential elements preventing student dropout. See, for example, Jeremy Finn, "Withdrawing from School," *Review of Educational Research* 59, no. 2 (Summer 1989): 117–42, doi.org/10.3102/00346543059002117. Recognition of the importance of belonging for student engagement and achievement has only grown over time. See Kelly-Ann Allen and Christopher Boyle, "School Belonging and Student Engagement: The Critical Overlaps, Similarities, and Implications for Student Outcomes, in *Handbook of Research on Student Engagement,* 2nd. ed., eds. Amy L. Reschly and Sandra L. Christenson eds., (Cham, Switzerland: Springer, 2022).
7. Jenny Anderson, "Loneliness Is Bad for Our Health. Now Governments Around the World Are Finally Tackling It," *Quartz,* October 9, 2018, https://qz.com/1413576/loneliness-is-bad-for-our-health-now-governments-around-the-world-are-finally-tackling-the-problem.
8. Julianne Holt-Lunstad, Timothy B. Smith, and J. Bradley Layton, "Social Relationships and Mortality Risk: A Meta-analytic Review," *PLoS Medicine* 7, no. 7 (2010): e1000316.

9. David Yeager, professor of psychology at Stanford University, interview with the authors, March 2023.
10. Geoffrey L. Cohen and Julio Garcia. Garcia, "Identity, Belonging, and Achievement: A Model, Interventions, Implications," *Current Directions in Psychological Science* 17, no. 6 (December 1, 2008): 365–69, doi.org /10.1111/j.1467-8721.2008.00607.x.
11. Pamela Cantor, child and adolescent psychiatrist, author on human potential, interview with the authors, March 2024.
12. Gregory M. Walton and Geoffrey L. Cohen, "A Brief Social-Belonging Intervention Improves Academic and Health Outcomes of Minority Students", *Science* 331, no. 6023 (2011): 1447–51.
13. "Helping Teens Thrive Emotionally and Socially w/ Lisa Damour," *The Psychology Podcast with Scott Barry Kaufman,* April 21, 2024, https:// scottbarrykaufman.com/podcast/helping-teens-thrive-emotionally-and -socially-w-lisa-damour.
14. Amy-Jane Griffiths, Elena Lilles, Michael J. Furlong, and Jennifer Sidhwa, "The Relations of Adolescent Student Engagement with Troubling High-Risk Behaviors," S.L. Christenson et al. eds., *Handbook of Research on Student Engagement* (Cham, Switzerland: Springer, 2012).
15. Shannon M. Suldo and Janise Parker, "Relationships Between Student Engagement and Mental Health as Conceptualized from a Dual-Factor Model," Reschly and Christenson, eds., *Handbook of Research on Student Engagement,* 2nd ed., (Cham, Switzerland: Springer, 2022), 217–38.
16. Ming-Te Wang and Stephen C. Peck, "Adolescent Educational Success and Mental Health Vary Across School Engagement Profiles," *Developmental Psychology* 49, no. 7 (July 2013): 1266–76, doi.org/10.1037/a0030028.
17. Sarah-Jayne Blakemore, *Inventing Ourselves: The Secret Life of the Teenage Brain* (New York: Public Affairs, 2018).
18. Erik H. Erikson, *Identity: Youth and Crisis* (London: Faber & Faber, 1974).
19. Martin E. Seligman and Steven F. Maier, "Failure to Escape Traumatic Shock," *Journal of Experimental Psychology* 74, no. 1 (1967): 1–9, doi.org/10.1037 /h0024514.
20. Yongsoo Kim et al., "Whole-Brain Mapping of Neuronal Activity in the Learned Helplessness Model of Depression," *Frontiers in Neural Circuits* 10 (February 3, 2016), doi.org/10.3389/fncir.2016.00003.
21. Joseph J. Taylor et al., "A Pilot Study to Investigate the Induction and Manipulation of Learned Helplessness in Healthy Adults," *Psychiatry Research* 219, no. 3 (November 2014): 631–37, doi.org/10.1016/j.psychres .2014.05.045.
22. Daihui Peng et al., "Altered Brain Network Modules Induce Helplessness in Major Depressive Disorder," *Journal of Affective Disorders* 168 (October 2014): 21–29, doi.org/10.1016/j.jad.2014.05.061.
23. Michael V. Baratta, Martin E. Seligman, and Steven F. Maier, "From Helplessness to Controllability: Toward a Neuroscience of Resilience," *Frontiers in Psychiatry* 14 (May 3, 2023), doi.org/10.3389/fpsyt.2023.1170417.
24. Baratta et al., "From Helplessness to Controllability."

25. Elliot Washor and Charles Mojkowski, *Leaving to Learn: How Out-of-School Learning Increases Student Engagement and Reduces Dropout Rates* (Portsmouth, NH: Heinemann, 2013), 36.

Chapter 5

EXPLORER MODE: PRODUCTIVE AND HAPPY

1. Johnmarshall Reeve and Hyungshim Jang, "Agentic Engagement," *Handbook of Research on Student Engagement*, 2nd ed., eds. Amy L. Reschly and Sandra L. Christenson (Cham, Switzerland: Springer, 2022), 95–107, doi.org/10.1007/978-3-031-07853-8_5.
2. Johnmarshall Reeve et al., "Enhancing Students' Engagement by Increasing Teachers' Autonomy Support," *Motivation and Emotion* 28, no. 2 (June 2004): 147–69, doi.org/10.1023/b:moem.0000032312.95499.6f.
3. Reeve and Jang, "Agentic Engagement."
4. Chris Dede and Lydia Cao, "Navigating a World of Generative AI: Suggestions for Educators," *Next level Lab*, 2023, https://bpb-us-e1.wpmucdn.com/websites.harvard.edu/dist/a/108/files/2023/08/Cao_Dede_final_8.4.23.pdf.
5. Matt Murray, "Future Of: Work | Davos," *Wall Street Journal*, video, August 6, 2019, https://www.wsj.com/video/events/future-of-work-davos/BE0D0E6C-87E1-4A3F-B4A4-8F6FA4BEA1B4?page=6.
6. Johnmarshall Reeve, professor at Australian Catholic University, interview with the authors, January 2024. See also Johnmarshall Reeve et al., *Supporting Students' Motivation: Strategies for Success* (Abingdon, Oxon: Routledge, 2022).
7. Dennis Shirley and Andy Hargreaves, *Five Paths of Student Engagement: Blazing the Trail to Learning and Success* (Bloomington, IN: Solution Tree Press, 2021).
8. Daphna Oyserman, professor of psychology at USC Dornsife, interview with the authors, February 2024.
9. Reeve et al., "Enhancing Students' Engagement by Increasing Teachers' Autonomy Support."
10. Johnmarshall Reeve, professor at Australian Catholic University, interview with the authors, March 2023.
11. We are broadly summarizing the focus of the study and updating the language to reflect the iterations Reeve and his colleagues developed over time as they refined the process of encouraging autonomy-supportive teaching. For example, at the outset Reeve and his colleagues did not use the term *explanatory rationale,* but rather "promote value in uninteresting activities" to describe a teaching practice that supports students' engagement. For the benefit of the reader, we have taken some liberties when describing this first study in order to illustrate the main findings of Reeve's full body of research. The specifics of this first study are detailed in Reeve et al., "Enhancing Students' Engagement by Increasing Teachers' Autonomy Support."
12. Reeve's work builds on that of many scholars before him, including Richard DeCharms's work on personal motivation when people feel they are not pawns of external forces but origins of their actions. Richard DeCharms, *Personal*

Causation: The Internal Affective Determinants of Behavior (New York: Academic Press, 1968).

13. Nathalie Aelterman et al., "Toward an Integrative and Fine-Grained Insight in Motivating and Demotivating Teaching Styles: The Merits of a Circumplex Approach," *Journal of Educational Psychology* 111, no. 3 (April 2019): 497–521, doi.org/10.1037/edu0000293. See also Reeve et al., "Enhancing Students' Engagement by Increasing Teachers' AutonomySupport"; and Reeve et al., *Supporting Students' Motivation.*
14. Aelterman et al., "Toward an Integrative and Fine-Grained Insight in Motivating and Demotivating Teaching Styles: The Merits of a Circumplex Approach."
15. Reeve and his colleagues identify seven teaching practices that work together to support agentic engagement: take the students' perspective, invite students to pursue their personal interests, present learning activities in need-satisfying ways, provide explanatory rationales, acknowledge and accept negative feelings, rely on invitational language, and display patience. For further details see Reeve et al., *Supporting Students' Motivation.*
16. Ellen Galinsky, *The Breakthrough Years: A New Scientific Framework for Raising Thriving Teens* (New York: Flatiron Books, 2024); and Aliza Pressman, "New Science on Navigating the Breakthrough Teen Years," *Raising Good Humans,* Apple Podcasts, March 15, 2024, https://podcasts.apple.com/ph/podcast/new-science-on-navigating-the-breakthrough-teen-years/id1473072044?i=1000649287474.
17. Mary Helen Immordino-Yang, professor of education, psychology, and neuroscience at the University of Southern California, interview with the authors, March 2023.
18. Mary Helen Immordino-Yang and Douglas R. Knecht, "Building Meaning Builds Teens' Brains," *Educational Leadership* 77, no. 8 (2020): 36–43.
19. Rebecca J. M. Gotlieb, Xiao-Fei Yang, and Mary Helen Immordino-Yang, "Concrete and Abstract Dimensions of Diverse Adolescents' Social-Emotional Meaning-Making, and Associations with Broader Functioning," *Journal of Adolescent Research*, preprint, April 29, 2022, 074355842210914, doi.org/10.1177/07435584221091498.
20. Rebecca J. Gotlieb, Xiao-Fei Yang, and Mary Helen Immordino-Yang, "Diverse Adolescents' Thinking Predicts Young Adult Psychosocial Outcomes via Brain Network Development," *Scientific Reports* 14, no. 1 (March 15, 2024), doi.org/10.1038/s41598-024-56800-0.

Chapter 6

NAVIGATING THE MODES: UNLOCKING CONSTRUCTIVE CONVERSATIONS

1. Herbert J. Walberg, "Improving the Productivity of America's Schools," *Educational Leadership* 41, no. 8 (May 1984): 19–27.
2. Michael M. Barger et al., "The Relation Between Parents' Involvement in Children's Schooling and Children's Adjustment: A Meta-Analysis,"

Psychological Bulletin 145, no. 9 (September 2019): 855–90, doi.org/10.1037/bul0000201.

3. Ian Leslie, *Curious: The Desire to Know and Why Your Future Depends on It* (New York: Basic Books, 2014), xxii.
4. Vitor Geraldi Haase, Amanda Paola Guimarães, and Guilherme Wood, "Mathematics and Emotions: The Case of Math Anxiety," *International Handbook of Mathematical Learning Difficulties: From the Laboratory to the Classroom,* ed. Annemarie Fritz, Vitor Geraldi Haase, and Pekka Räsänen (Cham, Switzerland: Springer, 2019), 469–503, doi.org/10.1007/978-3-319-97148-3_29; and Alana E. Foley et al., "The Math Anxiety-Performance Link," *Current Directions in Psychological Science* 26, no. 1 (February 2017): 52–58, doi.org/10.1177/0963721416672463.
5. Jo Boaler, *Limitless Mind: Learn, Lead, and Live without Barriers* (New York: HarperOne, 2022).
6. Mary Helen Immordino-Yang, professor of education, psychology, and neuroscience at the University of Southern California, interview with the authors, March 2023.
7. Immordino-Yang interview.
8. John Hattie and Kyle Hattie, *10 Steps to Develop Great Learners: Visible Learning for Parents* (Abingdon, Oxon: Routledge, 2022).
9. Project Zero, "Project Zero's Thinking Routine Toolbox," Harvard Graduate School of Education, 2022, https://pz.harvard.edu/thinking-routines.

Chapter 7

FINDING THE SPARK: SUPPORTING YOUR KID THROUGH PASSENGER MOMENTS

1. Kyung Hwa Lee et al., "Neural Responses to Maternal Criticism in Healthy Youth," *Social Cognitive and Affective Neuroscience* 10, no. 7 (October 22, 2014): 902–12, doi.org/10.1093/scan/nsu133.
2. John Hattie, *Visible Learning: The Sequel: A Synthesis of over 2,100 Meta-Analyses Relating to Achievement* (London: Routledge Taylor & Francis Group, 2023).
3. Hattie, *Visible Learning.*
4. Piers Steel, "The Nature of Procrastination: A Meta-analytic and Theoretical Review of Quintessential Self-Regulatory Failure," *Psychological Bulletin* 133, no. 1 (January 2007): 65–94, doi.org/10.1037/0033-2909.133.1.65.
5. Paula Szuchman and Jenny Anderson, *It's Not You, It's the Dishes: How to Minimize Conflict and Maximize Happiness in Your Relationship,* (New York: Random House, 2012).
6. Ronald Dahl, distinguished professor in the School of Public Health at the University of California, Berkeley, interview with the authors, January 2024.
7. David Yeager, *10 to 25: The Science of Motivating Young People: A Groundbreaking Approach to Leading the Next Generation—and Making Your Own Life Easier* (London: Avid Reader Press, 2024).

8. Ronald E. Dahl et al. "Wanting to Matter and Learning to Care: A Neurodevelopmental Window of Opportunity for (Pro) Social Learning?" (*forthcoming*); and William R. Stixrud and Ned Johnson, *The Self-Driven Child: The Science and Sense of Giving Your Kids More Control over Their Lives* (New York: Penguin Books, 2019).
9. "Aliza Pressman Breaks Down Popular Parenting Techniques," *Today,* June 14, 2024, https://www.today.com/video/aliza-pressman-breaks-down-popular-parenting-techniques-212993093634.
10. Angran Li and Daniel Hamlin, "Is Daily Parental Help with Homework Helpful? Reanalyzing National Data Using a Propensity Score–Based Approach," *Sociology of Education* 92, no. 4 (August 2, 2019): 367–85, doi.org/10.1177/0038040719867598.
11. David Yeager, *10 to 25.*
12. There is a large body of evidence supporting the effectiveness of autonomy-supportive parenting approaches, including in the domain of homework and academic help. See, for example, Wendy S. Grolnick et al., "Parental Provision of Academic Structure and the Transition to Middle School," *Journal of Research on Adolescence* 25, no. 4 (2015): 668–84, doi.org/10.1111/; and Janine Bempechat et al., "Parental Influences on Achievement Motivation and Student Engagement," in *Handbook of Research on Student Engagement,* 2nd ed., eds. Amy L. Reschly and Sandra L. Christenson (Cham, Switzerland: Springer, 2022), 403–30.
13. Stixrud and Johnson, *The Self-Driven Child.*
14. "Coaching Resources for Teachers," Graydin Coaching, accessed June 27, 2024, https://www.graydin.com/teacher-resources.
15. Wendy S. Grolnick, Professor of Psychology, Clark University, interview with authors, July 2024. Grolnick's work of autonomy-supportive parenting demonstrates the power parents have including in boosting motivation and student engagement in school.
16. Johnmarshall Reeve, professor at Australian Catholic University, interview with the authors, March 2023.
17. Johnmarshall Reeve, professor at Australian Catholic University, interview with the authors, January 2024.
18. Reeve, March 2023 interview.
19. Jal Mehta and Sarah M. Fine, *In Search of Deeper Learning: The Quest to Remake the American High School* (Cambridge, MA: Harvard University Press, 2020).
20. Mehta and Fine, *In Search of Deeper Learning,* 5.
21. Karen Johnson Pittman et al., *Preventing Problems, Promoting Development, Encouraging Engagement Competing Priorities or Inseparable Goals?* (2003; repr. Washington, DC: Forum for Youth Investment, March 2005), https://citeseerx.ist.psu.edu/document?repid=rep1&type=pdf&doi=bb0242e5f61e3ec0b2de95594fc7e9bb2605dbb2.
22. Kelly Young, founder of Education Reimagined, interview with the authors, March 2023.

23. Jennifer Gonnerman, "Kalief Browder, 1993-2015," *The New Yorker*, June 7, 2015.
24. Jeter Children's Publishing, "Jeter's Leaders," accessed May 12, 2024, http://www.jeterchildrenspublishing.com/jetersleaders.php.
25. Nina Steenberghs et al., "Peer Effects on Engagement and Disengagement: Differential Contributions from Friends, Popular Peers, and the Entire Class," *Frontiers in Psychology* 12 (September 27, 2021), doi.org/10.3389/fpsyg.2021.726815.
26. William Damon, *The Path to Purpose: How Young People Find Their Calling in Life* (New York: Free Press, 2009).
27. Peter L. Benson, *Sparks: How Parents Can Ignite the Hidden Strengths of Teenagers* (San Francisco: Jossey-Bass, 2008).
28. Susanne Schweizer, Ian H. Gotlib, and Sarah-Jayne Blakemore, "The Role of Affective Control in Emotion Regulation During Adolescence," *Emotion* 20, no. 1 (February 2020): 80–86, doi.org/10.1037/emo0000695. See also Sarah-Jayne Blakemore, *Inventing Ourselves: The Secret Life of the Teenage Brain* (New York: Public Affairs, 2018).
29. Fred Johansson et al., "Associations Between Procrastination and Subsequent Health Outcomes Among University Students in Sweden," *JAMA Network Open* 6, no. 1 (January 4, 2023), doi.org/10.1001/jamanetworkopen.2022.49346.
30. Johansson et al., "Associations Between Procrastination and Subsequent Health Outcomes Among University Students in Sweden."
31. Shari Tishman and David Perkins, "Episode 2: Mighty Metacognition," *Thinkability* podcast, February 27, 2022, https://thinkability.substack.com/p/episode-2-mighty-metacognition. See also Deanna Kuhn and David Dean, "Metacognition: A Bridge Between Cognitive Psychology and Educational Practice," *Theory into Practice* 43, no. 4 (2004): 268–73, doi.org/10.1353/tip.2004.0047.
32. We developed the Learning to Learn Cycle from Thomas O. Nelson and Louis Narens, "Why Investigate Metacognition?," *Metacognition*, (April 7, 1994), 1–26, doi.org/10.7551/mitpress/4561.003.0003; James Mannion and Kate McAllister, *Fear Is the Mind Killer: Why Learning to Learn Deserves Lesson Time—and How to Make It Work for Your Pupils* (Melton, Woodbridge, UK: John Catt, 2020); Arthur P. Shimamura, "Toward a Cognitive Neuroscience of Metacognition," *Consciousness and Cognition* 9, no. 2 (June 2000): 313–23, doi.org/10.1006/ccog.2000.0450; and Kuhn and Dean, "Metacognition."
33. Alia J. Crum, Peter Salovey, and Shawn Achor, "Rethinking Stress: The Role of Mindsets in Determining the Stress Response," *Journal of Personality and Social Psychology* 104, no. 4 (2013): 716–33, doi.org/10.1037/a0031201.
34. David S. Yeager et al., "A Synergistic Mindsets Intervention Protects Adolescents from Stress," *Nature* 607, no. 7919 (July 6, 2022): 512–20, doi.org/10.1038/s41586-022-04907-7.
35. "Dr. Lisa Feldman Barrett: How to Understand Emotions," Huberman Lab Podcast, posted to YouTube, October 16, 2023, https://www.youtube.com/watch?v=FeRgqJVALMQ.
36. Lisa Damour, "Lisa's New Book! The Emotional Lives of Teenagers," *Ask Lisa*

podcast, episode 107, February 21, 2023,https://drlisadamour.com/resource/lisas-new-book-the-emotional-lives-of-teenagers.

37. Kelly McGonigal, *The Upside of Stress: Why Stress Is Good for You, and How to Get Good at It* (New York: Avery, 2016). See also Trevor Ragan, "Rethinking Stress," The Learner Lab, July 11, 2023, https://thelearnerlab.com/rethinking-stress/.
38. Ana Homayoun, *Erasing the Finish Line: The New Blueprint for Success Beyond Grades and College Admission* (New York: Hachette, 2023).
39. Patrick Brischetto, "England Penalty Shootout History: Three Lions' Record at World Cups and Other Major Tournaments Ending on Penalties," *Sporting News,* December 10, 2022, https://www.sportingnews.com/us/soccer/news/england-penalty-shootout-record-world-cup-history/aqnm0cdyj1orqjbxg9s9lcgz.
40. Michael Barber, *Accomplishment: How to Achieve Ambitious and Challenging Things* (London: Penguin Books, 2023), 51–55.
41. This class was called Knowledge Integration and Tools for Success (KIT).
42. Elise Ecoff, chief education officer Nord Anglia Education, interview with the authors, July 2023.
43. Giada Di Stefano et al., "Learning by Thinking: How Reflection Can Spur Progress Along the Learning Curve," Harvard Business School NOM Unit Working Paper No. 14–093, September 14, 2023, doi.org/10.2139/ssrn.2414478.

Chapter 8

BALANCING THE DRIVE: SUPPORTING YOUR KID THROUGH ACHIEVER MOMENTS

1. Gordon L. Flett, "An Introduction, Review, and Conceptual Analysis of Mattering as an Essential Construct and an Essential Way of Life," *Journal of Psychoeducational Assessment* 40, no. 1 (December 16, 2021): 3–36, doi.org/10.1177/07342829211057640.
2. We developed these criteria by combining concepts of mattering from Gregory Elliott, Suzanne Kao, and Ann-Marie Grant, "Mattering: Empirical Validation of a Social-Psychological Concept," *Self and Identity* 3, no. 4 (October 2004): 339–54, doi.org/10.1080/13576500444000119; Ronald E. Dahl et al. "Wanting to Matter and Learning to Care: A Neurodevelopmental Window of Opportunity for (Pro) Social Learning?" *Developmental Cognitive Neuroscience* (in press); and Ronald Dahl, University of California, Berkeley, interview with the authors, June 2024.
3. Morris Rosenberg, "Disposition Concepts in Behavioral Science," *Qualitative and Quantitative Social Research: Papers in Honor of Paul F. Lazarsfeld,* ed. Robert K. Merton, James S. Coleman, and Peter H. Rossi (New York: Free Press, 1979), 245.
4. Alicja R. Sadownik, "Bronfenbrenner: Ecology of Human Development in Ecology of Collaboration," *(Re)Theorising More-Than-Parental Involvement in Early Childhood Education and Care,* ed. Alicja R. Sadownik and Adrijana Višnjić Jevtić (Cham, Switzerland: Springer, 2023), 83–95, doi.org/10.1007/978-3-031-38762-3_4.

5. Richard Weissbourd et al., *On Edge: Understanding and Preventing Young Adults' Mental Health Challenges* (Cambridge, MA: Harvard Graduate School of Education, Making Caring Common Project, 2023), https://mcc.gse.harvard.edu/reports/on-edge.
6. Jennifer Breheny Wallace, *Never Enough: When Achievement Culture Becomes Toxic—and What We Can Do About It* (New York: Portfolio/Penguin, 2023).
7. Weissbourd et al., *On Edge.*
8. Liz Mineo, "Over Nearly 80 Years, Harvard Study Has Been Showing How to Live a Healthy and Happy Life," *Harvard Gazette*, April 11, 2017, https://news.harvard.edu/gazette/story/2017/04/over-nearly-80-years-harvard-study-has-been-showing-how-to-live-a-healthy-and-happy-life.
9. Christina D. Bethell, Narangerel Gombojav, and Robert C. Whitaker, "Family Resilience and Connection Promote Flourishing Among US Children, Even Amid Adversity," *Health Affairs* 38, no. 5 (May 2019): 729–37, doi.org/10.1377/hlthaff.2018.05425; and Christina Bethell et al., "Positive Childhood Experiences and Adult Mental and Relational Health in a Statewide Sample," *JAMA Pediatrics* 173, no. 11 (November 2019): e193007, doi.org/10.1001/jamapediatrics.2019.3007.
10. Wallace, *Never Enough.*
11. William Damon, *The Path to Purpose: How Young People Find Their Calling in Life* (New York: Free Press, 2008), 33.
12. Martin E. P. Seligman, *Learned Optimism* (New York: A.A. Knopf, 1991).
13. Weissbourd et al., *On Edge*, 26.
14. William Deresiewicz, *Excellent Sheep: The Miseducation of the American Elite and the Way to a Meaningful Life* (New York: Free Press, 2014).
15. Rebecca J. Gotlieb, Xiao-Fei Yang, and Mary Helen Immordino-Yang, "Diverse Adolescents' Transcendent Thinking Predicts Young Adult Psychosocial Outcomes via Brain Network Development," *Scientific Reports* 14, no. 1 (March 15, 2024), doi.org/10.1038/s41598-024-56800-0.
16. Mary Helen Immordino-Yang, professor of education, psychology and neuroscience at the University of Southern California, interview with the authors, June 2024.
17. Roger E. Beaty et al., "Creativity and the Default Network: A Functional Connectivity Analysis of the Creative Brain at Rest," *Neuropsychologia* 64 (November 2014): 92–98, doi.org/10.1016/j.neuropsychologia.2014.09.019.
18. Xiao-Fei Yang et al., "Looking Up to Virtue: Averting Gaze Facilitates Moral Construals via Posteromedial Activations," *Social Cognitive and Affective Neuroscience* 13, no. 11 (2018): 1131–39, doi.org/10.1093/scan/nsy081; Immordino-Yang, interview with the authors, March 2023.
19. Roger E. Beaty et al., "Default and Executive Network Coupling Supports Creative Idea Production," *Scientific Reports* 5, no. 1 (June 17, 2015), doi.org/10.1038/srep10964.
20. Adam E. Green et al., "The Process Definition of Creativity," *Creativity Research Journal* (November 17, 2023), 1–29, doi.org/10.1080/10400419.2023.2254573.
21. Organization for Economic Cooperation and Development, *PISA 2022 Results,* vol. 3: *Creative Minds, Creative Schools* (Paris: OECD Publishing, 2024),

https://www.oecd.org/en/publications/pisa-2022-results-volume-iii_765ee8c2-en.html

22. Immordino-Yang, interview, March 2023.
23. Sarah Zoogman et al., "Mindfulness Interventions with Youth: A Meta-Analysis," *Mindfulness* 6, no. 2 (January 15, 2014): 290–302, https://doi.org/10.1007/s12671-013-0260-4.
24. Scott Barry Kaufman and George A. Bonanno, "Jerome L. Singer (1924–2019)," *American Psychologist* 77, no. 1 (January 2022): 147, doi.org/10.1037/amp0000889; and Rebecca L. McMillan, Scott Barry Kaufman, and Jerome L. Singer, "Ode to Positive Constructive Daydreaming," *Frontiers in Psychology* 4 (2013): 5, doi.org/10.3389/fpsyg.2013.00626.
25. Benjamin W. Mooneyham and Jonathan W. Schooler, "The Costs and Benefits of Mind-Wandering: A Review," *Canadian Journal of Experimental Psychology / Revue Canadienne de Psychologie Expérimentale* 67, no. 1 (March 2013): 11–18, doi.org/10.1037/a0031569.
26. McMillan, Kaufman, and Singer, "Ode to Positive Constructive Daydreaming."
27. William R. Stixrud and Ned Johnson, *The Self-Driven Child: The Science and Sense of Giving Your Kids More Control over Their Lives* (New York: Penguin Books, 2019), 135.
28. James Nottingham, founder of The Learning Pit, interview with the authors, Jan 2022.
29. James W. Stigler et al., *The TIMSS Videotape Classroom Study: Methods and Findings from an Exploratory Research Project on Eighth-Grade Mathematics Instruction in Germany, Japan, and the United States* (Washington, DC: U.S. Department of Education, Office of Educational Research and Improvement, 1999). For the summary, see "Highlights from the TIMSS Videotape Classroom Study / National Center for Education Statistics," HathiTrust, 6, accessed March 26, 2024, https://babel.hathitrust.org/cgi/pt?id=uiug.30112047041246&seq=1.
30. World Population Review database, "PISA Scores by Country 2024," accessed March 24, 2024, https://worldpopulationreview.com/country-rankings/pisa-scores-by-country.
31. Nottingham interview.
32. David Noonan, "Failure Found to Be an 'Essential Prerequisite' for Success," *Scientific American* 31, no. 1 (October 30, 2019): 15, https://doi.org/10.1038/scientificamericanmind0120-15.
33. John Brandon, "James Dyson on How [to] Invent Insanely Popular Products," *Inc.*, January 15, 2016, https://www.inc.com/john-brandon/james-dyson-on-how-entrepreneurs-need-to-innovate-not-just-invent.html.

Chapter 9

FROM PUSHBACK TO PROGRESS: SUPPORTING YOUR KID THROUGH RESISTER MOMENTS

1. Christina Bethell, professor of public health at Johns Hopkins University, interview with the authors, July 2023.
2. The benefits of parental empathy to children are manifold. Empathy also

benefits parents, but it doesn't come cost-free. See Erika M. Manczak, Anita DeLongis, and Edith Chen, "Does Empathy Have a Cost? Diverging Psychological and Physiological Effects within Families," *Health Psychology* 35, no. 3 (2016): 211–18, doi.org/10.1037/hea0000281.

3. Lynn Fainsilber Katz, Ashley C. Maliken, and Nicole M. Stettler, "Parental Meta-emotion Philosophy: A Review of Research and Theoretical Framework," *Child Development Perspectives* 6, no. 4 (May 9, 2012): 417–22, doi.org/10.1111/j.1750-8606.2012.00244.x.
4. Kelly E. Buckholdt, Katherine M. Kitzmann, and Robert Cohen, "Parent Emotion Coaching Buffers the Psychological Effects of Poor Peer Relations in the Classroom," *Journal of Social and Personal Relationships* 33, no. 1 (December 11, 2014): 23–41, doi.org/10.1177/0265407514562560.
5. John Mordechai Gottman, Lynn Fainsilber Katz, and Carole Hooven, *Meta-emotion: How Families Communicate Emotionally* (London: Routledge Taylor and Francis Group, 2013).
6. U.S. Department of Education, "U.S. Education Department's Office for Civil Rights Releases New Civil Rights Data on Students' Access to Educational Opportunities During the Pandemic," press release, November 15, 2023.
7. Richard Weissbourd, *Caring for the Caregivers: The Critical Link Between Parent and Teen Mental Health* (Cambridge, MA: Harvard Graduate School of Education, Making Caring Common Project, 2023), https://static1.squarespace.com/static/5b7c56e255b02c683659fe43/t/64ac08af6f3dc8123d9b3c45/1688996016873/Caring+for+the+Caregivers_final.pdf.
8. Michael Bungay Stanier, *The Coaching Habit: Say Less, Ask More and Change the Way You Lead Forever* (Toronto: Box of Crayons Press, 2016).
9. Daren Dickson, chief culture officer, Valor Collegiate Academies, interview with the authors, March 2023.
10. "Reimagining Student Engagement with Dr. Amy Berry," Powerful Learning, YouTube, January 27, 2024, https://www.youtube.com/watch?v=s7eBvpKqIuo.
11. E. Thomsen et al., *Student Reports of Bullying: Results from the 2022 School Crime Supplement to the National Crime Victimization Study* (Washington, DC: U.S. Department of Education, National Center for Education Statistics, 2024), https://nces.ed.gov/pubs2024/2024109rev.pdf.
12. "Attachment & Emotionally Focused Therapy—Dr Sue Johnson," YouTube, May 23, 2024, https://www.youtube.com/watch?v=C6_qOoQRLd8.
13. Rebecca Winthrop, Youssef Shoukry, and David Nitkin, *The Disengagement Gap: Why Student Engagement Isn't What Parents Expect* (Washington, DC: Brookings Institution and Transcend, 2025).
14. Daphna Oyserman, Deborah Bybee, and Kathy Terry, "Possible Selves and Academic Outcomes: How and When Possible Selves Impel Action," *Journal of Personality and Social Psychology* 91, no. 1 (2006): 188.
15. Daphna Oyserman, *Pathways to Success Through Identity-Based Motivation* (New York: Oxford University Press, 2015).
16. Oyserman, Bybee, and Terry, "Possible Selves and Academic Outcomes," 188.
17. Daphna Oyserman, "When Does the Future Begin? A Study in Maximising

Motivation," Aeon Ideas, April 22, 2016, https://aeon.co/ideas/when-does-the-future-begin-a-study-in-maximising-motivation.

18. John L. Holland, "A Theory of Vocational Choice," *Journal of Counseling Psychology* 6, no. 1 (1959): 35–45, doi.org/10.1037/h0040767.
19. John L. Holland, *Making Vocational Choices: A Theory of Careers*, Prentice-Hall Series in Counseling and Human Development (Englewood Cliffs, NJ: Prentice-Hall, 1973).
20. Amy Lunday, "Obituary: John Holland, 89, Studies Personalities in Workplace," *JHU Gazette,* December 15, 2008, https://pages.jh.edu/gazette/2008/15dec08/15holland.html.

Chapter 10

EXPLORING: SUCCESSFULLY NAVIGATING A LIFETIME OF LEARNING

1. Amy Berry, *Reimagining Student Engagement: From Disrupting to Driving* (Thousand Oaks, CA: Corwin, 2023).
2. Carmen Arellano, teacher at Kramer Elementary School, interview with the authors, February 2024.
3. Emily Brokaw, assistant principal at North Lake Early College High School, interview with authors, October 2023.
4. Amy Berry, senior research fellow, Australian Council for Educational Research, University of Melbourne, interview with the authors, May 2023.
5. Alison Gopnik, *The Gardener and the Carpenter: What the New Science of Child Development Tells Us About the Relationship Between Parents and Children* (New York: Farrar, Straus and Giroux, 2016).
6. John Jumper et al., "Highly Accurate Protein Structure Prediction with Alphafold," *Nature News,* July 15, 2021, https://www.nature.com/articles/s41586-021-03819-2.
7. Todd Rose, CEO of Populace.org, interview with the authors, July 2024.
8. Rebecca Winthrop, Adam Barton, and Eileen McGivney, *Leapfrogging Inequality: Remaking Education to Help Young People Thrive* (Washington, DC: Brookings Institution, 2018).
9. To bring to life the story of Paulo Freire, we relied on a number of sources and used our imagination to give some colorful details to help the reader engage with the narrative. We have endeavored to indicate where imagination entered the picture with words such as "we imagined." We relied on the following sources: Myles Horton and Paulo Freire, *We Make the Road by Walking: Conversations on Education and Social Change,* ed. Brenda Bell, John Gaventa, and John Peters (Philadelphia: Temple University Press, 1990); Paulo Freire, *Pedagogy of the Oppressed,* trans. Myra Bergman Ramos (New York: Herder and Herder, 1970); Nadine Nelson and Julian Chen, "Freire's Problem-Posing Model: Critical Pedagogy and Young Learners," *ELT Journal* 77, no. 2 (April 2023), doi.org/10.1093/elt/ccac017; Moacir Gadotti, *Reading Paulo Freire: His Life and Work,* trans. John Milton (New York: State University of New York

Press, 1994); and Carol Hills, "Teaching Literacy in 40 Hours: Looking Back at Paulo Freire's Groundbreaking Work," *The World*, October 1, 2021, https://theworld.org/segments/2024/04/04/teaching-literacy-in-40-hours-looking-back-at-paulo-freires-groundbreaking-work.

10. Horton and Freire, *We Make the Road by Walking*, 65.
11. Horton and Freire, *We Make the Road by Walking*, 89.

Ending the Tech Wars:

BOOSTING REAL ENGAGEMENT

1. Jordan Shapiro, *The New Childhood: Raising Kids to Thrive in a Digitally Connected World* (London: Hodder and Stoughton, 2020).
2. Matti Vuorre, Amy Orben, and Andrew K. Przybylski, "There Is No Evidence That Associations Between Adolescents' Digital Technology Engagement and Mental Health Problems Have Increased," *Clinical Psychological Science* 9, no. 5 (May 3, 2021): 823–35, https://doi.org/10.1177/2167702621994549.
3. Gloria Mark, *Attention Span: A Groundbreaking Way to Restore Balance, Happiness and Productivity* (Toronto, Ontario, Canada: Hanover Square Press, 2003).
4. This innovative survey used software to track kids notifications. See Jenny S. Radesky et al., *Constant Companion: A Week in the Life of a Young Person's Smartphone Use* (San Francisco: Common Sense, 2023), https://www.commonsensemedia.org/sites/default/files/research/report/2023-cs-smartphone-research-report_final-for-web.pdfhttps://www.commonsensemedia.org/sites/default/files/research/report/2023-cs-smartphone-research-report_final-for-web.pdf.
5. UNESCO, *Global Education Monitoring Report 2023: Technology in Education—A Tool on Whose Terms?* (Paris: UNESCO, 2023), https://unesdoc.unesco.org/ark:/48223/pf0000385723.
6. Charlotte Skau Pawlowski, Jonas Vestergaard Nielsen, and Tanja Schmidt, "A Ban on Smartphone Usage During Recess Increased Children's Physical Activity," *International Journal of Environmental Research and Public Health* 18, no. 4 (February 16, 2021): 1907, doi.org/10.3390/ijerph18041907.
7. Candice L. Odgers, "The Great Rewiring: Is Social Media Really Behind an Epidemic of Teenage Mental Illness?" *Nature*, March 29, 2024; Drew P. Cingel, Michael C. Carter, and Hannes-Vincent Krause, "Social Media and Self-Esteem," *Current Opinion in Psychology* 45 (June 2022): 101304, doi.org/10.1016/j.copsyc.2022.101304.
8. Jennifer Breheny Wallace, *Never Enough: When Achievement Culture Becomes Toxic—and What We Can Do About It* (New York: Portfolio/Penguin, 2023).
9. Jonathan Rothwell, "Teens Spend Average of 4.8 Hours on Social Media per Day," Gallup.com, February 9, 2024, https://news.gallup.com/poll/512576/teens-spend-average-hours-social-media-per-day.aspx.
10. Anne G. Wheaton et al., "Short Sleep Duration Among Middle School and High School Students—United States, 2015," *Morbidity and Mortality*

Weekly Report 67, no. 3 (January 26, 2018): 85–90, doi.org/10.15585/mmwr.mm6703a1.

11. Ut Na Sio, Padraic Monaghan, and Tom Ormerod, "Sleep on It, but Only If It Is Difficult: Effects of Sleep on Problem Solving," *Memory and Cognition* 41, no. 2 (October 6, 2012): 159–66, doi.org/10.3758/s13421-012-0256-7.
12. Ben Carter et al., "Association Between Portable Screen-Based Media Device Access or Use and Sleep Outcomes," *JAMA Pediatrics* 170, no. 12 (December 1, 2016): 1202, doi.org/10.1001/jamapediatrics.2016.2341.
13. Radesky et al., *Constant Companion.*
14. Amie M. Gordon, Wendy Berry Mendes, and Aric A. Prather, "The Social Side of Sleep: Elucidating the Links Between Sleep and Social Processes," *Current Directions in Psychological Science* 26, no. 5 (October 2017): 470–75, doi.org/10.1177/0963721417712269.
15. Cara A. Palmer et al.,"Sleepy and Secluded: Sleep Disturbances Are Associated with Connectedness in Early Adolescent Social Networks," *Journal of Research on Adolescence: The Official Journal of the Society for Research on Adolescence* 32, no. 2 (2022): 756–68, doi.org/10.1111/jora.12670.
16. Faith Orchard et al., "Clinical Characteristics of Adolescents Referred for Treatment of Depressive Disorders," *Child and Adolescent Mental Health* 22, no. 2 (July 15, 2016): 61–68, doi.org/10.1111/camh.12178.
17. Faith Orchard et al., "Clinical Characteristics of Adolescents Referred for Treatment of Depressive Disorders."
18. Max Stossel, Social Awakening website, accessed May 12, 2024, https://www.socialawakening.org.
19. "172 Max Stossel: Unleashing the Power of Words and Storytelling," Noble Warrior with CK Lin, YouTube, June 28, 2023, https://www.youtube.com/watch?v=N5PazS1ad4I.
20. Tristan Harris, "A Call to Minimize Distraction & Respect Users' Attention," Google presentation, 2013, http://www.minimizedistraction.com.
21. Daren Dickson, chief culture officer, Valor Collegiate Academy), interview with the authors, March 2023.
22. Amanda Ripley, "Can Teenage Defiance Be Manipulated for Good?," *New York Times,* September 12, 2016, sec. The Upshot, https://www.nytimes.com/2016/09/13/upshot/can-teenage-defiance-be-manipulated-for-good.html.
23. Alison Link, founder of The Leisure Link, interview with the authors, July 2023.
24. Link interview.
25. Elizabeth Weybright, associate professor of human development at Washington State University, interview with the authors, July 2023.
26. Linda Caldwell, professor emeritus at Penn State University, interview with the authors, June 2023.
27. There are a range of digital tools that help students with dyslexia. We chose to highlight Read&Write because, at the time of writing, it is one of the most common in more than half of U.S. K to 12 schools. It was free for teachers, and, most importantly, students we interviewed described using it. The founder of the Read&Write tool was also on the Center for Universal Education's Leadership Council that Rebecca manages.

28. Monica Anderson, Michelle Faverio, and Eugenie Park, *How Teens and Parents Approach Screen Time,* Pew Research Center, March 12, 2024, https://www.pewresearch.org/internet/wp-content/uploads/sites/9/2024/02/PI_2024.03.11_Teens-and-Screens_REPORT.pdf.
29. Susan Rivers, co-lead and chief scientist at The History Co:Lab, interview with the authors, June 2023.
30. danah boyd, *It's Complicated: The Social Lives of Networked Teens* (New Haven, CT: Yale University Press, 2015).
31. Andrew Goodrich, "Peer Mentoring and Peer Tutoring Among K—12 Students: A Literature Review," *Update: Applications of Research in Music Education* 36, no. 2 (April 29, 2017): 13–21, doi.org/10.1177/8755123317708765.

Index

About the Authors

JENNY ANDERSON is an award-winning journalist who spent more than a decade at *The New York Times* before pioneering coverage on the science of learning at *Quartz.* She writes a column for *Time;* contributes to other major media outlets, including *The New York Times* and *The Atlantic;* and moderates at high-level events, including the World Economic Forum and SXSW EDU. She lives in London with her husband, two daughters, and dog, Tiggy.

REBECCA WINTHROP is a senior fellow and director of the Center for Universal Education at Brookings and an adjunct professor at Georgetown University. She leads global studies on how to better support children's learning and is a sought-after speaker and adviser by education policymakers, UN agencies, business leaders, and philanthropic and nonprofit organizations. She lives in Washington, D.C., with her husband, two sons, and dog, Chewie.